Macao, 22 April 1996

For Don and Beth,
with much admiration
and gratitude,

The Shadow of Ulysses

The Shadow of Ulysses

Figures of a Myth

PIERO BOITANI

TRANSLATED BY
ANITA WESTON

CLARENDON PRESS · OXFORD

Oxford University Press, Walton Street, Oxford OX2 6DP

Oxford New York

Athens Auckland Bangkok Bombay
Calcutta Cape Town Dar es Salaam Delhi
Florence Hong Kong Istanbul Karachi
Kuala Lumpur Madras Madrid Melbourne
Mexico City Nairobi Paris Singapore
Taipei Tokyo Toronto

and associated companies in
Berlin Ibadan

Oxford is a trade mark of Oxford University Press

Published in the United States
by Oxford University Press Inc., New York

First published 1994

British Library Cataloguing in Publication Data

Data available

Library of Congress Cataloging in Publication Data
Boitani, Piero. [Ombra di Ulisse. English]
The shadow of Ulysses: figures of a myth / Piero Boitani;
translated by Anita Weston.
p. cm.
includes bibliographical references.
I. Odysseus (Greek mythology) in literature. I. Title.
PN57.03B6513 1994
809'.93351—dc20 93–34541
ISBN 0–19–812268–3

3 5 7 9 10 8 6 4 2

Printed in Great Britain
on acid-free paper by
The Ipswich Book Co Ltd,
Ipswich, Suffolk

To Bernice
a Francesco
per Giulia

PREFACE

Two days before I began the lectures on which this book is based, the American space shuttle *Discovery* launched the European Space Agency probe *Ulysses* on a long flight directed, one newspaper announced, 'like Dante's hero' towards 'the unchartered distances ... of the uninhabited world behind the sun'. Such a coincidence had to mean something. It summarized the gist of my whole subject, this 'mad flight' not beyond the Pillars of Hercules, but through interplanetary and interstellar space, which clearly fulfilled in the present a myth and a poem of the remotest past. This pattern of prophecy and fulfilment was precisely what I wanted to talk about. I was fascinated by the way literature, with its weight of being and existing, dovetails into history, the world of becoming; by the moments when they make contact, and the long periods when they conduct a dialogue across a distance.

To pick up their echo I needed a narrative which, while following one basic direction, would be mostly interested in the side roads; one which was less interested in the statues along the way than in the shadows cast by the traveller. This is the reason I talk about shadows, and one particular shadow: the one which starts from Odysseus' journey to Hades and spreads its long cone, in various forms, down to the present day. This was also the reason I opted for a long essay rather than a more organic treatment. There are as many studies as there are incarnations of Ulysses, and a truly complete one would now have to be around the length of the average encyclopaedia. What I wanted to do was touch on a number of problems, make a few suggestions, arouse curiosity, and open up a few gaps which readers would be stimulated to fill with their own reflections.

To fabricate my tale I had to become what I (shamelessly) call an 'impure' reader. The Impure Reader—who will be with us in a number of the following chapters—is not so much she or he who goes to bed with her or his books (though she or he will do that, too, with all the enjoyment associated with the activity), but above all one who already knows the plot and the end of the story, and deliberately chooses a position in time and space, history and ideology, from which to exercise her or his *voyeurism*. My Impure Reader is also someone who has duly fallen in love with theory, but has survived the affair because, to use Paul Valéry's and Frank Kermode's term, she or he has an insatiable appetite for poetry. Lastly, the Impure Reader is also restless: one who, in spite of everything, is concerned with the problem of interpretation and the history of interpretations, with their meaning as reflections—and at times as creative figurations—of aesthetic, moral, religious, ideo-logical, cultural, and material positions or situations. As a reader, and a Roman reader at that, I am totally impure. Puritanical readers, beware!

As for my female readers: William Golding once remarked in conversation that anyone who prefers the *Odyssey* to the *Iliad* has a woman's heart. I don't actually agree with him, far less with Samuel Butler who went so far as to posit a female (and Sicilian) authoress of the poem. I do realize, though, that a reading of Ulysses' adventures from the point of view of, say, Circe, or Calypso, Anticlea, Nausicaa, Euriclea, or Penelope (or Molly Bloom) would perhaps be 'newer' than my 'new' male account (but see now M. A. Katz, *Penelope's Renown*, Princeton, NJ, 1991). My interests were a little different. I hope, though, that the part on Wallace Stevens's Penelope testifies to the fact that, if Golding should happen to be right after all, I have to an extent had Tiresias' experience; it leaves us more whole, and leaves us more hope, and it would be an honour, albeit only through poetry, to be a part of the gentle sex.

This essay grew out of a long-standing obsession, pursued through much reading and travelling, with my old 'flame', if Dante will forgive this perverting of his term, Ulysses. It would never have been written, however, without three separate occasions which forced me to translate this obsession into a relatively cohesive thought-process.

In 1986 Cormac Ó Cuilleanáin invited me to conduct a seminar at Trinity College, Dublin, on Canto XXVI of the *Inferno*. To him, then, I owe the initial impetus, and a number of ideas and suggestions made over the years.

In 1989 the University of Virginia, Charlottesville, invited me to give a lecture on any theme in Italian literature which had applications in comparative literature. I chose 'Beyond the Sunset: Dante's Ulysses in Another World' (now published in Virginia's *Lectura Dantis*). For this invitation I am deeply grateful first of all to

Tibor Wlassics, but also to Barbara Nolan, A. C. Spearing, and Herbert Tucker. Particular thanks to Alastair Fowler who at the end of that lecture came up and said, 'You are, of course, writing a book on the subject?' I hadn't thought about it, but began to.

The following year the University of California, Berkeley, invited me to fill the chair of Italian Culture for the Fall semester. One of the far-from-onerous duties involved was to hold three lectures on, again, a subject from Italian and comparative literature. I took Ulysses again, this time looking at it as a mythical and literary problem with a good deal of existential and historical spin-off. This would have been onerous indeed without the kindness, advice, and continual exchange of ideas with my Berkeley colleagues and friends: Robert Alter, Gian Paolo Biasin, Stephen Botterill, Louise Clubb, Gustavo Costa, Phillip Damon, Stephen Greenblatt, Charles Muscatine, Dana Smith, Ruggero Stefanini, Brian Stock, and Kenneth Weisinger.

One debt I can never repay: that towards Bernice Joseph, who offered months of extraordinarily generous hospitality in her beautiful house on Presidio Heights, San Francisco, evenings of careful listening and quiet wisdom, and days of exploring the 'Wild West' and the wonderful Californian coast with Ulysses in mind. To her, then, first of all, this book is dedicated.

Once back in Rome, I decided to write it: in the form of an essay, in Italian, and for an educated but neither specialist nor strictly academic public. Carla Carloni from *Il Mulino* had no hesitation in accepting what was no more than an idea based on a short typescript in English, and I am most grateful for her enthusiasm.

For structural, stylistic, and personal reasons, the actual writing was more complicated than I had expected. Its completion was due to the friends—Barbara and Francesco Calvo, Paola and Giorgio Piacentini, and Carlo Biancheri—who helped in all three areas. In a very particular way, this book is the product of twenty-five years' friendship with Francesco Calvo, who has followed Ulysses and myself with patience, wisdom, and affectionate severity: to him too, then, the work is dedicated.

I could not, even if I wanted to, forget that I wrote the book while my wife was carrying our daughter Giulia; all things considered, both father and mother had a safe delivery. My thanks to Joan are subsumed in the dedication to Giulia, for whom I wish a longer and less restless life than her companion-in-gestation.

It would be impossible to mention all those who had some part in the birth-process of this study, but thanks for their comments and insights must go to Richard Ambrosini, Pamela and David Benson, Patrick Boyde, Robert Clark, Lidia Curti, Agostino Lombardo, Franco Marenco, Jeffrey Robinson, and Christian Zacher; colleagues of the Associazione Italiana di Anglistica, for feedback on my Venice lecture; and students and friends at the Universities of Rome, Perugia, and Connecticut.

P. B.

Rome
6 November 1991

PREFACE TO THE
ENGLISH EDITION

WHEN Oxford University Press decided to publish this book in English, Andrew Lockett, their Literature editor—to whom I am most grateful for his patience and understanding—seemed to take it for granted that, having written all my work in English for over fifteen years, I would translate it myself. But this book, after a long and painstaking dithering between the two languages, was conceived in Italian, and to prepare my own translation would have meant writing another book—something which, for all my love of Ulysses, I had neither the energy nor the inclination to do.

The words of one language do not just designate objects that can be transferred on to another verbal system: they create patterns of thinking, arguments, and images; they shape and are determined by their 'implied' readers. In short, I needed a translator, one who would transfer the dialect of my tribe and my own style into a different register, who would adjust the tone for non-Italian readers, and, collaborating with the author, make those changes, cuts, and additions to the text which were clearly needed for an English-speaking audience.

Traduttore, however, not *traditore*: the book had to remain substantially the same in its structure, argument, metaphorical texture, and above all voice, carrying at least some of the personal urgency the author had written into the original.

I was lucky. I found a translator, Anita Weston, who could do just that, creating a style—if she will allow me to so put it—of our own. Nothing like a translation can reveal the vices and emptiness of a text. As far as I am concerned, Anita Weston has quietly suppressed the former and filled up the latter, and I am very grateful to her for what she has done.

The English-speaking reader should, however, bear in mind that, quite intentionally, this is not a piece of purely academic, scholarly work. It is an *essay*—on myth, poetry, and history— destined for a cultured audience, who for instance will not need (and might have resented) heavy annotation and long biblio- graphical references. I decided to keep notes to a minimum, citing only unfamiliar primary texts and those critical works I allude to in my argument, or which have in some way inspired me; for this, and for any errors that may have slipped through the net even after the translator's corrections, I take full responsibility.

In the eight months since its first appearance in Italian (*Il Mulino*, 1992), this volume has been read by friends, colleagues, and reviewers. All of them have made useful suggestions for improvement. I have incorporated some of these and would thus like to thank Maurizio Bettini, Corrado Bologna, Beniamino Placido, Silvano Sabbadini, Jonathan Steinberg, and one of the readers who went through an earlier draft of the book for Oxford University Press.

P. B.

Rome
6 January 1993

CONTENTS

NOTE ON TEXTS AND TRANSLATIONS

THE editions used for all major authors are the standard ones: thus, for example, for Greek and Latin classics the Loeb series; for Italian writers the 'Classici Ricciardi', for French authors the 'Bibliothèque de la Pléiade', etc. English-speaking readers will not need to be told where to find the standard editions of their major writers. Other editions are indicated in the footnotes.

The text of Dante's *Commedia* is that established by G. Petrocchi (Milan, 1966–8), the English translation by John D. Sinclair (Oxford, 1961). The text of the *Odyssey* I use throughout was published by the Fondazione Lorenzo Valla and Arnoldo Mondadori (Milan, 1981–6). The English translation is Richmond Lattimore's (New York, 1975), at times modified, like Sinclair's *Commedia*, for greater fidelity to the original. All other English translations, unless otherwise specified in the notes, are Anita Weston's and mine.

NOTE ON THE COVER ILLUSTRATION

THE cover illustration comes from the so-called 'pictorial Odyssey', a fresco in a room of a villa on the Esquiline Hill in Rome, dating from the latter part of the first century BC. It is now preserved in the Sala delle Nozze Aldobrandini in the Vatican Museum, but belongs to the Biblioteca Apostolica Vaticana, by whose permission it is reproduced here. The scene it represents is that of Book XI of the *Odyssey*, the arrival of Ulysses and his companions in the 'other world' of Hades and their encounter with the shades of the dead. Ever since I was a boy, however, I dreamt that it also 'prefigured' the arrival of Columbus in the New World and his meeting with the 'Indians'.

The present book, then, is deeply indebted to that picture. Its faded blues and their contrast with the great overarching rock (a Dantean 'dark mountain' indeed), and the faintly glowing ghosts surrounded by obscurity, all appealed to me and played into my hands. Wasn't this familiar, ancient Roman fresco of a Greek mythological scene vaguely 'foreshadowing' a Turner?

Introduction
Wonder: Poetry and History

son di lor vero umbriferi prefazi

They are shadowy forecasts of their truth

In the middle of the sufferings which are to lead both to his tragic end and to his immediate fame throughout Europe as the precursor of a new sensitivity and modern literature, Goethe's anguished hero, the young Werther, notes in his 'diary' that he would sometimes stand for hours and watch a river, following it with the mind's eye into remote realms of adventure. His imagination would find itself suddenly checked, but, impelled to move further on, would finally lose itself in the contemplation of invisible distances. The cultured Werther immediately finds the classical parallel: 'Similarly limited and similarly happy were our magnificent patriarchs! Similarly childlike their sentiments and their poetry!' he exclaims with nostalgia. Then, by way of explanation, he hits on the apposite parallel: 'When Ulysses speaks of the boundless sea and endless earth, it is equally true, human, tender, intimate and mysterious.'[1]

Goethe, like others before and since, was fascinated by the *Odyssey*. In 1779, in the Alps, he would recite passages of it to the shepherds, and brace himself for the climb to the glaciers by thinking of Ulysses. In 1786, in Venice, he compares himself with his hero, and toys with the idea of writing a play about Ulysses' stay among the Phaeacians. In Palermo, he notes in the *Italian Journey* under 7 April 1787, he rushes to buy an *Odyssey* to reread in the light of the world he is discovering in Sicily. The public gardens of the coastal city of Palermo seem to him the tangible reflection of Alcinous' enchanted island, and the colours of the natural world in Sicily the incarnation of the *Urlandschaft*, the original, ideal Homeric landscape, just as the poem's characters appear as the

---

[1] J. W. Goethe, *Die Leiden des jungen Werther* (Munich, 1978), 73 (2. Buch. Am 9 Mai). And see H. Trevelyan, *Goethe and the Greeks* (Cambridge, 1941), 76–8, 159–69.

embodiment of the *Urmensch*—primeval man in a state of uncontaminated wisdom. The *Odyssey*, he later writes to Schiller, 'shines' for him not simply as a poem, but as Nature itself.

Goethe never finished his play on Ulysses and Nausicaa, but Homer's hold on him was to last throughout his life, and is obvious in all his work. This book is an attempt to explain why and how, 200 years after Werther and almost in the year 2000, Ulysses can still seem 'true, human, passionate, intimate and mysterious'.

Ulysses represents what some contemporary critics would define a 'discourse' of Western civilization; for historians, a *longue-durée* 'imaginary'[2]—in other words, an archetype of myth which comes to constitute a consistent cultural *logos* in history and literature. Ulysses represents the 'archaeology' of the *European* image of man, to paraphrase Bernard Andreae,[3] and in this sense is profoundly different from the Jewish Jonah or the Oriental Sinbad who otherwise share a number of characteristics with him. From the beginning Odysseus reveals himself as open to the future: to his many disguises in Homer, and to the transformations in poetry which his myth and its first literary text stimulate with their excesses and their evocative gaps.

Ulysses is simultaneously ancient and modern: an ideal observation-point from which to measure the similarities and differences between the 'alterity' of the past and the 'modernity' of the present,[4] both in historico-cultural terms and in that dimension of the 'true, human, passionate, intimate and mysterious' Werther speaks of. I shall be continually returning to these two aspects of the alterity–modernity polarization; to decide what the words of the past mean to us, and whether what they say and how they say it still has significance for the inhabitants of the third millennium seems

---

[2] For both concepts see *La Nouvelle Histoire*, ed. J. Le Goff (Paris, 1979).

[3] B. Andreae, *Odysseus: Archäologie des europäischen Menschenbildes* (Frankfurt, 1982). And see M. Horkheimer and T. W. Adorno, 'Odysseus oder Mythos und Aufklärung', in *Dialektik der Aufklärung, Philosophische Fragmente* (Frankfurt, 1969); E. Jünger, 'Der gordische Knoten', in *Sämtliche Werke*, vol. vii (Stuttgart, 1980); C. Schmitt, 'Die geschichtliche Struktur des heutigen Welt-Gegensatzes von Ost und West', in *Freundschaftliche Begegnungen: Festschrift für Ernst Jünger* (Frankfurt, 1955); E. J. Leed, *The Mind of the Traveler* (New York, 1991); P. Scarpi, *La fuga e il ritorno: Storia e mitologia del viaggio* (Venice, 1992); M. W. Helms, *Ulysses' Sail: An Ethnographic Odyssey of Power, Knowledge, and Geographical Distance* (Princeton, NJ, 1988).

[4] For the terms of the discussion see H. R. Jauss, *Alterität und Modernität der mittelalterlichen Literatur* (Munich, 1977), and *New Literary History*, 10 (1979).

to me the prime duty of anyone reading or inviting others to read today. Ulysses, the hero of continuity and metamorphosis,[5] can perhaps bridge for every citizen of Europe, and the offspring of its civilization all over the world, the two banks of time between which we all live.

Ulysses travels so well through time because he starts out as a sign—in cultural terms, the sign of an entire episteme. When Tiresias prophesies Odysseus' last journey towards the country without ships and salt (see Chapter 1), enjoining him to carry an oar on his back, he becomes the symbol of all sea-based civilizations: the *nomos*—the custom and law—of the oceans as against that of the earth.[6] From this moment, every time he undertakes that journey it is as a sign. Every culture is free to interpret him as such within its own sign-system, according him values rooted on the one hand in the mythical features of Odysseus as a character, and on the other in the ideals, problems, and philosophical, ethical, and political horizons of the individual civilization.

The present book attempts to follow the evolution of the sign through its various phases: Classical, Medieval, Renaissance, Romantic, and Modern, sometimes drawing on (and briefly discussing) the concepts of 'typology' and 'canon'.[7]

A typology is, for example, that which Italian culture generates in the Renaissance and which remains valid until the early twentieth century: Dante's Ulysses anticipates Christopher Columbus and constitutes the precursor of modern episteme and science. A canon is a historical or literary sequence (of the 'imaginary') which has been consecrated by tradition and the cultural, educational, and political institutions: in Italy, between the nineteenth and the twentieth century, the typology in question became 'canonical' in poetry, criticism, and education. Typologies and canons are far from changeless, but it would be absurd to deny their cultural value and dynamics: like museums, they speak of the past to visitors from the present, and the more clearly to those who wander freely from one room to another, ignoring the pre-established itinerary.

---

[5] E. Canetti, 'Medea und Odysseus', in *Die Gerettete Zunde* (Munich, 1977), part 3, 'Wien'; 'Der Beruf des Dichters', in *Das Gewissen der Worte* (Frankfurt, 1981), 283–4.

[6] C. Schmitt, *Der Nomos der Erde* (Cologne, 1950); and 'Die geschichtliche Struktur des heutigen Welt-Gegensatzes von Ost und West'.

[7] See *Canons*, ed. R. von Hallberg (Chicago and London, 1984); F. Kermode, *History and Value* (Oxford, 1989).

Ulysses is a sign because he expresses a sense without denoting a meaning. The distinction is from Frege,[8] the founder of modern mathematical logic, who posits that the meaning of a proper name is 'the object we indicate by it', while its 'representation' is totally subjective, the 'sense' being somewhere between the two. The example Frege gives is of interest here. 'The sentence "Odysseus was set ashore at Ithaca while sound asleep" '—he writes—'obviously has a sense. But since it is doubtful whether the name "Odysseus", occurring therein, has a meaning; it is also doubtful whether the whole sentence has one.' Ulysses is a real but non-objective image, received by the subject but not subjective: rather like the image of the moon seen through the lens of a telescope. Setting aside logical metaphor, Ulysses is, as Tennyson will say, a *name*: potentially one, No-body, and one hundred thousand. It is then left to the various Werthers and Goethes to give it meaning.

We are not analysing 'Ulysses' from a logical or linguistico-formal standpoint, however, but reading his adventures in poetry. While in logic it is the 'truth-value' of a sentence which interests us, 'in hearing an epic poem', Frege continues, 'apart from the euphony of the language we are interested only in the sense of the sentences and the images and feelings therein aroused. The question of truth would cause us to abandon aesthetic delight for an attitude of scientific investigation.' Readers of the present work will not want to be party to such a cruel metamorphosis, far less forgo their readerly *jouissance*. The aim is quite the reverse: if, as Frege states, it is the search for truth which drives us from sense to meaning, we shall try to effect this by reading in the images and feelings the 'meaning' attributed to Ulysses whenever history and poetry meet.

Frege himself points the way, suggesting in a note that 'signs having only sense' be called 'images' or 'figures' (*Bilder*). This is precisely the case with the figure of Ulysses (I shall shortly return to the other meaning of the term used throughout the present text), who from the beginning of his mythical and literary existence constitutes a model and 'multiform' (*polytropos*) form of human life which is full of potential.

[8] G. Frege, 'Sinn und Bedeutung', *Zeitschrift für Philosophie und philosophische Kritik*, 100 (1892), 25–50. Eng. trans. 'Sense and Reference', *The Philosophical Review*, 55 (1948) 207–30.

Odysseus is presented in the third line of the *Odyssey* as a paradigm of knowledge of the world and self through suffering: 'Many were they whose cities he saw, whose minds he learned of, | many the pains he suffered in his spirit on the wide sea.' By the time of the Roman Empire he had already, as we shall see in the first chapter, become an icon of experience, science, and wisdom. Ulysses is also the supreme engineer and craftsman of *tekhne*: the maker of a wooden horse, raft, and his own marriage-bed, and an expert sailor. Throughout the Trojan Wars and his long return, in all literary accounts from Sophocles to Shakespeare, he reveals himself a master of rhetoric, of language as survival-kit, or a political arm with which to persuade, cheat, illude, possess, and dominate (in Dante the desire for knowledge, oratory, and navigational skills are virtually all one). Lastly—and it is this which most interests us in the present context—in his *metis* and *aletheia*,[9] in the astute art of knowledge which links him with Athene and the truth which associates him with Apollo, Odysseus is a model of poetry.

The *Odyssey* takes shape from the protagonist's own words. In Book XI, when he tells Alcinous of his adventures and his visit to Hades (to which we shall shortly return), Alcinous praises his 'sound sense' which, instead of 'making up lying stories, from which no one could learn anything', gives 'form' to his 'narration'. 'Expertly, as a singer would do, you have told the story (*mythos*)', Alcinous compliments him. The effect of Odysseus' poetry is more startling even than that produced by Demodocus, the bard of the Phaeacians, who produces joy or tears, and similar to that of Phemios, the Ithacan, who 'enchants' his listeners with stories of the return of the Achaians to their homeland. When Ulysses ends his tale of Hades and the dead, the Phaeacians sit in stunned silence, 'held in thrall by the story all through the shadowy chambers': Alcinous wishes to stay awake for the whole night listening to the 'wondrous deeds' and misadventures Odysseus recounts so well.

Wondrous deeds: they bewitch like the poetry of Phemios or the song of the Sirens (the words used in all three cases have the same

---

[9] G. Chiarini, *Odisseo: Il labirinto marino* (Rome, 1991), 101–44. For Odysseus as master of lies, see M. Lavagetto, *La cicatrice di Montaigne: Sulla bugia in letteratura* (Turin, 1992), 5–33. For Odysseus as politician, see H. Münkler, *Odysseus und Kassandra: Politik im Mythos* (Frankfurt, 1990).

root, *thelgein*),[10] like the *Odyssey* with its theme of the *nostos*—the return narrated by the Ithacan poet and the protagonist himself. 'The gods themselves spun the destruction of peoples,' Alcinous exclaims when Odysseus weeps at Demodocus' accounts of the Trojan disasters, 'for the sake of the singing of men hereafter.' Poetry is born from the spell cast over the listener: it is the aim of destiny and History.

This poetics will later be substantially altered by Pindar, who declaims against the 'prodigies' and 'tales shot through with many-coloured lies' and sustains the value of 'truth', only to return to the *Odyssey*, however, as the one comparable model for his own poetry. In the seventh *Nemean* he suspects that the tale of Odysseus outshines the deeds it narrates on account of Homer's 'sweet singing'. The *mythoi* of art bewitch and cheat, Pindar insists; yet Homer's (and therefore Odysseus') 'lies' and 'winged cunning' contain a special *semnon*—something sacred, august, venerable, and majestic. It is this that Werther and Goethe are to admire, and what Benjamin, in our own century, calls 'aura'.[11]

For ancient and classical Greece Ulysses constitutes the supreme and unified model of episteme and poetry. The cultural context of a distant era finds a poetic text to mirror it: a text which, itself the product of wonder, produces fascination and silence. Our path moves between these two extremes, and here we encounter our guiding element: wonder, which unites poetry, philosophy, and science, and links the ancient Ulysses with the modern. 'Of poetry wonder must be the end,' states the Baroque poet Marino, echoing a doctrine common to all eras. For Plato and Aristotle, wonder was the original and perennial source of the love of knowledge (of philo-sophia), because humankind is fascinated by circumambient phenomena, finds itself plunged into uncertainty and ignorance, and therefore philosophizes, in the search for causes and principles (the modern age extends the definition to include science).

---

[10] P. Pucci, *Odysseus Polutropos* (Ithaca and London, 1987), 191–213. On enchantment and the 'terror of fables', see R. Calasso, now in his *I quarantanove gradini* (Milan, 1991), 487–97.
[11] On Pindar, see C. Segal, *Pindar's Mythmaking* (Princeton, NJ, 1986). On 'aura', see W. Benjamin, 'Das Kunstwerk im Zeitalter seiner technischen Reproduzierbarkeit', in *Schriften*, vol. i, (Frankfurt, 1955), 372–3, 461.

But wonder is also the beginning of poetry. The lover of legend, myth, and story-telling (the *philomythos*), Aristotle states in the *Metaphysics*, with a dig at Plato, 'is in some sense a lover of true knowledge (*philosophos*), myth comprising things of wonder'. One of Aristotle's medieval commentators, Thomas Aquinas, goes further. A great architect of the scholastic episteme, Aquinas inverts the sequence and has Aristotle say that 'the philosopher is in some sense a *philomythes*, a lover of fabulous myth: a quality proper to poets'. The philosopher is compared with the poet, he goes on, since 'both are concerned with things of wonder'.

We could summarize as follows: *en arkhe*, in the beginning was (and is) wonder, the source of *logos* and *mythos*. What unites philosophy, science, and poetry is the desire which human beings as such, by nature, have to know. Dante, poet-philosopher and inventor of one of the most memorable Ulysses myths, gave voice to this impulse with extraordinary force. In the *Convivio* he gives the blueprint for what is almost a medieval theory of the sublime:

Ché lo stupore è uno stordimento d'animo per grandi e maravigliose cose vedere o udire o per alcuno modo sentire: che, in quanto paiono grandi, fanno reverente a sé quelli che le sente: in quanto paiono mirabili, fanno voglioso di sapere di quelle.

For awe is a certain bewilderment of the mind at seeing great and wonderful things, or feeling them in some way. These, in so far as they are great, make him who feels them reverent towards them; in so far as they appear wonderful, they make him who feels them desirous of knowing them.[12]

This 'voglia' Dante speaks of seems to me the only state of mind uniting the inhabitants of his Limbo (who live, like us Moderns, 'sanza speme in disio', without hope in desire) with the ardour of his Ulysses, condemned to Hell, the 'desio' which 'bends' both Dante and the reader to listen to Ulysses, and the desire for truth which moves humankind towards Heaven.[13] Our journey in the present work, as Chapters 2 and 8 will make clear, is between these cardinal points.

The vision of wonder outlined above is the basis for the entire

---

[12] *Convivio*, IV. xxv. 5; trans. W. W. Jackson, *Dante's Convivio* (Oxford, 1909).

[13] On this problem see F. Ferrucci, *Il poema del desiderio: Poetica e passione in Dante* (Milan, 1990).

book: wonder permeates the verses of Homer, Tasso, and Leopardi, the diaries of Columbus and Darwin, and the novels of Conrad; it is the main characteristic of Ulysses as 'figure'; it is our only access, as children of the age of anxiety and poverty, to poetry and a knowledge of both the past and our own age: it is the only possible key to a reading of modernity in alterity, and vice-versa.

Naturally, the wonder which emerges through the following pages has its darker side. From the start, as we have just seen, it rubs shoulders with spells and incantations; when Ulysses meets it, it often becomes perplexity, horror, comic stupor, or terrified perturbation—the reaction produced by what Freud calls *das Unheimliche*, the uncanny and the 'disturbing'. Desire is not always joy: it can also be tension, suffering, division, and an awareness of the absurd; and when desire contains no vital impulse the human recipient is stultified and consumed by boredom. In brief, the wonderful landscapes of Goethe and the *Odyssey* also have their areas of shadow.

Any critical study of myth, poetry, and history—of the wonders and horrors we encounter—can only evolve in the awareness that we ourselves are shadows. Ulysses' journey through time and literature is a journey, like that of our own existence, towards Hades: from being to non-being, from this world to the next, from life to death. This is his endless voyaging, at the end of which he finds himself on the threshold between the two continents. On the plane of becoming, light does of course re-enter the tale, only to become shadow in the imagination: the light of the journey of life towards the Earthly Paradise, towards the New World which appears increasingly 'other'—the movement of history which is forever darkening and breaking off. Ulysses is suspended on the *limen* which unites and divides the eras: on the Conradian shadow-line which is our ontological and historical horizon.

Poetry and history meet in the existential shade. This dark cone helps us to understand and go beyond the Aristotelian distinction between history as an exposition of real facts within the 'particular', and poetry as an account of possible events within the 'universal'. Poetry, Aristotle states, 'is at once more philosophical and more serious than history'. Positing a category of the 'imaginary' is not sufficient to establish a link which will maintain the universal value of the one without losing the particularity of the other; a more organic, more 'intimate and tender' connection is needed: hence the present study's concept of 'shadow', in its 'figural' meaning.

In a celebrated essay Erich Auerbach demonstrates how the Christian and medieval vision of history, the arts, and interpretation is dominated by the concept of *figura*, or *umbra*. An Old Testament character or event 'prefigures' and prophesies a character or event in the New: Jonah's three days in the belly of the whale 'anticipates' Christ's three days in the tomb. Jonah is a figure or *typos* of Christ; Christ 'fulfils' Jonah, as it were:

> Figural interpretation establishes a connection between two events or persons, the first of which signifies not only itself but also the second, while the second encompasses or fulfils the first. The two poles of the figure are separate in time, but both, being real events or figures, are within time, within the stream of historical life. Only the understanding of the two persons or events is a spiritual act, but this spiritual act deals with concrete events whether past, present, or future, and not with concepts or abstractions.[14]

This prophetic concept of history also permeates the art and literature of the Middle Ages, the Renaissance, and the Reformation. In the *Divine Comedy*, the character Virgil 'fulfils' the Virgil of history as Dante knew him. Christopher Columbus sees his own exploits as the fulfilment of the words of Isaiah. The Puritans fulfil the prophecy of the New Jerusalem by founding the Holy City in America.

Might it not be possible to read myth, poetry, and history in the same way, reaching the imaginary of the past through its own categories, and extending it where necessary to take the modern vision of the world into account? Ulysses becomes just such a figure (Auerbach's definition neatly complements Frege's): a mythical and literary character whom commentators, poets, and historians read rhetorically and prophetically as a *typos*—a shadow which is transformed and extends over the Western imagination. To adapt Beatrice's words in *Paradiso* XXX, Ulysses is the 'shadowy forecast' of poetic truth and historical reality, in which he is then incarnated, marking all its crucial moments, its 'crises'.

The present study returns continuously to the interrelations between myth, poetry, and history, and between rhetoric and the

---

[14] E. Auerbach, 'Figura', in his *Scenes from the Drama of European Literature* (Manchester, 1984), 53. For another type of shadow, which borders on the 'other', see M. Trevi and A. Romano, *Studi sull'ombra* (2nd edn., Venice, 1990).

imaginary.[15] Each chapter has a section on the existential dimension of the shadow, and one on the figural, where a mythologico-historico-literary 'intertext' is created. The intention is not to trace exhaustive or conclusive correspondences, but to arouse interest (or wonder) in the readers, stimulating personal reflection and nudging them gently towards the recognition that the 'pleasures of reading' [16] are many, and that there may exist such a thing as a poetry of history.

Born out of the 'secret' contained 'in the word', and out of our desire to understand the mystery of the text, interpretation has made a shade of Ulysses.[17] Even in the *Odyssey* he is, as Werther observes, *geheimnisvoll*—full of the arcane. What on earth does Tiresias mean when, predicting for him a calm death in 'splendid old age', he adds that it will arrive 'ex halos': 'out of the sea' or 'far from the sea'? Why are the Sirens introduced as fascinating creatures who, according to Circe, are at the same time surrounded by images of death which Ulysses will fail to see? Homer's poem is prodigal with 'excessive' and contradictory information, raising questions it refuses to answer—excesses and gaps which creative and philosophical interpretation rushes to explain and fill. The Roman and Dantean Ulysses attempt to give different answers to the questions raised by Homer; the Renaissance Ulysses interprets Dante's; Baudelaire's traveller 'reads' Homer, Dante, and Columbus. Each text contains a mystery, and each poem is the interpretation of another poem in the light of history and existence.

Interpretation is the reader's central problem, hence the emphasis on it in the present study. Interpretation is both 'infinite' and 'limited'.[18] It grows with the understanding each individual acquires in life and letters, meditating—in a process of re-cognition—on that individual's desire within his or her own

---

[15] On myth and literature, see F. Ferrucci's discussion, 'Il mito', in *Letteratura italiana*, gen. ed. A. Asor Rosa, vol. v (Turin, 1986), 513–49. Ferrucci creates and destroys myth in his beautiful novel *Il mondo creato* (Milan, 1986), where God himself vainly attempts to explain to Dante that Ulysses represented man in his highest values. In the following chapter God takes part in Columbus's expedition. See also F. Ferrucci, *L'assedio e il ritorno* (2nd edn., Milan, 1991).

[16] R. Alter, *The Pleasures of Reading in an Ideological Age* (New York, 1989).

[17] F. Kermode, *The Genesis of Secrecy* (Cambridge, Mass. and London, 1979). My discussion also owes something to H. R. Jauss, *Question and Answer* (Minneapolis, 1989).

[18] P. C. Bori, *L'interpretazione infinita* (Bologna, 1987); U. Eco, *I limiti dell'interpretazione* (Milan, 1990). See also the essays by C. Segre and R. Antonelli in vol. iv of *Letteratura italiana*, gen. ed. A. Asor Rosa (Turin, 1985).

conscience. Since this growth is potentially infinite in the life of the individual and in humanity's life within history, interpretation also, potentially, has no end. It has limits, however: in the text and in its linguistic texture, in the surrounding context, and in the *intentio operis*. One of my possible conclusions will be the silence of interpretation, although four other possibilities, given the infinite potential of reading, are also suggested: laughter, horror, words, and enigma.

The text is readable, knowable, and enjoyable: it is also divided and in the final analysis ineffable. The present study takes a series of such texts, in the hope that they will at least give pleasure and provoke disquiet. 'A reader is no different from Ulysses, who descends to Hades and offers blood or, to speak non-metaphorically, a part of his vital essence to the ghosts, the characters met face to face in the very act of reception.'[19] Thus a reader is, as we shall see in Chapter 5, fundamentally restless. Anyone proposing such a descent, and intending to act as guide—the critic or commentator— is in the exact position of Dante's Virgil: not an 'omo certo' but a feeble shadow. No certainty is guaranteed, beyond critical 'imperfection' and a bewildering search within the realm of the human. The critic is guided by one hope: that the reader will understand— as Statius tells Virgil in Dante's *Purgatorio*—the love (or desire) that informs us all 'when [we] forget our emptiness and treat shades as solid things'.

---

[19] E. Raimondi, *Ermeneutica e commento* (Florence, 1990), 48.

1. Shadows: Figuralism and Prophecy

And the sun set, and all the journeying-ways were darkened.
The ship made the limit, which is of the deep-running Ocean.

I WOULD like to start with two 'substantial' shadows. One emerges from Ulysses' story of his adventures during his ten years' return from Troy to Ithaca, recounted in the *Odyssey*: the shadow of the journey to Hades and death. The other is the shadow which seeps quietly out of the myth, covering the whole of our culture: the Ulysses who is reincarnated, in different forms and bearing different values, in poetry and history through the centuries, from Homer to the present day. This constant presence and its continuing hold over the imagination are signs that it represents our destiny as human beings.

The two dark shapes meet continuously on the horizon of this destiny, as if moving along a perennial shadow-line. The literary tradition and the hereafter, poetry and death, are superimposed, interconnected, and revealed each as the extreme aspect of the other. We can begin with a passage which, belonging both to the beginning and almost the end of the present account, to the most remote and simultaneously the most immediate past, to Homeric antiquity and to the twentieth century, is a direct testimony to the continual meeting of the two shadows in poetry and in time:

> And then went the ship,
> Set keel to breakers, forth on the godly sea, and
> We set up mast and sail on that swart ship,
> Bore sheep aboard her, and winds from sternward
> Bore us out onward with bellying canvas,
> Circe's this craft, the trimcoifed goddess.
> Then sat we amidships, wind jamming the tiller,
> Thus with stretched sail, we went over sea till day's end.
> Sun to his slumber, shadows o'er all the ocean,
> Came we then to the bounds of deepest water,
> To the Kimmerian lands, and peopled cities
> Covered with close-webbed mist, unpierced ever
> With glitter of sun-rays

Nor with stars stretched, nor looking back from heaven
Swartest night stretched over wretched men there.
The ocean flowing backward, came we then to the place
Aforesaid by Circe.

The reader will recognize these as the first lines of Canto XI of the *Odyssey*, narrating the hero's journey to the threshold of Hades and then the *nekyia*, the evocation of the dead. A number of particulars deserve our attention. Odysseus departs from Circe's shores and sails westwards until, as the original puts it, the sun sets and the ways are plunged into shadow. He then reaches the 'limits of the Ocean'; a thick fog and black night reign over the land of the Cimmerians. In Greek *zophos*, significantly, means both 'west' and 'darkness'. Immediately afterwards Odysseus follows the course of the ocean and reaches the gates of Hades. He later turns back and sails north-east, thereby completing within just one day what has been called 'a mythical, clockwise circumnavigation'. On his outward journey he is directed towards the 'confines of the cosmic dominion of life and death'.[1] In the *Iliad* (xiv. 201), the ocean is called *theon genesis*, the origin of the gods; hence, moving towards its outmost limits and sailing on this immense river which surrounds the earth, Odysseus sets sail towards the beginning of the cosmos: towards the confine between being and non-being. There, on Montale's 'opposite bank', he finds Hades, inhabited by the *psykhai*, those shades, those breaths without nerves, 'breaths without matter or voice betrayed by darkness'[2] which are the dead; from their apppearance and the words they pronounce he discovers 'das Sein des Gewesenen':[3] the being of having been, a shadowy essence, a 'being-in-death' and 'being-in-the-past' which differs from our mortal passage, and is blind, deaf, and mute towards it, until the smoking blood of the victims restores memory, eyes to recognize, language, and infinite sadness.

This, then, is our first shadow: a journey, precisely, 'per umbram ad umbras', towards the realm of myth, but open towards the horizon of our mortal existence, our death; a journey westwards, towards the sunset. When celebrating Theron in the third

[1] This and the preceding quotation are from A. Heubeck, in *Odissea*, vol. iii (Milan, 1983), 259–64.

[2] E. Montale, 'I morti', in *Ossi di seppia: L'Opera in versi*, ed. R. Bettarini and G. Contini (Turin, 1980), 93–4.

[3] W. Otto, *Theophania* (Frankfurt, 1975), 52.

Olympian, Pindar states that the name of the tyrant of Agrigento, the winner of the race, has reached the *eskhatia*, the margin or limit, covering the distance 'from his home to the Pillars of Herakles'. 'All that is beyond', Pindar comments 'neither the ignorant nor the wise may cover'. In the fourth *Nemean* this is reiterated: 'No man may pass to that *zophos*—the darkness of the west—which lies beyond Gadeira.' Metaphorically, then, in the 'discourse of myth',[4] to sail beyond Gibraltar means passing an ontological threshold and passing the limit assigned to humankind, towards a transnatural darkness. The limits to knowledge and life, the two trees forbidden to humanity at the entrance to the Garden of Eden, to the east, are thus immediately established. It is hardly surprising, in a civilization based on the sea, that it is again the metaphor of navigation which represents, in the mouth of Pindar himself in the third *Nemean*, the divine prescription:

> To travel further is not easy
> Over the untrodden sea beyond the Pillars of Herakles.
> Them the god-hero placed to witness to all
> Of the limit of sailing.
> He broke monstrous beasts in the sea
> And alone tracked the currents in the shallows
> Till he came to the bounds which send men home,
> And made the earth known.[5]

Knowledge of the world has very precise 'nautical' confines which coincide with the 'limit' posed by the well-known witness of the Pillars, 'markers' placed by Heracles 'beyond which men may not trespass'. Here lies the extreme boundary 'which sends men home', the 'end of the return'. Yet myth—and poetry—are unequivocal: Odysseus, hero *par excellence* of the *nostos*, the return which turns upon itself like a symbolic labyrinth,[6] sailed beyond this final bourn, towards darkness. From this shadow he then returned, alive, to the world of the living, to tell Alcinous of the dead 'expertly, as a singer would do'.

Even then, however, through the Phaeacians' long, unsleeping night, the *mythos*—the marvellous tale caught in the second in which it turns into myth before our very 'ears'—fails to remove the

---

[4] P. H. Damon, 'Dante's Ulysses and the Mythic Tradition', in W. Matthews (ed.), *Medieval Secular Literature: Four Essays* (Berkeley and Los Angeles, 1965), 25–45.

[5] Trans. C. M. Bowra, *The Odes of Pindar* (Harmondsworth, 1969).

[6] G. Chiarini, *Odisseo: Il labirinto marino* (Rome, 1991), 67–101.

shadow from Odysseus' account; it deepens in memory, presenting it in a blinding, spell-binding light. The 'sound sense' of the hero (and of the poet), in giving form to the narration, immediately follows up the journey to Hades with another, more disquieting breath from the tomb: the Sirens who, reclining in the meadow, prevent the return of all who listen to their 'clear song'. They are announced by a total, breathless calm and divinely stilled waves; in this absolute if momentary immobilizing of time and space, in the total silence imposed on the world of mortals by the wax poured into his companions' ears, the honeyed sounds from their mouths offer Odysseus, tied to the mast, pleasure and wisdom; they promise the song of the Trojan disasters and a knowledge of all 'that occurs on the fertile earth'. They are surrounded, however, as Circe had warned, by 'a heap of the bones of rotting men, with shrivelled skin'.

This, then, constitutes the largest, densest, and most paradoxical shadow Odysseus has so far faced. Like Demodocus, King Alcinous' poet, whose account of the quarrel between Odysseus and Achilles and of the wooden horse moved Odysseus to tears, the Sirens sing of him and of his own past; like the Muses of the *Iliad* and of Hesiod, they are all-knowing. Poetry is the tenacious memory of oneself and the world: individual and universal knowledge. This is why it seduces, coming to us in silence, in solitude, when sea and sky are suspended in a dead calm, in a heaven-sent vigil imposed by the divine 'demon'.[7]

We have, however, been warned: inside the glance which, in poetry, we turn in upon ourselves, inside the knowledge poetry offers, sits death, the ultimate truth, 'what's bred in the bone'. The final sleep is glimpsed, like a veiled face, in the stilled waves; poetry breathes from the threshold, a frail and dangerous bridge between the two sides. Anyone who, unknowing, listens to its voice and 'draws near', as Circe puts it, can never return, like the traveller venturing beyond the Pillars of Hercules: 'that man | . . . has no prospect of coming home and delighting | his wife and little children as they stand about him in greeting'. He remains 'enchanted', the desire for knowledge leaving him as good as dead to all domestic affections. This is the message the apparently limpid

---

[7] See G. Steiner, *Real Presences* (London and Boston, 1989), 137–232, esp. pp. 197–8.

Homer leaves for posterity and which, through the following pages, we would do well to bear in mind.

We should equally remember the other aspect of the image: in spite of everything, Ulysses *wants* to hear, be seduced, and listen to the voice of beauty and death while still alive. Unharmed, without a glimpse of putrefying flesh, he moves beyond poetry; providentially bound fast, he sails beyond the 'binding' singers and abandons the 'virgin daughters of the chthonic world', as Euripides calls them; he continues on his way, wandering for years through the lands of the fantastic, but obstinately bent on home, life, and reality.

Nor, lastly, should we ignore the final shadow the episode casts in our direction—the enigma and division it opens up on the future. Precisely what Odysseus learns from the Sirens, the actual text, secret in its concise clarity, never tells us, throwing a veil over its revelation and forcing us and centuries of hermeneutics to interpret it in varying degrees of allegory, just as I myself, in a sense, have done in the last few paragraphs. Who exactly are the Sirens? Obscure beings of the subterranean world, as Plato has it in the *Cratilus*? Or, as he proposes in the *Republic* with exemplary sublimation and implicit self-deconstruction, celestial beings who intone the music of the spheres in the world of the future—hence, for a later period, 'angels'? Symbols of earthly desire and the pleasure of the senses, courtesans or prostitutes, as Hellenism believed, or icons of knowledge like the *doctae sirenes* Ovid celebrates? And what were the Septuagint translators of the Bible thinking of when, in one of Job's most terrible lamentations, they had him say 'seirenes' instead of 'jackals', so that his invective against God reads: 'I am a brother to sirens and a companion to ostriches. My skin is black upon me, and my bones are burned with heat'? Were they connecting Homer's enchantresses with the mounds of bones surrounding them? Even Jerome, who in the Vulgate always avoids the word, puts into Isaiah's mouth, in a fit of Judaeo-Greek syncretic exoticism, an oracle on Babylon according to which the wretched city will be inhabited by dragons, ostriches, and 'pilosi' (possibly satyrs), and all its 'houses of pleasure' by sirens!

We here face another shadow, born out of the deepest Homeric darkness, which shrouds interpretation in questions and lengthens over the narratives of future centuries. I shall come back to this shortly. For the moment I want to look at another sort of projection, related to hermeneutics but more specifically literary. The passage I quoted at the beginning is not simply the opening of Canto XI of Homer's *Odyssey* but also a (subtly perverse) English translation, filtered through the sixteenth-century Latin of Andreas Divus and modelled on the rhythm of a twentieth-century version of the old English poem *The Seafarer*. With this 'translation' Ezra Pound, a figure so central to modernity, begins his most ambitious work, *The Cantos*. The most abstruse, exciting, and magmatic 'epic' poem of our century begins with the journey to Hades. The shadow of death, then, not only returns but is a prelude to all the events narrated in the poem, as if all exploration had to be based on a knowledge of the last world.

What Pound does is also significant as a passage from Homer reprocessed through reworkings of successive periods, like a concretion of literary sediment or the literary shadow—the shadow of a shadow—which Canto XI of the *Odyssey* projects through time to 1923–30. It indicates a tradition which is still vital, and an interconnection between literature, death, and life which is so profound that Western poetry has accepted it as inevitable.

The heart of the shadow has an even darker core. Beginning *The Cantos* with the *nekyia*, Pound puts between himself and Homer not just Andreas Divus and *The Seafarer*, but above all Dante, whose *Inferno* is, obviously, the account of a descent into the lowest depths of Hades, and whose whole *Commedia* is an evocation of the hereafter: the description, as the Letter to Cangrande states regarding the literal meaning of the poem, of the 'status animarum *post mortem*'. Pound will in fact return to Dante later on, recalling the 'whirlpool' of his Ulysses in Canto XX and, when speaking of the circumnavigation of Africa by the Carthaginian Hanno, the Pillars of Hercules in Canto XL.

We can now take one step back. Tiresias' prophecy in Canto XI of the *Odyssey* should ideally be placed between the beginning of the same Canto and the *Divine Comedy*,[8] its importance being such that Penelope makes Odysseus repeat it (Canto XXIII) at the crucial moment when, after twenty years of separation and

[8] D. Thompson, *Dante's Epic Journeys* (Baltimore and London, 1974); E. Bloch, 'Odysseus Did Not Die in Ithaca', in G. Steiner and R. Fagles (eds.), *Homer* (Englewood Cliffs, NJ, 1962), 81–5; R. Calasso, *Le nozze di Cadmo e Armonia* (Milan, 1988), 389–417.

abstinence, husband and wife finally head for the bed made from the olive-tree. The gist, readers will remember, is as follows: after his return to Ithaca and his revenge against the suitors, Odysseus will have to face, as he himself tells Penelope, 'an unmeasured, long, laborious trial', setting out for a final journey and carrying an oar on his back; he must continue his journey until he reaches a land where the inhabitants know neither salted food, nor the sea, nor oars, 'which act for ships as wings do'. He will recognize the place by a 'very clear sign' because another wayfarer (*allos hodites*) will take this for a winnowing-fan—an agricultural implement. He must then offer suitable sacrifices to placate Poseidon's wrath definitively, this ensuring that death will come *ex halos*, 'in the ebbing time of a sleek old age'.

We know that, from antiquity on, the Greek expression *ex halos* has given rise to a series of conjectures as to Odysseus' death, since its prophetic ambiguity indicates both 'outside, far from the sea' and 'out of the sea', thus prefiguring either a peaceful passing away in old age, or the death by water of an old man. Now, this 'excess of information' (Tiresias has no need to specify where Odysseus' death will come from), with the 'conditional' quality of the prophecy—what one critic has called its 'degree zero'[9]—open up a chasm of secrecy which readers of successive ages, whether poets or commentators, have tried to fill with new stories or what in a biblical Hebrew context would be called *midrash*: an unending interpretative-creative reading.

So it is that, from Eugamnon's *Telegony* to Dictys, Servius, and others up until Eustathius in the twelfth century of our own era, Odysseus dies many and various deaths *ex halos*. At the same time, in keeping with the prophecy of the last, long, mysterious voyage, Odysseus' wanderings about the globe extend continuously. Some, like Theopompus, send him to Etruria; others, like Solinus, maintain he founded Lisbon (Ulixabona); Tacitus has it that Ulysses sailed in the Atlantic and founded Asberg, in Germany; Strabo thinks it appropriate that 'the adventures narrated about him should be placed beyond the Pillars of Hercules, in the Atlantic'. Lastly, he becomes the traveller *par excellence*: the proverbial wanderer whose destinations are increasingly surrounded

---

[9] J. Peradotto, 'Prophecy Degree Zero: Tiresias and the End of the *Odyssey*', in B. Gentili and G. Paioni (eds.) *Oralità: Cultura, Letteratura, Discorso* (Rome, 1985), 429–59.

by uncertainty, to the limits of the great, greatly desired and greatly feared unknown. Seneca rather rhetorically asks whether Ulysses journeyed 'beyond the world known to us'. As a titbit for his *Attic Nights*, a learned friend of Aulus Gellius gives him an exhaustively erudite book he had composed of 'mera miracula', a list of curiosities and wonders including the question whether Ulysses had travelled over the 'internal sea', as Aristarchus would have it, or the 'external' one, as Crates insists.[10]

The shadow swiftly returns. Beside the entrance to the Portico of the Cnidians, in the Sanctuary to Apollo in Delphi, the celebrated Polignotus, in the fifth century BC, painted two scenes: on the right, the conquest of Troy and the departure of the Greeks, and on the left the *nekyia*. In the mysterious *Alexandra*, the even more mysterious Lycophron states that 'after suffering such hardship, Odysseus returns to *Hades* (from which there is no return) never having enjoyed one peaceful day in his whole life'.[11] The centre of the circle Odysseus described in twenty years of war and exploits was Ithaca; at the centre of the circle of the second half of his life lies the world of the dead. 'Circular' Odysseus is becoming a 'linear' Ulysses, whose definitive *telos* is Hades.

All this, note, is going on in a period, between Hellenism and the full splendour of the Roman Empire, in which the figure of Odysseus-Ulysses is undergoing a number of allegorical inter-pretations centring, possibly on account of archaic links with Athene and Apollo, on an emblem of patience, virtue, political wisdom, eloquence, reflectiveness, action, and 'theoretical curi-osity', of knowledge and research—the model or *Vorbild* of man, 'new' in Homeric terms, 'European' in hindsight, and 'Graeco-Roman' in classical terms, consecrated at the highest level, in Tiberius' admirable 'Odyssey' sculptured in a grotto in Sperlonga.[12] Tiberius was obsessed with the Ulysses myth; Suetonius tells how he would quiz grammarians as to what the Sirens usually sang, a

---

[10] For references in the above paragraph see W. B. Stanford, *The Ulysses Theme* (2nd edn., Ann Arbor, Mich., 1968), 154, 87–8, 258 nn. 16 and 17. For further evidence, see now M. Corti, *Percorsi dell'invenzione* (Turin, 1993), 114–24.

[11] Lycophron, *Alexandra*, 812–14.

[12] B. Andreae, *Odysseus: Archäologie des europäischen Menschenbildes*. For the other references see also P. Faure, *Ulysse, le Cretois (XIIIe Siècle avant J.C.)* (Paris, 1980), chs. 6 and 7; and for 'theoretical curiosity', H. Blumenberg, *Der Prozess der theoretischen Neugierde* (Frankfurt, 1973), 68–9 and nn.

question later picked up by Sir Thomas Browne (and Edgar Allan Poe) as an example of delighted humanity's potential for conjecture.

This constitutes a central, significant meeting-point between poetry, myth, philosophy, hermeneutics, the ethos of an entire civilization, and power. It is even more significant if one considers that the various traditions surrounding Odysseus' travels mentioned so far—oblique and resistant germinations of the wanderings which fill Books IX–XII of the *Odyssey*, for which Tiresias' prophecy provides fertile and boundless soil—are beginning to interweave at a time when geographical exploration is increasing together with the store of knowledge as evidenced in the work of Strabo, Pliny, Ptolemy, and others.

History and myth, as we shall continue to see, meet at decisive points in human affairs, and pose the problem of their reciprocal relations with some urgency. As readers of these real and imaginary events, it is our duty at least to ask, if we cannot answer, what, for example, a Pliny would make of Hercules' 'markers', since he certainly knew about the Carthaginian Hanno's circumnavigation of Africa, about the Canaries, and about the Roman expedition on Atlas; or how a Seneca would have reacted to Homer's prophecy of a land without knowledge of ships and the sea, having himself recounted, in the *Naturales Quaestiones*, of the expedition commissioned by Nero to find the sources of the Nile. These are not idle questions: they help keep the echo of Tiresias' prophecy alive, and remind us how much it says and fails to say—in short, they make us experience poetry in history.

The post-Homeric traditions mentioned briefly above quite explicitly represent a written, post-oral tradition (the example of Aulus Gellius is significant here). If we wished to consider them, as Hans Blumenberg does with the 'stock of myths' 'optimized' by the cumulative elaboration of story-tellers and listeners, as the results of a process of natural selection in what he calls a 'Darwinism of words',[13] we should imagine them as excessive growths of a species at a given stage of natural history. The many versions of Odysseus' death bequeathed us by antiquity would then appear to modern observers like the fossils of the innumerable dinosaurs which walked the earth at that time. With the end of antiquity a new ice-

---

[13] H. Blumenberg, *Work on Myth*, trans. R. M. Wallace (Cambridge, Mass. and London, 1985), 164–72.

age, a spectacular drought, or a vast earthquake (metaphor apart, the dark centuries of the incipient Middle Ages) wiped them from the face of the earth, leaving only voices, fears—shadows, in fact—which will obsess the successive age.

Tiresias' prophecy in *Odyssey* XI seems to me to contain both the impulse for future growth and the germ of the final selection. A closer look reveals a number of curious points. First: in Tiresias' words, in the future of the final voyage, Odysseus, the No-body of Canto IX, appears as an unknown and unrecognized wayfarer—a *hodites* whose identity is of no relevance—and at the same time as the representative of a whole civilization, based on ships and the sea. What happens to him is what Tiresias described of his own encounter with the wayfarer and the resulting misunderstanding, in which non-recognition acts as a 'most clear sign' of recognition. By depriving him, however momentarily, of his name and personal 'history' in the poem, while maintaining and emphasizing his rôle as traveller and universalizing its significance, Homer opens the way for future semiotizations of Odysseus. He makes him into a sign which is able to receive a signified whenever it meets a signifier. Future eras, as we have seen and shall continue to see, 'recognize' themselves in that sign, attributing to it the meaning of their own moment in history—their own   *kairos*—and their own system of values. Odysseus thus becomes the representative of the different civilizations.

Secondly: the oars, the symbols of Homer's sea civilization and of Odysseus' last voyage, are called in a kenning 'wings for ships', a key image which, as we shall see, is to echo resolutely through future ages.

Thirdly, an inevitable question remains to be asked: are we really sure Homer might have conceived of a country where an oar can be mistaken for a winnowing-fan, and where land *Kultur* can survive without sea *civilitas*? To what heart of darkness is he alluding? Is it not, perhaps, the 'other' he is presenting here, while exploding the signs of his own episteme? Is he not shifting Odysseus' final horizon into a hinterland which is so 'hinter' as to be unreachable, and thus prefiguring a never-ending journey?

In other words, I propose a triple reading of the text: as the beginning of the mystery concerning Odysseus' final voyage, generating new narratives on the theme (and thus a 'genesis of secrecy' of the kind so entrancingly theorized and described by

Kermode),[14] and at the same time as the *typos* or *figura* of subsequent texts, and thus a pre-figuration in the ancient Christian and Auerbachian sense of the term, as a character or episode in the Old Testament which 'announces' and is 'fulfilled' ('so that the Scriptures may be fulfilled') by another character or episode in the New.[15] However—and this is my third reading—these subsequent texts *fulfil* Homer's text at the crucial junctures, the critical moments of history.

If, then, as Harold Fisch says, myths are subject to change under the pressure of history,[16] I would suggest that literature too, by anticipating circumstances, 'foretells' them and shapes that 'imaginaire' which in turn conditions events in actual history. In this sense it is perfectly correct to speak of the intersection of word and world at turning-points in time; of the past which 'remembers' the future, of poetry which adapts to future events and contributes to their form and meaning, transmitting the memory of them after their enaction. By borrowing the medieval and Renaissance view of history, and the rhetoric which was an integral part of their mind-set, we can go beyond the merely rhetorical value historicism attributes to poetry and restore its rightful place in history. At the same time it becomes possible to appreciate the 'poetry of history', and look beyond the Aristotelian distinction between *historia* as an exposition of facts from the point of view of the 'particular', and *poiesis* as the 'more serious and philosophical', because more 'universal', account of events which could happen and which are possible within the logic of the probable and the necessary.

For an example we can go back to our specific *mythos*. In the following chapters I shall use it in the way I have just described, but let me immediately sketch in the two main directions I shall follow. The 'excess' provided by Homer, the gap left empty in the *Odyssey*, can be filled by opposite oscillations. There are two possible aims or 'ends' to Odysseus' journey, both anticipated in antiquity. One is Lykophron's, which is the 'other' world *par excellence*: Hades, the reign of death. The second contains a gleam of hope. Various Roman writers, as noted above, ask themselves whether Ulysses

---

[14] F. Kermode, *The Genesis of Secrecy* (Cambridge, Mass. and London, 1979).

[15] E. Auerbach, 'Figura', in his *Scenes from the Drama of European Literature* (Manchester, 1984).

[16] H. Fisch, *A Remembered Future: A Study in Literary Mythology* (Bloomington, Ind., 1984). I am indebted to the whole of Fisch's book.

travelled within the confines of the known world or beyond. Tibullus, who mentions both possibilities, expresses the second in what to me seem emblematic terms: 'legend', he writes, may have placed his journeys within a 'novus orbis'—another, *new* world.[17] In actual fact, both in history and in poetry, Ulysses is to move continuously between the two worlds, the other and the new. At an existential level he will pass the ontological limits of the Pillars and head towards our common destiny; a transgressor of being, he will move tragically towards non-being. At a figural and historical level, at the opportune moment Ulysses will set sail, with a host of modern navigators, towards the New World.

These, however, are the limits of the pendulum swing. The 'other' and the 'new' are too close not to touch and produce ambiguity, superimpositions, contradictions, and shadow-lines. The other world can also be that of eternal life after death: the Elysian Fields, or the nostalgically dreamt-of Eden. The new world will possess a profoundly existential dimension, an America of life and the spirit, a Paradise which, being literally Earthly, will excite extraordinary enthusiasm in the individual and collective European breast.

To conclude this chapter and anticipate the next, we shall now follow our hero on his existential path towards the other world of death. In his important *Work on Myth*, Hans Blumenberg takes Odysseus' mythical quality to lie not only in the fact that 'his return to his native place is a movement of the restoration of meaning', but also in the particular achievement of the *nostos*, against 'the most incredible resistances, and indeed not only those of external adversities but also those of internal diversion and silencing of all motivations'. Attempting an explanation for Odysseus' transformation into Ulysses, Blumenberg maintains that, as the 'figure of suffering that culminates in success', Odysseus is exposed 'to criticism and correction, first by the Platonists, then also by Dante, and most of all by the modern despisers of the "happy ending" as a symptom of a possibly "whole" world'.[18]

His reconstruction of this process of 'criticism', which is obviously somewhat different from the process of prefiguration and

[17] *Panegiricum Messallae*, 79–81.
[18] Blumenberg, *Work on Myth*, 75–6. See also his *Prozess der theoretischen Neugierde*, 85–9.

fulfilment proposed above, is based on the Stoics' allegorical interpretation of the myth, and Plotinus' 'violence' to Homer's text in his montage of the *Iliad* and the *Odyssey*. In the *Enneads* Circe and Calypso represent the world of the senses in which Odysseus 'is not content to linger' and from which he cries out all his desire to 'flee to the beloved fatherland'. 'The fatherland to us', Plotinus states, 'is there whence we have come.' In other words, Odysseus is no longer simply returning to Ithaca and his family, but to his eternal Father.

In indicating the general drift of the mythological discourse on Odysseus in ancient philosophy, Blumenberg moves in a linear fashion which necessarily ignores the poetic parentheses and overlooks Tiresias' prophecy and all its consequences. But he also ignores a passage in Plato which, within philosophical terms alone, is absolutely crucial to the 'Platonizing' allegorizations. Precisely at the moment when, for the first time, as has often been underlined, philosophy makes a deliberate effort to replace *mythos* with *logos*, Odysseus appears in quite a different light.

At the end of the *Republic* a 'tale' is told which is explicitly and significantly distinguished from Alcinous' *apologues*, the proverbially fantastic stories in Books IX–XII of the *Odyssey*: the famous story of Er. In this complex and enigmatic passage where Plato expounds his views about life after death, punishments, rewards, and the reincarnation of the soul, Odysseus is the last character to appear on stage, almost as if to close the curtain on the immense performance of the *Republic*. With little left to select from, all the other spirits having already taken their pick, his soul has to choose its lot for its next incarnation:

Disenchanted of ambition by the recollection of former toil, his soul searched for a considerable time for the life of a private man devoid of all care. Not without difficulty did he find it, cast aside and neglected by all other souls; but on seeing it he said that he would have done the same had his lot been first instead of last; and with contentment he received it.

I hope I will be forgiven for taking Plato's story somewhat literally and literarily. In this most impure of readings Odysseus chooses, then, the sort of life Achilles' soul, in the *nekyia* of *Odyssey* XI, had said he preferred to reigning over the dead ('I had rather follow the plough as thrall to another man'). He makes, too, what from the context of Book X of the *Republic* must be read as an extreme, but not completely philosophically mistaken choice (Proclus himself praises it as the best).[19] Oppressed by the remembrance of his labours and travels—or, as we can now say twenty-five centuries later, weary of the burden of suffering thrust upon him by generations of poets, readers, and commentators— Odysseus renounces ambition, suffering, and all the trappings of a hero, and opts for the life of a common man. He no longer wishes to be a myth, or even the 'new' man proposed by Homer and celebrated by classical culture, but simply an *idiotes*, a private individual. Potentially, typologically, he is already 'everyman', the Leopold Bloom of the future;[20] almost the prototype of anti-myth.

We find our protagonist, then, becoming another figure, the *typos* of future characters: surfacing from the great sea of *mythos* up into *logos*, but with the language of the former still clinging to him. He is suspended emblematically between life and death, poetry and prose, narrative and interpretation: between two cultures. The poetic model, Homer, has produced a mythical and philosophical type which both colludes and collides with the archetype: Plato undermines the whole epistemic paradigm of the preceding age. We must not forget that this is the only time in antiquity that Odysseus appears, albeit temporarily, as an inhabitant of the 'other' world, a being of death, a shadow. It is this death, and this shadow, which transforms him into a stranger; possibly the unrecognized wayfarer of Tiresias' prophecy.

---

[19] *Commentaire sur la République*, trans. A. J. Festugiere, vol. iii (Paris, 1970), 279–80.

[20] Stanford, *The Ulysses Theme*, 117. Stanford's is the most exhaustive account of the Ulysses theme in Western literature, followed by R. B. Matzig, *Odysseus: Studie zu antiken Stoffen in der modernen Literatur, besonders im Drama* (St Gallen, 1949). See now *Odysseus/Ulysses*, ed. Harold Bloom (New York and Philadelphia, 1991). For further references, see J. Davidson Reid, *The Oxford Guide to Classical Mythology in the Arts, 1300–1990s* (New York–Oxford, 1993), s.v. 'Odysseus', pp. 724–54, especially 752–4.

2. Shipwreck: Interpretation and Alterity

> Tu nota; e sì come da me son porte,
> così queste parole segna a'vivi
> del viver ch'è un correre a la morte.

> Take note, and just as I speak these words to you,
> so should you teach the living
> of life which is a hurtling towards death.

MORE than one thousand, five hundred years separate Dante from Plato, and more than two thousand, probably, from Homer, and we can discount the possibility that he had direct knowledge of either the *Republic* or Canto XI of the *Odyssey*. But it is this world, indicated by Tiresias' prophecy and the myth of Er, which I believe is the best key to an understanding of Dante's Ulysses. I propose to read *Inferno* XXVI within the frame of a *longue-durée* mythical tradition,[1] and to add my first tragic shadow to the many layers already identified in the story, enveloping them all, as it were, in a swathe of darkness.

Let us pause, firstly, to consider the episode as a whole. There is an initial darkening of the scene when Dante and Virgil enter the eighth *bolgia* (xxvi. 25–33):

> Quante il villan ch'al poggio si riposa,
>   nel tempo che colui che 'l mondo schiara
>   la faccia sua a noi tien meno ascosa,
> come la mosca cede a la zanzara,
>   vede lucciole giù per la vallea,
>   forse colà dov'e' vendemmia ed ara;
> di tante fiamme tutta risplendea
>   l'ottava bolgia, sì com'io m'accorsi
>   tosto che fui là 've 'l fondo parea.

As many as the fire-flies which the peasant resting on the hill—in the season when he that lights the world least hides his face from us and at the hour when the fly gives place to the gnat—sees along the valley below, in the fields, perhaps, where he gathers the grapes and tills; with so many

---

[1] P. H. Damon, 'Dante's Ulysses and the Mythic Tradition', in W. Matthews (ed.), *Medieval Secular Literature: Four Essays* (Berkeley and Los Angeles, 1965), 25–45.

flames the eighth ditch was all gleaming, as I perceived as soon as I came where the bottom was in sight.

The splendid simile of the peasant resting on the hill isolates, in a summer-evoking succession of insects, a setting sun and incipient twilight which contrasts and enhances the glow of the flames enveloping and consuming the spirits of the fraudulent counsellors. Darkness pervades Ulysses' story, metaphorically and literally. Having reached the Pillars of Hercules, he and his companions 'turn the stern to morning', i.e. depart at dawn, but also, of course, westward, implicitly turning the prow towards night. From this moment on, the only light which filters into the narrative, through Ulysses' own memory, is that of the moon and stars:

> Tutte le stelle già de l'altro polo
> vedea la notte, e 'l nostro tanto basso,
> che non surgea fuor del marin suolo.
> Cinque volte racceso e tante casso
> lo lume era di sotto da la luna,
> poi che 'ntrati eravam ne l'alto passo . . .
> (xxvi. 27–32)

Night then saw all the stars of the other pole and ours so low that it did not rise from the ocean floor. Five times the light had been rekindled and as often quenched on the moon's under-side since we had entered on the deep passage . . .

The sun must certainly have shone in that part of the world, but no mention is made of it. Ulysses now sails 'di retro al sol', following the sun, and traditional exegesis, from east to west; but he also sails, metaphorically, 'behind' ('di retro') the sun. The boundless 'alto mare aperto' which Ulysses had sailed into through the Mediterranean has now become an ocean of the night.

To understand quite what shores of existence Ulysses is travelling towards, we should now follow up the narrative's metaphorical movement into darkness with some biographical facts. After more than a year near Gaeta, Ulysses leaves Circe (his departure-point has a very particular significance, as we shall see) as it were 'nel mezzo del cammin', in the middle of the way of his life: a married man, with a son and elderly father. When they reach the Pillars, Ulysses and his companions are 'vecchi e tardi', old and slow. The crossing of the western Mediterranean, from Sardinia to 'l'uno e l'altro lido' (the one shore and the other), and 'as far as

Spain, as far as Morocco', beyond Seville on the one hand and
Ceuta on the other, takes him within the space of a few lines from
maturity to old age. In his speech to persuade his men to venture
further, Ulysses underlines this aspect with pathos but not without
ambiguity. After 'a hundred thousand perils', they have reached, he
states, the 'occidente'. This is certainly the geographical west but
also, as Cristoforo Landino had already grasped, the stage of
decline in human life. Ulysses stresses the point; with an expression
which struck Tasso with its evocative power,[2] he calls the present
moment a 'tanto picciola vigilia | d'i nostri sensi ch'è del
rimanente': what is left now is a wake of the senses, a last, brief
flicker of consciousness and life: a 'vigil' of death. To move from
the 'alto mare aperto', the open deep, to the 'foce stretta', the
narrow outlet, means facing the ultimate bottleneck of life, reaching
the supreme threshold between living and dying. 'Foce' is precisely
the word Thomas Aquinas uses in *Paradiso* XIII to describe the
place, the 'harbour' where the 'bark' of human life can unexpectedly
'perish' after a 'straight and swift' navigation across the entire sea.
To enter the outlet is to risk terminal shipwreck.

Dante's Ulysses, then, departs from Circe and sails towards
darkness, the extreme limit of old age, the Ocean, and the
Antipodes. I cannot for one moment believe that Dante was
unaware, far less uncomprehending, of what some of his 'authorities'
spelt out so clearly. To go back a little: in his commentary on *Aeneid*
VI, Servius maintains that Homer 'feigns' that Ulysses, having
abandoned Circe, sailed 'in one night' (and 'night' is particularly
evocative for my reading), arriving 'in extrema Oceani parte'. In the
Fabulae, Hyginus recounts that Ulysses left Circe and travelled
'towards Lake Avernus', 'descending into Hades'. In the *Georgics*,
Virgil describes the southern hemisphere as 'seen' only by the
murky Styx and the 'profundi Manes'; there, he adds, perhaps
'night keeps sempiternal silence, shadows thickening within its
curtain'. Finally, the 'land of darkness' has, ever since Job, been the
land 'of the shadow of death', where 'light is as darkness' and from
which no one is allowed to return.

Dante, of course, is well aware of this; at the beginning of the

---

[2] *Dante con L'Espositioni di Christoforo Landino et d'Alessandro Vellutello*, ed. F.
Sansovino (Venice, 1596), fo. 131; *La Divina Commedia postillata da T. Tasso* (Pisa,
1830), *ad loc.*

Purgatorio (i. 130–2), in a deliberate allusion to his Ulysses, he says he has, with Virgil, reached the 'desert shore'

> che mai non vide navicar sue acque
> omo, che di tornar sia poscia esperto.

that never saw any man sail its waters who afterwards had experience of return.

Ulysses' 'alto passo' corresponds, quite clearly, to the 'passo | che non lasciò già mai persona viva' (the 'pass which never yet let any go alive') which Dante turns to gaze on in *Inferno* I, when, having escaped shipwreck, he finds himself 'on the shore, out of the open sea': not just the 'dark wood' of sin, but also 'that undiscovered country, from whose bourn | No traveller returns'. Lotman's description of Ulysses as 'Dante's original double'[3] is indeed feasible of the Dante who in the *Commedia* embarks on a voyage to the world of the dead.

Several of the 'semiological models' Avalle applies to Ulysses' journey[4] lead to this world, as does the oars–wings kenning Dante inherits from a tradition which is not only Latin but which goes back, as we have seen, to *Odyssey* XI:

> 'de' remi facemmo ali al folle volo'

we made of the oars wings for the mad flight

In short, the 'flying ship', like all human craft on the sea of existence, is headed for the undiscovered shore.[5]

But the point hardly needs labouring. The shadow of death is already there, openly evoked, right at the beginning of the episode. When Virgil nails the 'ancient flame' to a story ('non vi movete', 'do not move on', he commands after an extremely ambiguous *captatio benevolentiae*) the injunction is clear. One of the two spirits must recount 'dove, per lui, perduto, a *morir* gissi'—where, when lost, he went to die. Ulysses' story is dictated by an inexorable narrative *telos* which is also *thanatos*: losing one's way means departing, and departing means death. Not death pure and simple, the mystery

---

[3] J. M. Lotman, *Testo e contesto: Semiotica dell'arte e della cultura* (Bari, 1980), 81–101, at p. 96. And see J. L. Borges, *Nueve ensayos dantescos* (Madrid, 1983), 113–18.
[4] D. S. Avalle, *Modelli semiologici nella Commedia di Dante* (Milan, 1975), 33–63.
[5] See E. Raimondi, *Metafora e storia* (Turin, 1970), 31–7; also J. Freccero, *Dante: The Poetics of Conversion* (Cambridge, Mass. and London, 1986), 15–24, 136–51.

which so many characters in the *Commedia* are given to touch upon, but a journeying, while dying, across the extreme threshold of the 'vigil', over the lost ways of *morir*.

And it means repeating the journey now, in the narrative. We understand why the 'greater horn of the ancient flame' undergoes first and foremost a tragedy of language, and begins to swoon and stammer, as if wearied by the wind. Ulysses' labour here consists in having to transform these lost ways of death into words and narrative; moving the tip of the flame about, 'come fosse la lingua che parlasse', as if it were the tongue that spoke, he is forced to eject his voice, 'gittar voce di fuori', and give painful birth to his own *récit de la fin*. 'The communication | Of the dead is tongued with fire beyond the language of the living', as Eliot puts it in 'Little Gidding', the fourth of the *Quartets*. This, then, is poetry's extreme limit, where it says the unsayable, expressing the *Erlebnis* of death.

Faced with Homer's Sirens, Odysseus (and we as readers with him) overcame the excruciating desire to surrender to the charm of this voice from the shadows. As always in myth, the image was of two separate figures: man and the supernatural singers. In Dante we see the beginning of the shadow within the figure: the point where poetry, death, and life meet, ejecting a voice, human but beyond the language of humans, which speaks in tongues of fire. Tossed by the wind, by a breath, an inspiration which is both pentecostal and infernal, wafted from Hell, at its most extreme limit poetry appears as a divine and diabolic spirit, a force which illuminates and destroys, reveals and consumes: flame.

I shall return to this aspect shortly, when examining the end of the canto. For the moment, note how tragic and tormented the birth of narrative is for Ulysses, an aspect poignantly and ironically underlined by Dante's evocation of St James's praise and condemnation of language in a significantly nautical image. Just as a ship, however large and wind-tossed, is steered by a tiny rudder, so the tongue, however small, is capable of immense feats; and just as fire, however circumscribed initially, can burn down a whole forest, so the tongue, which is fire, 'inflameth the wheel of our nativity, being set on fire by hell'.[6] Inevitably, the conclusion has to be silence; when the *récit de la fin* becomes *fin du récit*, the flame (Canto XXVII, 1–2) stands 'erect' and 'quiet' 'having ceased to

------

6 James 3:6, Douay-Rheims Bible.

speak', all passion spent, placated by having said, dead to narrative, to tragedy, and to life.

Our problems, however, are not over: in a sense, as problems of interpretation, i.e. questions to the text, they are only just beginning. Virgil's peremptory order specifies a 'where' (where, being lost, he went to die) which remains unanswered both in Ulysses' account and in the *Commedia* in general until the first canto of the *Purgatorio*. Where does Ulysses go to die? He himself does not know; indeed, he knows very little in general about this final voyage even while actually undertaking it. Ulysses knows himself, of course, and acknowledges that his 'ardore . . . a divenir del mondo esperto | e de li vizi umani e del valore' ('passion . . . to gain experience of the world and of the vices and the worth of men') overcame all family ties, all earthly love, and all desire of the return home which so obsessed Homer's Odysseus. At a factual level, he knows he set out 'per l'alto mare aperto', and that he sailed westwards across the Mediterranean; and he knows, at an ethical level, that man should not 'pass beyond' the markers set by Hercules.

When, however, Ulysses enters the 'foce stretta' of Gibraltar, all geographical co-ordinates and material knowledge cease, and with them all sense of ethics and of self. His flight is now 'folle', mad. The world that lies beyond is, simply, 'di retro al sol' and 'sanza gente', unpeopled. All the human vices and values he so desired to learn of seem forgotten. Now, 'at this so brief vigil of [the] *senses*', Ulysses wants to gain *experience* of the uninhabited darkness. Painfully conscious of the diminished sensitivity of old age, he wants to test and touch with his own hands the hollow course of the sun.

Old and slow as he is, Ulysses cannot hope to return alive from that world. 'Fandi fictor',[7] word-smith and spinner of yarns, he can, perhaps, with his 'little speech' deceive those companions he himself has elevated to a brotherhood ('O frati!') and in whom he seems to be choosing one sort of society, the cameraderie of the scientific expedition, over that of father, wife, and child. But on the threshold of his own consciousness he must be aware that what awaits him beyond Hercules' 'markers' is death. Deep within himself, Ulysses yearns for the life of non-being, and yearns for

---

[7] G. Padoan, *Il pio Enea, l'empio Ulisse* (Ravenna, 1977), 170–204.

life-in-death. Man's 'semenza', his seminal, Adamic origin and destiny is to live not as a brute, but with the awareness of death: simultaneously supreme *virtù* and *conoscenza*.

Significantly, this eager and narratively ineluctable movement towards dying and knowing, initially recorded with all the precision of the seasoned explorer, is then lost (losing oneself being an essential part of Virgil's predestined plot) in an ever-widening void. The course is west, then, 'always gaining on the left', south-west. The southern sky is already visible, while the northern disappears beneath the watery floor ('marin suolo'). Points of reference in space, so abundant earlier (Sardinia, Spain, Morocco), now disappear. They give way to time, suddenly urgent after the indefinite interval which, in the Mediterranean, had consumed the whole second half of Ulysses' life. The vigil is suddenly terribly short: five moons, a five-month journey.

Then, out of the literally blue, the surprise. In the distance there appears a mountain, which the experienced sailor describes as 'dark because of the distance', and notes as seemingly the highest he has ever seen. Now, this mountain, which readers of the *Commedia* will discover (probably from the notes) is Mount Purgatory, represents the 'great stony mountain' which rears its head in Propp's folk-stories to signal the world of the dead.[8] Ulysses should be the first to recognize it, and be ready for the last, desired step. But in his wish to know and experience death, he is a man to the last: 'denn nah am Tod sieht man den Tod nicht mehr | und starrt *hinaus*', in Rilke's words—when death is close we fail to see it, and stare fixedly outwards.[9] And precisely in accordance with Rilke's maxim, Ulysses allows himself, momentarily, to labour under the greatest of illusions. The captain and his crew, almost as if they had reached a true Cape of Good Hope, actually *rejoice*. For them this is no longer the other world but, as Ulysses himself says, *another* world, the *nova terra*: Tibullus' *novus orbis*. For one moment Ulysses exults, believing he has discovered the New World which classical, Old and New Testament prophecy had dreamt of: a new beginning of time, life, and human happiness.

The misunderstanding—and all its tragic irony breaks over readers the moment they realize that the mountain is precisely that

⁸ E. Raimondi, *Metafora e storia*, with reference to V. Propp, *Les Racines historiques du conte merveilleux*, trans. L. Gruel-Apert (Paris, 1983).
⁹ R. M. Rilke, *Duineser Elegien*, viii. 22–3.

topped by the Earthly Paradise—is, however, resolved immediately: 'Noi ci allegrammo, e tosto tornò in pianto' ('We were filled with gladness, and soon it turned to lamentation'). Death's implacable precision flings the other world open before the new one, making the one rise from the other against all expectations, but logically, in accordance with the iron law which Aristotle had been the first to see as ruling the tragic *mythos*. On the verge of ultimate knowledge, at the moment when Ulysses is about to discover where 'per lui, perduto, a morir gissi' ('being lost, he went to die'), the divine whirlwind rises from the new land, strikes the ship, makes it spin round three times with all the waters, lifts the stern aloft, plunges the prow down, and closes the ocean's seal over him. The wind which earlier on had 'wearied' the flame is finally replaced by the terrible, uncanny 'whirlwind' of the Other, which, as in Jeremiah, 'comes forth' against the king and all the Gentiles of the world *a summitatibus terrae* (from the *mountains* of the earth) and, in apparently nameless and silent but wrathful and dreadful voice, tones down all wretched, mere human speech: 'com' altrui piacque' ('as the Other willed'). He, the Other Poseidon unexpectedly turned Yahveh, but still Nameless, is the prime and only cause, the 'pleased' witness of what, to paraphrase another of Blumenberg's titles, with tragic irony becomes a 'shipwreck *with* spectator'.[10]

I will at this point be reproached for offering a 'romantic' reading (though I would prefer to call it existential) of Dante's Ulysses, and for ignoring the more or less firm conclusions which critics have reached in their interpretations of the episode: the fact, for example, that Ulysses is the 'impious' antagonist of the 'pious' Aeneas (but, in answer to Virgil who, in the world, had written 'alti versi' about the son of Anchises, Ulysses replies that he left Gaeta '*prima* che sì Enea la nomasse', before Aeneas so named it, almost underlining, with Dante's pen, his own independent precedence); or that Dante the pilgrim is a 'new Ulysses' who reaches not only the desert shore of Purgatory, but also the point from the Empyrean from which he witnesses his character's 'varco folle', his mad passage, himself becoming an Argonaut, a transhumanized Glaucus over whose head divine waters close (and, 'folle' or otherwise, the memory of Ulysses' flight will stay with him to the

---

[10] H. Blumenberg, *Schiffbruch mit Zuschauer* (Frankfurt, 1979).

very threshold of the beatific vision). I will be accused of neglecting Ulysses' *megalopsykhia*, his magnanimity, his 'curiositas' and 'fol hardement', the fact that he embodies pagan wisdom (which ultimately fails because devoid of Christian grace), and that he is the symbol of a purely human *philo-sophia*.[11]

My answer to these objections is that they are almost certainly groundless. I would first point to the need for a human-centred interpretation. Any reader of *Inferno* XXVI feels the pain and urgency of Ulysses' story, and its relation to our own existence between being and non-being, and between desire, illusion, and destiny. The message we receive from Dante's Ulysses can be subsumed in Beatrice's words to Dante on that same summit of Purgatory, in that earthly Paradise which Ulysses has unwittingly glimpsed:

> Tu nota; e sì come da me son porte,
> così queste parole segna a' vivi
> del viver ch'è un correre a la morte.

Take note, and just as I speak these words to you, so should you teach the living of life which is a hurtling towards death.

(Purgatorio, xxxiii. 52–4)

Secondly, as 'disinherited minds', who, like the inhabitants of Dante's Limbo, 'sanza speme vivemo in disio', how can we avoid reading Ulysses in this way, now, in our 'destitute time'?[12] We cannot wipe out the shadow: the text and our crisis (in the sense of

---

[11] For the many interpretations of *Inferno* XXVI, see the bibliography in the *Enciclopedia Dantesca*, vol. v (Rome, 1976), 808–9, and E. Esposito, *Bibliografia analitica degli scritti su Dante 1950–1970* (Florence, 1990), ii. 655–66. Interpretations indirectly discussed in the present chapter, besides those of Freccero and Padoan quoted above, are the following: A. Pagliaro, *Ulisse: Ricerche semantiche sulla Divina Commedia* (Messina and Florence, 1967), 371–432; F. Forti, *Magnanimitade: Studi su un tema dantesco* (Bologna, 1977), 161–206; J. A. Scott, *Dante Magnanimo: Studi sulla 'Commedia'* (Florence, 1977), 117–93; G. Mazzotta, *Dante, Poet of the Desert* (Princeton, NJ, 1979), 66–106; R. Mercuri, *Semantica di Gerione* (Rome, 1983); A. A. Iannucci, *Forma ed Evento nella Divina Commedia* (Rome, 1984), 147–88; A. M. Chiavacci Leonardi, 'The New Ulysses', in P. Boitani and A. Torti (eds.), *Intellectuals and Writers in Fourteenth-Century Europe* (Tübingen and Cambridge, 1986), 120–37; G. Carugati, *Dalla menzogna al silenzio* (Bologna, 1991); M. Picone, 'Dante, Ovidio e il mito di Ulisse', *Lettere Italiane* (1991), 500–16. See also T. Barolini, *The Undivine Comedy: Detheologizing Dante* (Princeton, NJ, 1992), 48–58, 105–15; G. Mazzotta, *Dante's Vision and the Circle of Knowledge* (Princeton, NJ, 1993), 135–53.

[12] E. Heller, *The Disinherited Mind* (London, 1952); M. Heidegger, 'What are Poets For?', in *Poetry, Language, Thought* (New York, 1971), 91–142.

krisis, a critical moment or breaking-point) meet in it as if it were their *kairos*, their natural time and season. My interpretation, emerging as it does at the 'right' moment, might perhaps open up vast possibilities for a meditation on the condition of hermeneutics in time. As free prisoners of our material and cultural world, or, as I shall argue in Chapter 7, when I come to contemporary incarnations of Ulysses, as the inevitable but still unappeased inheritors of an interpretative destiny, we cannot simply bury our heads in the sand before the inescapable necessity of Dante's story. Medieval alterity, the difference in conditions and mentality which separate us from Dante's times, is also part of the flesh and blood of modernity. There is simply no escaping from this: Dante's Ulysses is no 'discarded image'[13] but the figuration of all that we are.

Nor can we avoid the complementary and even wider chasm of alterity which Ulysses opens up by mentioning, a name without a name, the 'altrui', pronouncing his last words with deeply disturbing obliquity:

> ché de la nova terra un turbo nacque
> e percosse del legno il primo canto.
> 　　Tre volte il fé girar con tutte l'acque;
> a la quarta ire in giù, com'altrui piacque,
> infin che 'l mar fu sovra noi richiuso.

for from the new land a storm rose | and struck the forepart of the ship. | Three times it whirled her round with all the waters, | the fourth time ... plunged the prow below, as Another willed, | until the sea closed over us.

The lines contain three real and grammatical subjects the very sequence of which is disturbing: 'turbo', 'altrui', and 'mare'. The first and third suggest impersonality: the initially 'open' place and object where Ulysses 'puts forth', the ocean is here transformed into an active horizon, a subject or natural agent which 'closes' in on man definitively and sends him to its depths, sub-jecting him. It is the law of chance and fate. But the 'whirlwind' intertextually (cf. Jeremiah) suggests divine action; the 'fu richiuso', taken as a passive, could imply an Agent; and the dative, the indirect 'altrui', puts the Unnamed, like some final ontological Shadow, as squarely responsible for the sinking.

---

[13] C. S. Lewis, *The Discarded Image: An Introduction to Medieval and Renaissance Literature* (Cambridge, 1964).

And since we readers are the real spectators of the shipwreck, from our vantage-point on this bank and shoal of time (and on that of the fourteenth century too, as we shall see), we are obliged to ask ourselves what unsounded depths of alterity are being suggested here, one second before the tongue of fire becomes forever silent, and what the meaning might be of that extreme resistance of culture and consciousness Ulysses puts up while recognizing his defeat. 'Com'altrui piacque': the parenthesis is a *sottovoce* challenge to Dante's own universe, in which God is not the 'other', and is not into the business of sinking pagan heroes. It is the poet's own tongue which ends up being set on fire by the greater horn of the ancient flame.

To experience poetry, then, is a dangerous business; playing with fire, we can get burnt, body and soul, in the 'whirlwind' the Other sometimes wraps round us, and which a writer every now and then manages to express with flaming tongue. We retreat, appalled, from the abyss; but we know (and shall know even more clearly in Chapter 7) that the unsurmountable block, the unresolvable contradiction has been experienced, at terrible cost, by those who spoke of the Canto of Ulysses in a Nazi concentration camp. It was there, in Auschwitz, that Primo Levi re-evoked Dante's lines and the 'something gigantic' which they revealed to him 'only now, in the intuition of a second, perhaps the why of our destiny, of our being here today'.[14]

If, on the other hand, we exercise our right to free will and choose to argue from *within* the logic of traditional interpretation—from the other side of the 'other', as it were—my reading of Ulysses, however impure, in no way excludes the orthodox ones: it actually complements and subsumes them in a rational and neatly philological fashion, while keeping well within the 'limits of interpretation'[15] and functioning as the mere recording of the dark shadow over Dante's story. In the light of this, the moralities and allegories I have mentioned, which grow out of a legitimate need to read the text within its cultural context and late-medieval episteme, within Dante's own 'system', acquire a doubly tragic resonance.

The *libido sciendi*, the limitless hunger to know non-being as if it

[14] P. Levi, *Se questo è un uomo* (Turin, 1971), 145.
[15] U. Eco, *I limiti dell'interpretazione* (Milan, 1990).

were being, and to experience life-in-death, leads to the opposite end. A misunderstanding, a *méconnaissance*, an ignorance (*agnoia*) which is repression, suppression, and profoundly human *hamartia* (error), penetrates Ulysses' psyche when he sights the dark mountain. Then, with his shipwreck, magnanimity, curiosity, and ancient and pagan wisdom all fall into the abyss. Dante's Ulysses is not simply another Adam who, as *Paradiso* XXVI will make clear, 'overpasses the bound' ('trapassar del segno'). It is not only the fruit of the tree of knowledge he wants to taste to throw off the brute and become fully human, since he rejoices at the sight of the mountain, and, calling it the 'nova terra', reveals the sudden illusion of believing himself to be on death's farther shore, in a new life. This was God's reason for expelling Adam from the Earthly Paradise: for his desire to know good and evil, and live in eternity, and so that he should remain 'other', and not become like Him. And perhaps Ulysses' 'altrui' may also at this point be read by some as the expression of a claimed, if not achieved, equality with the only 'other' worthy of consideration.

What a terrible irony that this Ulysses, the reincarnation of the *dios Odysseus* who survived so many shipwrecks and returned from Hades, cheating death, should be sunk by the storm of the one true God just when within sight of the mountain at the top of which lies the Garden of Eden, where man had lived without 'virtute' and without 'conoscenza', but also without death! What a singular superimposition and interweaving of myths (from the very beginning of the episode: the ascent of Elijah's chariot in the eyes of Elisha, and the pyre of Eteocles and Polynices); what an astonishing anachronism for what T. S. Eliot considered, not without reason, a 'simple romance', a 'well-told seaman's yarn'![16]

The more we read the story, the more we feel the unbearable tensions that are built into it. The more, too, we understand why its interpreters, its pure readers, have divided sharply into two opposed factions, the 'hawks' and the 'doves'. There is no escape, then, from the problem of interpretation. Let me briefly summarize the extreme positions, reserving the right to draw my own conclusions and expound my own allegories.

Three mythical and literary traditions, all equally authoritative, were available to Dante when embarking on his account of Ulysses.

---

[16] T. S. Eliot, *Dante* (London, 1965), 25.

In the first, the Greek hero is a trickster, a teller of tall stories, a sharp-talker. This is Ulysses as read by Virgil in the *Aeneid*, by Ovid in the *Metamorphoses*, by Statius in the *Achilleis*, and by a score of later writers: Dictys, Benoît de Sainte-Maure, Guido delle Colonne, and so on. There is no doubt that Dante, too, had Ulysses condemned to Hell on account of his deceit: as Virgil clarifies in his presentation of the ancient flame, it was for the 'agguato del caval', the ambush of the Trojan horse, and for the stratagems by means of which, with Diomedes, he took Achilles from Deidamia, and stole the Palladium.

Now, a number of interpreters, with solid philology on their side but a possibly over-developed sense of ideological rigour, border-ing on integralism, go one step further. Ulysses' supreme deceit, they maintain, is intellectual: that he sets out for the 'alto mare aperto' as an old man, in that phase of our 'etade' when, as that other great spirit of fraud, Guido da Montefeltro, declares in the following canto, with echoes of the Dante of the *Convivio*, 'ciascun dovrebbe | calar le vele e raccoglier le sarte' ('every man | should lower the sails and gather in the ropes'); that he fraudulently convinces his companions to pass beyond the Pillars with his 'orazion picciola'; that, even without going beyond Aristotle, i.e. pagan philosophy, true knowledge is not that of the senses, the 'esperienza' 'd'i nostri sensi' constituting a mere 'wake', a vigil of higher forms of knowledge; that, according to St Augustine, a number of philosopher-navigators reach the port of the 'vita beata' only by avoiding the 'enormous mountain' of an excessive desire for glory and knowledge; that Ulysses, both in pagan and Christian terms, commits the sin of hubris; and that he is condemned for that flight which he himself recognizes as 'folle'.

All this is perfectly true as far as Ulysses' *life* is concerned, but less so when we consider his eternal damnation. If Ulysses is in the eighth *bolgia* of the eighth circle because of the 'art' of deceit, God drowned out his earthly life because he was reaching the land where no post-lapsarian mortal, with the exception of Dante Alighieri, is allowed. Let me stress that other characters of the *Inferno*, like Francesca or Ugolino, are put to death by their fellow human-beings, a cuckolded husband, and a treacherous bishop. Ulysses stands alone—hardly a minor detail—in being killed directly, and with no idea of an Eden or a Purgatory, by a god he does not know.

The wings of the doves, on the other hand, like Ulysses' oars, soar above this mythical-ontological prohibition of the Pillars of Hercules and, in ultra-humanistic, Romantic fashion, draw on a second tradition. In this, Ulysses is the embodiment of virtue and wisdom and the noble pursuer of knowledge: in a word, the 'classical' ideal we looked at in the first chapter. Cicero, Horace, and Seneca, but also Fulgentius, and in the Middle Ages Bernard Silvestris and Giovanni del Virgilio, Dante's friend and contemporary, all speak of Ulysses in these terms. Dante himself, possibly more closely following Bernard (who, in commenting on Virgil apropos of Ulysses, has much to say about the different natures and ends of men as opposed to beasts), makes his hero remind his companions (so that he becomes a paragon of man's 'passion . . . to gain experience of the world'):

> Considerate la vostra semenza:
> fatti non foste a viver come bruti,
> ma per seguir virtute e canoscenza.

Take thought of the seed from which you spring: | you were not born to live as brutes, | but to follow virtue and knowledge.

In the following chapters I shall try to show how literary versions of these two opposed readings are conditioned by, and in turn interpret, historical circumstances. For a text-focused moment, let me observe that whilst the Dante who begins the *Convivio* with the memorable Aristotelian sentence, 'All men by nature desire to know', would have agreed whole-heartedly with Ulysses' 'passion'; and whilst the character Dante of the *Commedia* is undoubtedly drawn to Ulysses by an overwhelming 'desio' ('vedi che del desio ver' lei mi piego', he tells Virgil; 'thou seest how I bend towards it with desire'), Dante the character and poet senses the extreme danger Ulysses represents for him, as he enigmatically announces at the beginning of the canto:

> Allor mi dolsi, e ora mi ridoglio
> quando drizzo la mente a ciò ch'io vidi,
> e più lo 'ngegno affreno ch'i non soglio,
> perché non corra che virtù nol guidi;
> sì che, se stella bona o miglior cosa
> m'ha dato 'l ben, ch'io stessi nol m'invidi.

I grieved then and grieve now anew when I turn my mind to what I saw, and more than I am wont I curb my powers lest they run where virtue does not guide them, so that, if favouring star or something better have granted me such boon, I may not grudge it to myself.

Lastly, Dante the poet has his hero drowned by God; Dante the judge condemns him to hell, and even Dante the character and author will later repeat that Ulysses' 'varco' was indeed 'folle'.

And, as if this were not enough, Dante the writer out-Ulysses Ulysses and plays on his hero a trick worthy of his own wiles. A third exegetic tradition exists, equally venerable and time-honoured, in which Ulysses tied to the mast before the Sirens is a 'prefiguration of Christ'.[17] Now, in the account of *Inferno* XXVI, neither Ulysses nor Dante nor Virgil makes any mention of the Sirens. In *Purgatorio* XIX, however, Dante himself dreams of a 'femmina balba, | ne li occhi guercia, e sovra i piè distorta, | con le man monche, e di color scialba', ('a woman, stammering, cross-eyed, and crooked on her feet, with maimed hands and of sallow hue') whom his own gaze transforms into a beautiful Siren, and who immediately begins to sing in such a way that the listener is rapt:

> 'Io son', cantava, 'io son dolce serena,
> che' marinari in mezzo mar dismago;
> tanto son di piacer a sentir piena!
> Io volsi Ulisse del suo cammin vago
> al canto mio; e qual meco s'ausa,
> rado sen parte; sì tutto l'appago!'

'I am', she sang, 'I am the sweet siren who beguiles the sailors in mid-sea, so great delight it is to hear me. I turned Ulysses, eager on his way, to my song, and he who dwells with me rarely departs, so wholly I content him'.

Here, again, is the irresistible call of the open sea; but this time the Siren manages to divert Ulysses from his wandering way ('cammin vago') or, as others have it, turns him off track, enamoured as he is of travelling ('del suo cammin vago': the two readings, dividing over the 'vago', are subtly different, the second re-emphasizing the desire for travel and knowledge evinced in *Inferno* XXVI). There is inevitable, and fierce, critical collision over this passage. Quite validly drawing on other passages in the *Commedia* and a respectable iconographic and allegorical tradition,

---

[17] See H. Rahner, 'Odysseus am Mastbaum', in *Symbole der Kirche* (Salzburg, 1964), 239–71; and his *Greek Myths and Christian Mystery* (New York, 1963), 353–86.

the majority sustains that the Siren stands for pleasure, lust, avarice, and gluttony: in a word, that the Siren and the 'femmina balba' represent the imperfect pleasures of this world and the fatal attraction they exert over unwary mortals. Others, following the 'moralization' of the character already established in the Middle Ages, identify the Siren-Woman with Circe (her intemperate swine becoming a distinctive feature of the signified), or even with Calypso. There is, lastly, a vocal minority which reads the Siren as 'cupiditas sapientiae', basing themselves on a passage in Cicero's *De finibus bonorum et malorum*, a work which Dante cites in the *Convivio*. Homer, Cicero says after translating the relevant lines of *Odyssey* XII, realized that his narrative would have appeared less than plausible if a man as great as Ulysses could be ensnared by a mere snatch of song ('si cantiunculis tantus irretitus vir teneretur'); 'it is knowledge the Sirens offer, and it is not to be wondered at if to a lover of knowledge this is dearer than his fatherland and his home' ('né dolcezza di figlio, né la pièta | del vecchio padre', Dante will have Ulysses say, 'not fondness for a son, nor duty to an aged father').

Dante, however, is more complex than his interpreters. He conjures up a 'holy' woman ('donna santa e presta'), to expose the beauty projected on to the 'femmina balba' by his own sub-conscious; at her request Virgil rends the Siren's garments revealing to Dante the belly, the smell of which wakes him. Basically Dante changes the ancient story of Odysseus and the Sirens almost beyond recognition (it will take a Kafka, as we shall see, to go further than this), making Ulysses succumb to extreme desire, be it of the flesh, the mind, or even of poetry. He is also teaching us a lesson in interpretation. The nightmare of the 'femmina balba' turns into an enthralling erotic dream when the protagonist's own gaze, 'as the sun revives cold limbs benumbed by the night', 'colours her wan features as love desires'. It is the dreamer's desire which reads beauty into the Siren, straightening the crippled body of the woman and endowing her with a tongue to speak and sing. The enchantress's appearance then changes once more when the dream becomes an allegory—i.e. when reason and wisdom emerge from Dante's sleeping consciousness to reveal the creature's ultimate ugliness.

If, then, as we could conclude from *Inferno* XXVI and *Purgatorio* XIX, poetry begins with a projection of 'desio' towards its object, and is able to burn the poet's tongue, it is still desire, the reader's, which succumbs to temptation. But interpreting, 'rending the garments' (which the poet himself can do), forces us to project these desires on to a rational reflection, a re-cognition.

We should recognize, then, that the Ulysses tradition is split, and that these divisions are clearly reflected in Dante's story. Dante begins the episode by asking Virgil who is inside the 'foco *diviso*', the cloven fire, and remains silent at the end. He begins with curiosity and wonder, and ends, significantly, in total silence. Equally significant, however, is his speaking of the episode throughout the *Commedia*, to the Empyrean, each time to place it squarely within the medieval epistemic model the poem embodies. All the contrasts to emerge from a reading of the text and context— between pagan knowledge and Christian wisdom; between the other and the new world, and between what Kenelm Foster calls the 'Two Dantes'[18]—all these differences, which a French critic would subsume under the *différance* accompanying any *écriture*, coexist not as the fractured atoms of a self-deconstructing universe, but in the tense metamorphosis of Dante's yearning as it enters his conscience.

Myth and narrative, however, are never completely outside history. Being and existing belong to each individual, but meet with the events of human becoming-in-time. If the ancient Ulysses is, as we have seen, a 'sign' which classical civilization interprets and fills with meaning at the moment of its apogee, projecting the journey prophesied by Tiresias to the limits of the known world, the timeless adventure of his medieval counterpart is obliquely touched by evocative shadows emanating from reality.

Let us go just a little further forwards in preparation for the next chapter, and enter into history. Dante's Ulysses, with his supreme transformation, his repressed desire and ineluctable dying, clearly marks a crisis: in a historical perspective, the transformation of consciousness which marks a whole age—as Blumenberg puts it, 'the epoch's incipient doubt about the finality of its horizon and its narrowness'.[19]

Two centuries before Christopher Columbus, in 1291, as Bruno

[18] K. Foster, *The Two Dantes* (London, 1977).

[19] H. Blumenberg, *Work on Myth*, trans. R. M. Wallace (Cambridge, Mass. and London, 1985), 79; and *Der Prozess der theoretischen Neugierde* (Frankfurt, 1973), 138–42.

Nardi recalls,[20] the Genoese Vivaldi brothers leave, never to be seen again, on a voyage beyond Gibraltar, 'ad partes Indiae' 'per mare Oceanum'. At the same time (and Maria Corti has suggested powerful analogies with the Ulysses episode),[21] the speculations of radical Aristotelians, the Averroists and the Modists, go even further, beyond all limits, sustaining, for example, the eternal nature of the world, the non-survival of the individual soul, the perfect happiness of intellectual contemplation on earth, and the self-referential nature of language. In brief, they sketch out what in the eyes of the constituted authorities (which, in 1277, in the person of Etienne Tempier, Bishop of Paris, condemned these and other propositions), and of a convert like Dante, must have seemed the end of Christian philosophy.

Dante's Ulysses seeks the 'terra incognita' and, having found the other world, believes he has sighted a new world. His existential adventure and desire to experience death end in an existential and cultural *méconaissance*. This unbearably tragic poetic model throws in doubt past and present visions of the world, considering them 'alterity'; it breaks open the circle of the *Odyssey* and the 'closed world' of the Middle Ages, transforming them into a linear, but not ascendant, itinerary, and into a potentially infinite universe which turns out to be a road leading only to Hell.[22] Thus this extraordinarily subversive Ulysses embarks on a final journey which, in the history of Western civilization, ideally 'fulfils' Tiresias' prophecy to Homer's Odysseus. Now, at the beginning of the fourteenth century, Ulysses stands on a triple threshold, that on which, in Dante's conscience, the death of the classical world, the end of Christian philosophy, and the advent of a new world finally clash.

[20] B. Nardi, *Dante e la cultura medievale* (Bari, 1942), 89–99.

[21] M. Corti, *Dante a un nuovo crocevia* (Florence, 1981); *La felicità mentale* (Turin, 1983); 'Le metafore della navigazione, del volo e della lingua di fuoco nell'episodio di Ulisse', in *Miscellanea di studi in onore di Aurelio Roncaglia* (Modena, 1989); and now 'La "favola" di Ulisse: invenzione dantesca?', in her *Percorsi dell'invenzione* (Turin, 1993), 113–45.

[22] A. Koyré, *From the Closed World to the Infinite Universe* (Baltimore and London, 1967).

3. *The* Nova Terra: *Typologies, History, and Intertextuality*

Or entra ne lo stretto e passa il corto
varco, e s'ingolfa in pelago infinito.

The ship now enters the strait, sailing through the short
passage, plunging into the infinite sea.

A MYTHICAL hero who seeks the highest goal of pagan, classical antiquity by trespassing beyond his own culture's ontological borders, a late-medieval philosopher who goes beyond the bounds of Christian wisdom, and a new Adam, the fourteenth-century Ulysses embodies, then, the tragic birth of the modern world. The fact that this crucial juncture is shrouded in the darkness of death seems to me highly significant, and we shall shortly come back to it. For the moment we can bask in a brief and intense respite from darkness while poetry wells up from its other ancient source, life: from men's perennial dreams and hopes, and from their enthralled wonder.

I shall be more concerned with history than in the previous chapters, first tracing the interpretation of Dante's Ulysses, in commentary and in poetry, from the fourteenth to the sixteenth century. The story's interpretation, its exegesis, again meets the events of history head on at a crucial moment, and when the new, vast, and real space beyond the Pillars of Hercules is finally opened up to Europeans, the 'song' it inspires strains to cancel out all shadow of non-being, to read the whole adventure in the light of nostalgia for the paradise lost, and of overwhelming existential desire for the paradise regained.

The meeting-point between interpretation, poetry, and history generates, as we shall see, a typological sequence in which Dante's Ulysses is the 'figure' and Christopher Columbus the 'fulfilment'; in which reality fulfils the 'scriptures' which prophesied it, constructing a rhetoric and myth which in one form or another the modern world recognizes as its own almost until the present day. Nothing here, however, is pure and simple, because people operating within effectual reality are as visionary as the poets, and 'make' history as if they themselves were writing a text. This will produce two further typological sequences, both focused around Christopher Columbus. In one he is 'announced' by the Argonauts and 'taken up' by philosophers, utopians, scientists, and poets. In the other he is at the centre of a biblical figuralism which interprets the New World literally as the Garden of Eden, thus taking us back to Dante's *nova terra*. If, then, history and poetry become intertexts, we must welcome them as such, enjoy their 'coupling', and revel in both the poetry of history, and the plot which events, problems, and words suggest.

We can now take up from where we left off in the previous chapter. In establishing his own canon and positing himself, indirectly but firmly, as the Moses of his Book, and in ultimate analysis as the *Auctor* and Other of the *Commedia*, Dante chooses for himself as pilgrim a different 'flight' from that of his own Ulysses, full of light and no longer 'folle' but wise in the orthodox and totalitarian Christian view of things, to the point of presenting himself, in *Paradiso* II, as an Argonaut who 'cantando varca' ('singing makes [his] passage') towards the infinite sea of being and of God. If, as Dante himself realizes, this voyage is not to all tastes, that undertaken by Ulysses, on the purely human level its most seductive parallel, is certainly not without its tragic tensions for the late-medieval episteme.

The first exegetes and interpreters of Dante's canon seem overcome by deep anxiety when faced with *Inferno* XXVI. Guido da Pisa, for instance, is clearly fascinated by the passion for glory and knowledge that makes Ulysses similar to the philosophers Secundus and Empedocles (an extremely interesting comparison in our context), but also reproaches him for his 'great cruelty' in neglecting the family to pursue a 'vagabunda inquisitio' of this world. Francesco da Buti condemns him for his 'ardour' to gain knowledge in that it proceeded, he says, not from virtue but from pride. Lana is very unforthcoming, and only points out that while Ulysses and his sailors looked for 'the harbour of safety (or salvation)', they found death. The Anonimo follows Horace and interprets Ulysses as 'the virtue of experience', seeing the 'other land' as that to which 'man cannot descend without danger of death'. The Ottimo, while underlining Ulysses' qualities as an orator, praises his 'ardour to search the world', which, as he mentions, was also highly approved by Plato; as for the 'volo', he maintains it was 'foolish' inasmuch as it is mad for any free man to submit himself to the dangers of a ship at sea. When the dark mountain appears, he balks: 'from here to the end of the chapter', he states, 'it is clear'.

Dante's own children provide interesting examples of timidity and suppression. Jacopo reads the journey across the Ocean as 'the mind's going through worldly operations, because of which [Ulysses] finally reached a dark height'. Pietro clearly feels he is handling hot stuff. In a studiedly neutral tone, he offers clues for the understanding of details in the episode, always careful to point out passages in Scripture and in Augustine which would help view Ulysses in a relatively negative light, though at the same time also praising Ulysses' 'sapientia'. Maybe Ulysses' neglect of his family was too near the bone for Dante's children. Maybe Pietro in particular did not want to pick a quarrel with the Church, which was highly suspicious of Dante and had already condemned the *Monarchia*. Whatever the reason, half-way through his exposition of *Inferno* XXVI, Pietro simply opts for open interpretation: 'Alia per te vide', he orders: look at the rest by yourselves.[1]

This silence is not just the first sign of the doubts and divisions which will dominate exegesis for centuries, but also a trace of the deep anxiety caused when the tongue of fire vibrates: almost ideological cowardice before the tragic shipwreck willed by the supreme alterity.

The choice of silence is particularly significant in the light of what happens in the same period, towards the end of the fourteenth century. When Benvenuto da Imola, after Boccaccio, and with similar Dantophiliac enthusiasm, embarks on his *Comentum* on the *Commedia*, Dante's Ulysses becomes a *new* cultural paradigm which he dovetails with and superimposes on the Homeric one as the latter surfaces again from considerable depths of time. Thus my second shadow, that which Odysseus-Ulysses throws over modern culture, reappears to stalk the scene.

---

[1] Guido da Pisa, *Commentary on Dante's Inferno*, ed. V. Cioffari (Albany, NY, 1974), 534–47; *Commento di Francesco da Buti*, ed. C. Giannini, vol. i (Pisa, 1858), 684; *Comedia . . . col Commento di Jacopo della Lana*, vol. i (Bologna, 1866), 425; *Commento . . . d'Anonimo Fiorentino del Secolo XIV*, ed. P. Fanfani, vol. i (Bologna, 1866), 555, 557; *L'Ottimo Commento della Divina Commedia*, vol. i (Pisa, 1827), 453–6; *Chiose alla Cantica dell'Inferno . . . scritte da Jacopo Alighieri*, ed. G. Piccini (Florence, 1915), 135; Pietro di Dante, *Commentarium*, vol. i (Florence, 1846), 227–38.

Benvenuto is acquainted with the plot of the *Odyssey* (and perhaps a bit more) as well as with Dares and Dictys. He can hardly believe, he writes, that Dante was unaware of what even children and the ignorant knew, namely, that both 'poetic' and 'historical' authorities had given very different accounts of Ulysses' death from that of *Inferno* XXVI. Far from reproaching Dante, however, he praises him for his 'industry' and 'invention', his 'new' fiction ('fingere *de novo*'), which have the precise aim of revealing Ulysses as the example of the 'vir magnanimus, animosus' (and thus *megalopsykhia* again appears as a viable ethical model) who had spared no toil, no danger, nor even life itself to acquire 'experientia rerum', and who 'had chosen to live gloriously for a short time rather than ignominiously for a long one'. In other words, Benvenuto understands the novelty of Dante's Ulysses and appreciates it. Even he, however, when it comes to glossing 'altrui', tries to let himself off the hook, adopting concepts from antiquity which were common currency in the Middle Ages, but giving them as alternatives and filtered through a different sensibility: 'scilicet'— he glosses the famous hemistich—'deo, fato vel fortunae'.[2] Equating fate or fortune with God means foregrounding all the impersonal indetermination of the 'other', but at the price of neutralizing all that is disquieting in it.

The great men of Benvenuto's own generation are more cautious, and oscillate between opposite poles. In the *De Casibus* Boccaccio, for example, like most early commentators, says that nothing can be known for certain about Ulysses' end. In the *Amorosa Visione* (A, XXVII), however, he goes back to Dante's version and, with a clever montage of *Paradiso* XXVI, *Purgatorio* I, and *Inferno* XXVI, declares that our hero so desired 'del mondo sentire'

> ché per voler veder trapassò il segno
> dal qual nessun poté mai in qua reddire.

'that he trespassed, because of his desire to see, beyond the sign | from which no-one has ever been able to return'.

The reading of the *Commedia* leads the poet-exegete, who will shortly afterwards be the first to hold public *Lecturae Dantis*, into an

---

[2] Benvenuto da Imola, *Comentum*, eds. G. W. Vernon and J. P. Lacaita (Florence, 1887), v. 279–94, at p. 293.

intertextual conflation of Ulysses, Adam, and Dante, in which Ulysses is the distinct loser.

Petrarch, the founder of Humanism, and therefore of a new canon, in the first of the *Familiares* sees himself as a new Ulysses, with more wanderlust than the first (and we shall shortly return to this significant identifying of any cultural innovation with the exploits of Homer's and Dante's hero). Further on in the same collection of letters he praises Ulysses, quoting Apuleius, as a 'man endowed with great wisdom' who reaches 'the height of virtue visiting diverse cities and making the acquaintance of diverse peoples'. As proof that the figural link is still active, the context is once more made up of references to both Homer and Dante (and others): to gain 'experientia' of the world, in order to return home 'wiser', Ulysses, 'rejecting all affections, neglecting his kingdom and his loved ones', 'preferred to grow old between Scylla and Charybdis', 'between'—and here comes my first shadow again— 'the black abysses of Avernus'; he 'travelled over lands and seas, nor did he rest until he had founded in the far-off west a city of his own name'. Petrarch, in his famous and controversial letter to Boccaccio regarding his relationship with his predecessor, sees Dante as a Ulysses whom 'the love of wife and children did not distract from his chosen path'.[3] However, just when Ulysses seems to be re-emerging as the model of the 'noble soul aspiring to noble deeds', the echo of *Inferno* XXVI qualifies the praise with an adverbial condemnation. In the *Trionfo della Fama* Petrarch celebrates Ulysses as he who 'longed to see *too much* of the world'— 'desiò del mondo veder *troppo*'.

These uncertainties soon cease, and the change becomes radical. By the fifteenth century Dante's Ulysses has consolidated his position in the *imaginaire* of Italian culture, to become not simply a new model, but a positive one. In Canto XXV of Luigi Pulci's *Morgante*, the demon Astaroth recounts the exploits of Rinaldo the knight to Malagigi. One of these is of particular importance in finally praising Dante's Ulysses:

> Poi vide i segni che Ercule già pose
> acciò che i navicanti sieno accorti
> di non passar più oltre, e molte cose
> andò veggendo per tutti que' porti

---

[3] Petrarch, *Familiares*, ix. 13, 24–7; xxi. 15, 8.

e quanto ell'eran più maravigliose,
tanto pareva più che si conforti
e sopra tutto *commendava* Ulisse
che per veder nell'altro mondo gisse.

He then saw the signs which Hercules placed | that navigators should
beware of going beyond, and many things | he saw, travelling from port to
port, | and the more marvellous they were, | the more he seemed to take
comfort | and above all praised Ulysses | who in his wish to see ventured
into the other world.

The *Morgante* was begun in 1461 and published in 1484, three
years before Bartholomeu Diaz rounded the Cape of Good Hope,
but when the Portuguese explorers had already gone a good way
south down the coast of Africa. If Pulci can still play on the two
meanings of 'other world', Astaroth soon afterwards refutes the
'ancient error' whereby the Pillars of Hercules mark the extreme
limit of human navigation, maintaining that the populated 'other
hemisphere' can indeed be reached.

With Ariosto no ambiguity is possible. In Canto XV of *Orlando
Furioso* Andronica prophesies the enterprises of modern explorers
to Astolfo (quite appropriately, since he is the slightly mad British
knight who—oh *folle volo!*—lands on the 'other world' of the
moon!). 'From the extreme lands of the west' (from Portugal and
Spain) 'new Argonauts and new Tiphys', Andronica proclaims—
inaugurating what, as we shall see, is to become the alternative
mythical model—will open up 'the way unknown to the present
day'. Others, like Vasco da Gama, will then 'turn round Africa' and
navigate across the border between the Atlantic and the Indian
Oceans, until they 'coast all the shores and nearby islands of the
Indies, Araby and Persia'. Others, following on Ulysses' trail, will
'leave the right and left banks which were built by Hercules', this
time no longer, ambiguously, 'behind the sun', but 'imitating the
round path of the sun' and finding *new* lands and a *new* world
('nuove terre e nuovo mondo').

The Renaissance, then, gives a shout of victory in consecration
of the resurrection of an intertextually Dantean, but new, Ulysses.
Reborn amidst the apparently frivolous knights, ladies, arms, and
love-affairs of romance, he becomes a necessary part of the poets'
enthusiasm for the marvellous and simultaneously real *present* in
which they find themselves living. Such is the profoundly liberating
joy at the opening up of the world and the imagination that, three

centuries later, Hölderlin is still full of it in the draft of his
'Kolomb'. In his search for a hero, the Pindaric German chooses
those same seas and, setting off for the home of Columbus in
Genoa, sees Anson, Vasco, and Aeneas, with Godfrey of Bouloigne,
Rinaldo, and Bougainville, trace a 'palpitating image of man' on the
horizon of expeditions which are simply 'attempts to clarify what
distinguishes the Hesperian world from that of the Ancients'.[4]

Death and the dark mountain disappear from the Ulyssian
horizon; in its place is the 'nova terra'. Camões writes the *Lusiads* in
celebration of Vasco da Gama and declares he has heard his fill of
Ulysses and Aeneas, although he mentions Ulysses' founding of the
city of Lisbon and, significantly, his 'lingua fraudulenta', his
fraudulent tongue.[5] Quevedo, who praises Columbus in a famous
epitaph, in another sonnet proclaims that not 'all the legions of the
wind' can imprison Ulysses.[6] Lastly, the most solemn and vibrant
consecration is to be found in an extraordinary passage in the
Gerusalemme Liberata where Rinaldo's wanderings are, at the
author's explicit declaration, to echo 'l'Odissea ne l'eccesso de la
meraviglia', to imitate the excess of wonder in the *Odyssey* and
where, if Sveno appears as a Christianized version of a Dantean
Ulysses, Ubaldo is a Homeric Odysseus turned Christian. A
passionate Dante reader, Tasso has Carlo and Ubaldo, led by
Fortune, sail westward, on the route of *Inferno* XXVI, through the
'short pass' of Gibraltar. There they encounter a stretch of water
which modern humanity knows is infinite, and which Tasso
describes with a wholly new note of sublime wonder, amazement,
and pleasure (xv. 23):[7]

> Or entra ne lo stretto e passa il corto
> varco, e s'ingolfa in pelago infinito.
> Se 'l mar qui è tanto ove il terreno il serra,
> che fia colà dov'egli ha in sen la terra?
>
> Più non si mostra omai tra gli alti flutti
> la fertil Gade e l'altre due vicine.
> Fuggite son le terre e i lidi tutti:
> de l'onda il ciel, del ciel l'onda è confine.

---

[4] F. Hölderlin, 'Kolomb', *Sämtliche Werke*, ed. D. E. Sattler, vol. i (Frankfurt, 1975),
111–17.   [5] Luis De Camões, *Os Lusiadas*, i. 3 and x. 24.
[6] Respectively in sonnets 266 and 299 (Parnaso 165, B and 194).
[7] For this paragraph see E. Raimondi, *Poesia come retorica* (Florence, 1980), 85–7 and
163–9; D. Della Terza, 'Tasso e Dante', *Belfagor*, 25/4 (1970), 395–418.

Now the ship enters the strait and sails beyond the short | pass, and
plunges into the infinite open sea. | If here the sea is so vast, here where
the earth encloses it, | what will it be there, where it embosoms the
earth?

No longer among the high waves | were fertile Gades nor the two nearby
shores to be seen. | Fled are the lands and shores: | wave with sky and sky
with wave confines.

When Ubaldo asks Fortune if no one has previously sailed over this
'boundless sea', and if, moving further into this new world, they will
meet any inhabitants, she replies that Hercules, not daring to
'tempt the deep ocean', after all his admirable exploits set down his
'markers', thus 'narrowing the boldness of the human mind within
too strict confines'. Ulysses, however, 'eager to see and know,
scorned those signs. He passed the pillars and set the daring flight
of his oars on the open sea; yet experience of the waves did not avail
him, for the voracious Ocean swallowed him up and, with his body,
his enterprise lay covered, so that it is still unknown to you' (xv.
25–6):

> ma quei segni sprezzò ch'egli prescrisse,
> di veder vago e di saper, Ulisse.
>
> Ei passò le Colonne, e per l'aperto
> mare spiegò de' remi il volo audace;
> ma non giovogli esser ne l'onde esperto,
> perché inghiottillo l'ocean vorace,
> e giacque co 'l suo corpo anco coperto
> il suo gran caso, ch'or tra voi si tace.

The 'bold flight' 'over the open sea' is itself a significant
counterpoint to *Inferno* XXVI, and explicit criticism of the limits of
medieval episteme (the narration is set fictionally at the time of the
Crusades, when Ulysses' last enterprise lies buried under the sea
and centuries of ignorance). But Fortune goes further: the time will
come, she adds, taking us back into prophetic discourse, when the
Pillars will no longer be 'markers' placed 'on that beyond which
man cannot pass' (xv. 30):

> Tempo verrà che fian d'Ercole i segni
> *favola vile* a i naviganti industri,
> e i mar riposti, or senza nome, e i regni
> ignoti ancor tra voi saranno illustri.

The time will come when the Pillars of Hercules will be mere fable to the industrious sailors; and the now unnamed, sheltered seas and realms unknown will be renowned among you.

Here comes Magellan sailing round the globe, in the 'boldest of all ships', no longer just 'di retro al sol', but emulating and *overtaking* it, circling round 'what the sea surrounds' and measuring the immense mass of the earth (xv. 30):

> Fia che 'l più ardito allor di tutti i legni
> quanto circonda il mar circondi e lustri,
> e la terra misuri, immensa mole,
> vittorioso ed emulo del sole.

Meanwhile a man from Liguria will launch himself on an 'unknown course', and set his 'lucky sails' no longer in 'foolish flight' but in a flight which Fame herself will be hard pushed to keep up with, towards a '*new* pole'. Nothing will keep this man's 'exalted mind', like Ulysses, 'within the narrow prohibitions of Abila'. And no 'threatening breath of wind' will now stop, as the divine whirlwind had, the race towards America. Dante's Ulysses is a 'sign', the *figura*; Christopher Columbus is the signified, the fulfilment. Let fame, Tasso concludes, sing of Hercules and Bacchus, and give no more than a hint of Columbus to posterity; for 'that will give him a lasting memorial most worthy of poetry and history' (xv. 31–2):

> Un uom de la Liguria avrà ardimento
> a l'incognito corso esporsi in prima;
> né 'l minaccievol fremito del vento,
> né l'inospito mar, né 'l dubbio clima,
> né s'altro di periglio o di spavento
> più grave e formidabile or si stima,
> faran che 'l generoso entro a i divieti
> d'Abila angusti l'alta mente accheti.

> Tu spiegherai, Colombo, a un novo polo
> lontane sì le fortunate antenne,
> ch'a pena seguirà con gli occhi il volo
> la fama c'ha mille occhi e mille penne.
> Canti ella Alcide e Bacco, e di te solo
> basti a i posteri tuoi ch'alquanto accenne,
> ché quel poco darà lunga memoria
> di poema dignissima e d'istoria.

The extraordinary power of poetry, to see other poems issue from it, as poetry itself had been born of previous poems! With this prophecy of nautical and poetic generations, within two centuries European culture seemingly heals its wound and wipes all guilt at its own Ulyssean transgression out of its consciousness. The darkness apparently fades away, the sun is now openly emulated, followed, and overtaken. The *reality* of the New World sinks Dante's nightmare, silences the tragedy of myth, and extinguishes the flame of Ulysses speaking from the depths of Hell.

The tale becomes History, and the story it tells is one of seduction. By taking up and transforming Ulysses' courageous and audacious gesture, his setting forth on the 'alto mare aperto', poetry now plunges into infinite seas: it feels the irresistible pull of the confine between water and sky, and rushes headlong into the waters which surround everything, in the 'unknown' and 'boundless' ocean which, as the seventeenth-century Jesuit Daniello Bartoli will say of its currents, 'runs, extends and throws out a part of itself, within itself almost generating a river'.[8] Literature responds to the epistemic infinity which the sea makes possible with the creation of a new sublime. Poetry has no intention, however, of losing itself in that infinity, but will in its turn 'surround' it with words, and will touch the new world with human intelligence, thereby revealing it.

Nor is this an unpeopled world, 'sanza gente', but, as Fortune tells Tasso's knights, 'it conceals thousands of islands and of kingdoms', all full of inhabitants and extremely fertile. 'The virtue which the sun infuses can nowhere be sterile': in the other world, poetry finds not death but warm, dazzling, teeming Life.

And, like ancient Odysseus, the new Ulysses, Christopher Columbus, returns. Du Bellay can once again exclaim: 'Heureux qui, comme Ulysse, a fait un beau voyage.'[9] The new transgressors, Faust and Don Juan, have as yet no need to face the 'alto mare aperto'. Those who are shipwrecked now, like the protagonists of *The Tempest* or, later, that new myth of puritan and economic modernity, Robinson Crusoe, find before them a brave new world

[8] Daniello Bartoli, 'Della Geografia Trasportata al Morale', in E. Raimondi (ed.), *Trattatisti e Narratori del Seicento* (Milan and Naples, 1960), 615.

[9] J. Du Bellay, *Les Regrets*, XXXI. And see G. H. Tucker, *The Poet's Odyssey: Joachim du Bellay and the Antiquitez de Rome* (Oxford, 1990).

to possess and construct, like new divinities, in their own image and
after their own likeness.

But let us pause for a moment in this glorious summer of the
Renaissance. The *Gerusalemme Liberata* goes back to 1575. In the
meantime at least one interpreter of the *Commedia*, Bernardino
Daniello, had already noted in his commentary on *Inferno* XXVI
that the 'opinion' of the ancients according to which the Pillars of
Hercules must not be crossed had been proved to be 'false and
vain' 'by the navigations of the moderns, who by virtue of the valour
and science they possess in things maritime greatly surpassed the
ancients, and discovered many parts of the earth not before known,
and many islands, which may truly be called a new world'. Warming
to his theme, Daniello (whose *Espositione* came out posthumously in
1568) takes a significant step, linking Dante's Ulysses to present
reality and at the same time, figurally, to a prophecy of classical
antiquity. When he reaches the terzina in which Dante describes
the increasing fullness of the southern sky, and the gradual
disappearance of the northern under the sea-bed, Daniello writes:

> Through these words the Poet seems to state that he is of the opinion
> that, beyond the Straits of Gibraltar, man might navigate in the direction
> of the other Pole and new regions, and places discovered by the moderns,
> and not known to ancient navigators. This opinion was similarly held by
> Seneca the Tragedian, who in one of his Tragedies, entitled Medea, states
> thus: venient annis Secula seris quibus Oceanus Vincula rerum laxet . . .
> the which we have witnessed, and each day we see brings the discovery of
> new earths and new worlds.[10]

In short, although he knows perfectly well that, according to Dante,
in the further reaches of that hemisphere stands the dark mountain
of Purgatory, Daniello still reads the literary model of the
Commedia as an anticipation of the contemporary episteme, and
proposes interpreting Dante's lines as a meeting-point or pivot
between the ancient *typos* and its modern fulfilment. Subject in
time to exegesis, poetry transforms reality into text: read within the
kairos, poetry is both prophesied and prophesying discourse.

In this way the world conforms to the myth in the most seductive
way possible. The prediction Daniello attributes to Seneca's *Medea*

---

[10] *L'Espositione di Bernardino Daniello da Lucca sopra la Comedia di Dante*, ed. R.
Hollander and J. Schnapp (Hanover and London, 1989), 120.

(and which ultimately derives from Virgil's Fourth Eclogue) proclaims, in the sixteenth-century reading of the passage, that 'the age shall come when the Ocean will release its hold on things, the Earth shall appear immense, Typhis [the pilot of the Argonauts] will find new worlds ['novos orbes'] and there shall be no "ultima Thule" to the land'. Now, this link of Daniello's between the events predicted by Seneca and modern discoveries is actually more than mere literary rhetoric. In the *Libro de las Profecías*, composed between 1501 and 1502, Christopher Columbus applies Seneca's lines to his own enterprise, and his son Ferdinand later reiterates that the words of *Medea* had been fulfilled by his father.[11]

Dante's Ulysses obviously has a place in this fascinating scheme of things. When Amerigo Vespucci, the man with whose name Europe will baptize the new land of America, enters the 'great gulf of the Ocean sea' for the first time (on an expedition begun, he tells Piero Soderini in a letter, on 10 May 1497), he discovers 'much *terra firma* and infinite islands, a great many of them inhabited'. He then immediately recalls that Dante had called the Ocean 'mare senza gente', and quotes 'chapter XXVI of the *Inferno*, where he feigns Ulysses' death'.[12]

Vespucci, in short, considers Dante's fictional, mythical, and existential geography 'real' but wrong, and corrects it in the light of his own 'discoveries'. He is ready to accept it, though, where it coincides with his own revelations and above all with his own wishes. Thus, in his letter of 18 July 1500 to Lorenzo di Pierfrancesco Medici about the journey of the preceding year, he recounts having sailed southwards, beyond the mouth of the present-day Amazon River, and the 'equinoctial line', until he 'held the one pole and the other at our farthest horizon' and lost sight of 'the north star'.

Vespucci's route is that of Dante's Ulysses, as he is contentedly aware. While, 'desirous of being he who marked the star of the firmament of the other pole', he is losing sleep every night star-gazing, he at one point sees four 'almond-shaped' stars, which bring to his mind the passage in *Purgatorio* I in which Dante, 'when he feigns rising out of this hemisphere to find himself in the other', describes 'quattro stelle | non viste mai fuor ch'a la prima gente'

[11] *Libro de las Profecías*, in Cristóbal Colón, *Textos y documentos completos*, ed. C. Varela (Madrid, 1989), 287. All quotations from Columbus are from this text.
[12] A. Vespucci, *Lettere di viaggio*, ed. L. Formisano (Milan, 1985), 38.

('four stars | only ever seen by the first people')—in other words those seen from the deserted shore of Mount Purgatory. Amerigo Vespucci, then, liked to see himself as a Ulysses and a Dante, and to read his travels in the light of those in the *Commedia*. He happily connects Dante's southern stars with the Southern Cross. Antonio Pigafetta, sailing with Magellan some years later, does exactly the same thing. Already in the sixteenth century the historian Pero Antón Beuter, of Valencia, with explicit reference to Dante, maintained that after the foundation of Lisbon Ulysses set off across the sea on the very journey the Spaniards were making to the Indies, possibly successfully; while the sailor and chronicler Pedro Sarmiento de Gamboa went one step further, actually stating, not long after this, that the ancient civilization of New Spain had been founded by Ulysses in person.[13]

In short, as soon as geographical discoveries get under the European skin, be it of sailors, poets, or scholars, they unexpectedly expand the imagination and start to be read *typologically*. Old texts are found to square with new reality.[14] The poetry of the past already contains the modern world. Dante's *nova terra* links Seneca and Columbus, the Purgatory and Vespucci; it bridges the gap between the sixteenth century and the time of the Crusades, and, to all effects, in the minds of Tasso, Daniello, and their like, it *invents* America. Those operating within the world see it in the light of prophecy and poetry, because it is these which give a meaning to life.

If this is a case of 'Darwinism of words', then natural selection has created a new species, a new Cro-Magnon: Dante's Ulysses, with whom, as Bruno Nardi puts it, the poet 'discovered the Discoverer'.[15] But the fact is that this Darwinism is not just of 'words', but of word-facts which rest on literary and Scriptural interpretation. Columbus's enterprise really is the most significant event of the Renaissance in European eyes. Francisco López de Gómara knows what he is talking about when in 1552 he proclaims

[13] G. Gliozzi, *Adamo e il Nuovo Mondo* (Florence, 1977), 199.

[14] Kepler, the meticulous theorizer of the planetary orbits, does not hesitate to translate Plutarch's *On the Face of the Moon* and to maintain, in his commentary, that the transatlantic continent west of Ogygia (for him Iceland)—a mythical continent modelled on Plato's Atlantis, from which, in the dialogue, a mysterious stranger arrives—is in fact America. J. Kepler, vol. viii of *Opera Omnia*, ed. C. Frisch (Frankfurt, 1870), nn. 97–8, 103–5 to Kepler's Latin trans. of Plutarch.

[15] B. Nardi, *Dante e la cultura medievale* (Bari, 1942), 99.

that 'the Discovery of the Indies, what we call the New World, is, excepting only the Incarnation and Death of our Lord, the most important event since the creation of the World'.[16] For Italian poets, the connection with Dante's Ulysses appears almost automatic, so naturally right, so neatly emblematic of the meeting of poetry and history within time as to seem even obvious to us, cynical, post-figural, post-modern experts of the fiction–reality divide.

As late as 1897, for example, Arturo Graf is still thinking along lines not unlike Tasso's. In his 'L'ultimo viaggio di Ulisse', published in the *Danaidi*,[17] he puts into his hero's mouth an 'orazion picciola' prospecting a route, not 'di retro al sol' and towards a world without people, but, 'dietro del corso del sol', the rising from the waters of another, larger, inhabited world. The arrival at the dark mountain is preceded by a passage drawing deliberately, down to the 'signs' of earth—a flock of birds, a branch still 'in green fronds dressed'—on Christopher Columbus's so-called *Diary of the First Voyage*. We should also take into account the extreme, but significant, case of Gaspare Finali. In 1892, during the celebrations of the fourth Columbus centenary, Finali, in ecstasy at the sight of the port of Genoa, suddenly comes up with the idea that the great Christopher was actually inspired by Dante's story, thereafter spending a number of years of his life trying to prove his theory.[18] In a manner which can only be described as romantico-positivistic, Finali tries to close the circle, to establish through textual and contextual evidence a relationship of cause and effect between fiction and event. He fails, of course, but he paradoxically represents the supreme example of the way in which the poets and exegetes of the Italian Renaissance have taught us, indeed conditioned us, to read historical facts as literary re-enactments of myth, as fulfilment of the imagination: in an inversion of the traditional view, as *signifiers* of *res fictae*.

Of course we all know that America is a strange invention,[19] from its name to the system of signs by means of which cartography

---

[16] López de Gómara, *Historia de las Indias*, quoted by A. J. Slavin, 'The American Principle from More to Locke' in F. Chiappelli (ed.), *First Images of America* (Berkeley, Los Angeles, and London, 1976), 140.

[17] A. Graf, *Le Danaidi* (2nd edn., Turin, 1920).

[18] G. Finali, *Cristoforo Colombo e il Viaggio di Ulisse nel Poema di Dante*, 'Collezione di Opuscoli Danteschi', vol. xxiii (Città di Castello, 1895).

[19] E. O'Gorman, *The Invention of America* (Bloomington, Ind., 1961).

imposes it on the general attention. The theological, ethical, legal, political, and anthropological problems this invention poses for the Old Continent have long been the subject of passionate, and ongoing, study.[20] It has provoked an interminable historiography, a weighty body of travel literature of the period, in all languages, and an almost uncontrollable poetic production in Latin and the vernacular within Italian, Spanish, Portuguese, French, and English cultures alone, in which references to the discovery of the new lands are fused with traditional subjects and incorporated into the most varied genres. I refuse, with a deliberately anti-historicist gesture, to sail over such limitless oceans. I shall simply take up again my account of the typologies within Italian culture.

In France and England, for example, the literature and the reality of the New World are one and the same thing. Pantagruel's journey in Rabelais's *Fourth Book* (1548–52) significantly comprehends 'the ancient journey of the Celts towards the utopian country of death and resurrection, colonial adventures of the period, and the itinerary of Jacques Cartier' in Canada.[21] To bring home to us just how close America is, Rabelais superimposes on to its geography a corporeal topography: 'Trou de Gibraltar', 'Bondes de Hercule'. Montaigne denies most emphatically that the New World has anything to do with either Plato's Atlantis or (pseudo) Aristotle's Carthaginians sailing across the Ocean. As far as he is concerned, in Book I of the *Essais* (1580), the Pillars of Hercules do not exist: they are simply the 'détroit de Gibraltar'. His answer to the discovery of 'cet autre monde', this 'pays infini', is that our eyes are bigger than our bellies, and human curiosity greater than understanding; that there will be other discoveries, and, quite rightly, that cannibals are not savages. Perplexed by the reality, he refutes the myth, reasons things out, and distinguishes between 'true' and 'false'.

In England, in 1516, Thomas More compares his traveller, Raphael Hythlodaeus, to Ulysses and Plato, making him a member of the Amerigo Vespucci expedition. More, going beyond ancient myth, projects on to the Utopia at the antipodes of Europe,

---

[20] I shall quote only the fundamental *First Images of America*, ed. F. Chiappelli, referring readers to F. Provost, *Columbus: An Annotated Guide to the Scholarship on His Life and Writings* (Providence, RI and Detroit, 1991).

[21] M. Bakhtin, *L'Œuvre de François Rabelais et la culture populaire au Moyen Age et sous la Renaissance* (Paris, 1970), 392–6, at p. 447.

described by his character, the dream of a perfect society: he introduces into European culture the 'American principle'[22] and transports 'a long-standing expectation of popular radicalism from the temporal perspective proper to millennialism to the spatial one suddenly opened up by the discoveries'.[23] One hundred years later, in 1625, Samuel Purchas publishes his *Pilgrimes* (presented as a *History of the World in Sea Voyages and Land Travel*), and opens his work with a 'large treatise of King Salomons navie sent to Ophir'. When, however, he comes to the travels of Odysseus and Aeneas, he declares himself 'weary of travelling in such loose sandy soile, where so few footprints and paths of truth are to be found'.[24] There is no room for Ulysses here: what matters is the actual exploration of the world by *Englishmen*, England's choice of a 'purely maritime existence',[25] and the historico-theological foundation, within a new figuralism, of the future colonial empire.

Italian writers seem to be both more imaginative and firmly conditioned by tradition, classicism, and literature. But their rhetoric has shaped our response to historical reality; to paraphrase Foucault, it is their *words* which have given life to *things* in the Western *imaginaire*.[26] They have established two typologies which constitute the lines of descent, the actual 'canons', of modern culture.

The first centres on the figural axis of Dante's Ulysses–Christopher Columbus, passing through Tasso to Tassoni and Chiabrera between the sixteenth and seventeenth centuries, to Parini in the eighteenth, down to Leopardi, in a revolutionized version, in the nineteenth. This is the line of victorious transgression, culminating in Parini's ode (1765) 'L'Innesto del Vaiuolo' significantly dedicated, in the positive spirit of the Enlightenment,

---

[22] Slavin, 'The American Principle from More to Locke'.

[23] F. Marenco, Introduction to *Nuovo Mondo; Gli Inglesi* (Turin, 1990), p. xvii.

[24] Samuel Purchas, *Hakluytus Posthumus or Purchas His Pilgrimes*, vol. i (Glasgow and New York, 1905), 194.

[25] C. Schmitt, 'Die geschichtliche Struktur des heutigen Welt-Gegensatzes von Ost und West', in *Freundschaftliche Begegnungen: Festschrift für Ernst Jünger* (Frankfurt, 1955). In his *Principall Navigations* (London, edn. of 1600, iii. 1 ff.), Hakluyt had already maintained that the 'Briton' Madoc, the son of the Welsh king Owen Gwynedd, had discovered the New World well before the Spaniards (supposedly in the twelfth century). The legend will be elaborately celebrated by Robert Southey in his poem 'Madoc' (1805).

[26] M. Foucault, *Les Mots et les choses* (Paris, 1966).

to the invention of the smallpox vaccine. Here Ulysses and Columbus are *typoi* of the paragon of modern *science*. Columbus, the 'pilot-hero', 'pulls down the feared Pillars of Hercules' by reasoning in terms of rational naturalism:

> Erra chi dice
> che natura ponesse all'uom confine
> di vaste acque marine,
> se gli diè mente onde lor freno imporre:
> e dall'alta pendice
> insegnogli a guidare
> i gran tronchi sul mare,
> e in poderoso canape raccorre
> i venti onde su l'acque ardito scorre.

He who says that nature imposed on man a limit of wide sea-waters errs, for she also gave him a mind by which he could rule over them. She taught him to guide great trees from the high mountains on to the sea, to catch the winds by means of powerful sails, whereby he boldly moves over the waters.

The line of argument recalls that whereby it is impossible to stop man from eating the fruit of the tree of knowledge if you plant it and give man a mouth. But in Parini's image Ulysses and his descendant, Columbus, have become the God of Genesis: like His Spirit, their ship moved 'upon the face of the waters'. The fruit of the tree of *life* has finally been picked and gulped down.

The second canon begins with those whom Dante would have considered the anti-types of Ulysses, Typhis or Jason, the Argonauts with whose journey he identifies his own through the infinite seas of paradise and of the *Paradiso*. Columbus and his son, as we have seen, believed that on 12 October 1492 Seneca's prophecy about the new Typhis had been fulfilled in this world. Giordano Bruno later reiterates the connection, while violently condemning discoverers and *conquistadores* for having 'found once more the means to disturb the peace of others', 'to propagate fresh follies and plant unthinkable madness where none existed', setting his own work, with its opening on to a limitless universe peopled with infinite worlds, against that of Typhis and Columbus. Tommaso Campanella extends the chain to include the newest and truest Typhis–Columbus, Galileo Galilei. Lastly, Marino, the most Baroque of poets, squeezes himself into the canon as its latest child: Typhis–Columbus–Galileo–Marino.[27] It is not a question of mere ornament: Bruno's and Campanella's philosophical and visionary fire burns quite literally, Marino's verbal and imaginative 'whirlwind' creates serious havoc, and Galileo's work is to revolutionize the traditional vision of the universe for ever. Transgression, in other words, has become norm, and acquired a wholly positive value. For centuries Gibraltar bore the sign 'Nec plus ultra'. In Bacon's *Instauratio Magna* (1620), Ulysses' ship appears behind the Pillars of Hercules accompanied by the motto: 'Many shall pass and science increase.' 'Curiosity', the very principle of modern knowledge, will override all prohibitions.[28] The New World is the Golden Fleece, and its discovery gradually constitutes the icon of all that is best and noblest in human intelligence.

This is confirmed in the nineteenth century in a poem from the New World itself. In Walt Whitman's *Passage to India*, published in 1871, the vision described above becomes grand and organic. Inspired by the opening of the Suez Canal, the completion of the American transcontinental railway, and the laying of transatlantic and transpacific telegraph cables, Whitman celebrates human evolution and its achieving of cosmic ends. For him the past is simply an anticipation of the present; the fables and myths which shine from afar, 'spurning the known', are the first instruments God himself uses for his plan:

> Passage to India!
> Lo, soul, seest thou not God's purpose from the first?
> The earth to be spann'd, connected by network,
> The races, neighbors, to marry and be given in marriage,
> The oceans to be cross'd, the distant brought near,
> The lands to be welded together.

Adam and Eve now make their appearance, descending from the gardens of Asia, followed by their numerous children who wander curiously around exploring the world, restless and unhappy. The passage to India stretches 'along all history, down the slopes, | As a

---

[27] See G. Costa, *La leggenda dei secoli d'oro nella letteratura italiana* (Bari, 1972), 124–39.

[28] H. Blumenberg, *Der Prozess der theoretischen Neugierde* (Frankfurt, 1973), 141 and nn. 220 and 221.

rivulet running, sinking now, and now again to the surface rising, |
A ceaseless thought'. It will be taken by Alexander and
Tamburlaine, merchants and sailors, Muslims, Venetians,
Byzantines, Arabs, and Portuguese. Suddenly the 'sad shade', the
'gigantic, visionary' ghost emerges, 'spreading around, with every
look a golden world, | Enhuing it with gorgeous hues': Christopher
Columbus. He appears (Whitman confirms the Admiral's own
messianic role) in the fullness of time, when 'the seed unreck'd for
centuries in the ground' 'in God's due occasion, | Uprising in
the night, sprouts, blooms, | and Fills the earth with use and
beauty'.

Finally, when all the seas have been sailed, in the wake of
captains, engineers, and scientists comes the 'Poet, worthy that
name', 'the true Son of God, singing his songs'. The secret will
then be revealed, and the earth, now fragmented and cold, will be
made whole again and 'completely justified'. But the moment has
in fact already come; the seas are 'all cross'd', and the poet-
prophet-Messiah is Walt Whitman himself, whose soul travels
backwards towards the 'primal thought', 'reason's earthly paradise',
and further still, towards 'wisdom's birth' and Creation; and
forwards, in a 'passage to more than India', on God's infinite seas:

> Passage to more than India!
> Are thy wings plumed indeed for such far flights?
> O soul, voyagest thou indeed on vogages like those?
> Disportest thou on waters such as those?
>
> .   .   .   .
>
> Sail forth—steer for the deep waters only,
> Reckless O soul, exploring, I with thee, and thou with me,
> For we are bound where mariner has not yet dared to go,
> And we will risk the ship, ourselves and all.

Humanity's first two ships, Ulysses' 'bark' and the 'shade of the
Argo' which Neptune admires at the summit of Dante's *Paradiso*, in
the end are one and the same ship. Poetry passes through history
and being.

The *nova terra*, then, is not just America, but primarily a country of
the imagination, man's approach to the supreme destiny of life here
and now. One last, surprising typological system, from the
'inventor' of the New World himself, will demonstrate this.

Christopher Columbus is dominated by a far more obsessive

figuralism than that attested by the poets.[29] After his third journey across the Atlantic, when in 1498 he reaches the continent of South America, he begins to think that the Indies are 'another world'. He is convinced, however, and sets out to prove it by reading the Scriptures and the Fathers in the light of his experience, that this is *literally*, *actually* the Earthly Paradise. And if, just if, it is not, then it may be an 'even greater marvel', perhaps a 'tierra infinita, puesta al Austro, de la cual fasta agora no se a avido noticia' ('an infinite land lying to the South, of which there has been no information until now'),[30] although immediately afterwards he repeats his steadfast conviction that this is indeed the Garden of Eden.

One or two years later, his typological and messianic mentality leads him to proclaim himself openly, in the Letter to Doña Juana, the 'messenger of the new heaven and the new earth described by St John in the Book of Revelation, following Isaiah'. In fact, in the famous 1502 letter to Ferdinand and Isabella, Columbus declares with humility and proud awareness that 'neither reason nor mathematics nor worldmaps have availed [him] in the execution of the enterprise of the Indies; in it that has simply been fulfilled which was spoken by Isaiah'. The passages our admiral has in mind are Isaiah 65: 17 and Revelation 21: 1. Both are visions of the new Jerusalem:

For behold, I create new heavens and a new earth; and the former things shall not be remembered, nor come into mind. But be ye glad and rejoice for ever in that which I create: for, behold, I create Jerusalem a rejoicing, and her people a joy. . . . They shall build houses and inhabit them; they shall plant vineyards and eat their fruit.   (Isaiah)

And I saw a new heaven and a new earth: for the first heaven and the first earth were passed away; and there was no more sea. And I John saw the holy city, new Jerusalem, coming down from God out of heaven, prepared as a bride adorned for her husband.   (Revelation)

The author of Revelation is certainly quoting Isaiah. Whether we consider the two passages, according to the Christian tradition, in typological relation to each other (the New Testament fulfilling the Old), or within Columbus's supposedly 'Hebrew' messianism, the fact remains that he makes them meet in himself. Christopher

---

[29] A. Milhou, *Colón y su mentalidad mesianica* (Valladolid, 1983).
[30] Colón, *Textos y documentos completos*, 218.

Columbus, then, feels that he has seen with his own eyes and touched with his own hands the new heaven and the new earth sighted by Dante's Ulysses. The New Jerusalem prophesied by Isaiah and Revelation is here and now.

In the *Mundus novus* (1503) Amerigo Vespucci proclaims that 'it is licit to call this a New World, because our ancestors had no knowledge of it and it is a new thing to all who hear of it'.[31] This is straight fact: exciting but also prosaic. Columbus lives and thinks on another plane. He believes that Española (Haiti) is Tarshish and Ophir, the places of fable which provided Solomon with the wealth to build his temple. After February 1502 he signs his papers not just with the usual 'the Admiral', but with the anagram of 'Christopher', meaning not 'the bearer of Christ', but 'Christo ferens', he who bears to the Christ, the Messiah. What he now has in mind is perhaps another passage from Isaiah (60):[32]

Who are these that fly like a cloud, and like *doves* to their windows? For the coastlands shall wait for me, the ships of Tarshish [the Indies] first, to bring your sons from afar, their silver and gold with them, for the name of the Lord your God ... Foreigners [the Spanish] shall build up your [Jerusalem's] walls, and their kings shall minister to you.

In dwelling on the reconstruction of the House of Jerusalem Columbus is motivated by political, utopistic, and messianic considerations. Even though he sees three 'sirens' (who, he wryly states, are not so beautiful as people depict them, 'for they look like men'), Columbus fails to make any connection with Ulysses, preferring to see himself as a prophet. Had he had more of a classical imagination, he would no doubt have realized that the 'pala como de fornero', the 'baker's peel', the paddle which he saw the natives use as an 'oar' for their canoes, in a sense fulfilled Tiresias' prophecy. Certainly, a number of questions about the Admiral's actions immediately spring to mind:[33] why, for example, take possession of something, the Indies, in the name of the Catholic Kings, if you believe it to belong to the Grand Khan; why give names to places which already have them; why call 'discoveries'

[31] *Mundus novus*, in *Raccolta di documenti pubblicati dalla Reale Commissione Colombiana nel Quarto Centenario della Scoperta dell'America* (Rome, 1892), iii. 2, p. 123, 8 ff.

[32] See J. Gil, *Mitos y utopias del descubrimiento: 1. Colón y su tiempo* (Madrid, 1989), 214–15. I owe a good deal to Gil's book.

[33] For which see S. Greenblatt, *Marvelous Possessions: The Wonder of the New World* (Oxford, 1991).

what, if these really be the Indies, should if anything be considered 'rediscoveries'; why immediately evaluate the Indians for their servant-potential; and why insist on seeing yourselves reflected in their eyes like beings from heaven? But, these considerations apart, it is his biblical 'vision', rather than the clearly ill-founded notion that by sailing westwards a shorter route to India could be found, which forces Columbus across the dreaded Atlantic four times.

This figuralism, based on a literal interpretation of biblical texts and a Scriptural reading of reality, lies behind the typologies Columbus and the whole of Western civilization have applied to the New World. Columbus's own son, Ferdinand, maintains that his father's name means 'dove', because he took the grace of the Holy Ghost to the New World he discovered, revealed the Son of God to the ignorant, like the Spirit 'in the shape of a dove' when John baptized Christ, and carried the olive-branch and baptismal oil over the waters of the ocean, like the dove of Noah's ark.[34] In the sixteenth century, the Jews read his name as a version of Isaiah's 'doves' and considered him a new Jonah, the 'dove' who embarks for Tarshish. By 1591 the Catholics, through Ulisse Aldrovandi, are corroborating this reading.[35]

In the *Libro de las Profecías* Columbus quotes a passage from a letter from the Genoese ambassadors to the Spanish kings (1492), in which the Calabrian abbot, Joachim of Flora, had predicted that 'he who was to rebuild Jerusalem and Sion would come from Spain'. He himself repeats the prophecy in his account of the fourth voyage (1503).[36] Nor is it accidental that the great Dominican Bartolomé de Las Casas, author of the *Historia de las Indias*, to whom we owe an enormous part of what we know of Columbus's exploits, writes that 'we must indeed believe that the Holy Ghost prophesied that those who would first convert these peoples would come out of Spain'.[37] If the notion of the American Indians' constituting the remnant of the ten lost tribes of Israel was widespread in the sixteenth century, Paul Claudel, in our own

---

[34] Quoted by P. Moffitt Watts, 'Prophecy and Discovery: On the Spiritual Origins of Christopher Columbus's "Enterprise of the Indies" ', *American Historical Review*, 90 (1985), 101.

[35] See J. Gil, *Mitos y utopías: 1*, 215–16.

[36] *Textos y documentos completos*, 288, 327.

[37] B. de Las Casas, *Historia general de las Indias*, ed. J. Perez de Tudela and E. Lopez Oto (Madrid, 1957), i. 127, p. 340b.

century, still believes that Columbus 'portait le Christ', and calls him 'la Colombe', the Holy Ghost in, so to speak, 'person'.[38]

While only touching on some of the more obvious aspects of the Columbus mystery, I may seem to have wandered miles from my theme just to prove that in 'Fourteen Hundred and Ninety-Two | Columbus sailed the ocean blue'. My actual purpose was a little different. My intention was certainly not to suggest that the 'discovery' of the New Continent, which came to completion only when the 'other' received the name 'America',[39] was the result of hazy geography, fantastic biblical exegesis, chivalric romances, and creative readings of the classics. What I did want to underline was that poetry and reality are historically related at least through typology, figuralism, and prophecy, and form a complex intertextual web without understanding and enjoying which we cannot even begin to approach wider methodological issues.

This means, implicitly but still urgently, that attention be paid to the ways and means whereby, in Jaussian terms, their alterity becomes our modernity. I shall try to explore some of these now and in the following chapters. It has to be said immediately that this process will in no way be a neutral affair: at each step, as the examples of Tiberius, Dante and his children, Columbus, and Purchas have proved, we shall stumble across ideological and political motivations.

Moreover, a nagging awareness that a choice is required here of our own 'impure' reading affects the very process of enquiry, acting like Heisenberg's principle of indetermination. The kind of question we ultimately have to ask is: whose side are we on? That of Ulysses, or Isaiah, or the Argonauts, Tasso, Columbus? Why? What—psychologically, culturally, historically, and politically—makes our predecessors and ourselves prefer one of these characters? And how does this inclination affect their and our interpretation of the past and its links with the present? It is these enquiries into power, and into the cultural, intellectual, but also personal consequences of poetry and its encounter with history, which should motivate and move us.

To understand the urgency of these questions it was necessary to

[38] See J. de Labriolles, 'Le Christophe Colomb de Paul Claudel', *Columbeis*, 2 (1987), 365–78.
[39] T. Todorov, *The Conquest of America: The Question of the Other*, trans. R. Howard (New York, 1984).

show both the similarities and the differences between the two typological systems, the one essentially biblical, the other substantially classical. At the centre of both lies the image of the Earthly Paradise, the *nova terra* within sight of which Dante's Ulysses is shipwrecked, and which Columbus claims to have, literally, rediscovered.

The idea is so exciting not simply in embodying the literal Land of Plenty and Eldorado (far from negligible factors, these, and destined to predominate more and more), but also, and above all, because it represents the myth of human happiness and innocence, our living without death but *with* knowledge, in a society which is to be built by throwing off, once and for all, the notion of original sin. Poetry, which comes from death, has naturally always talked about what is basically the other aspect of its origins and its *telos*—Life. Hence Dante's lines, spoken by Matelda, about the Earthly Paradise, with all their terrible, twofold nostalgia, for the condition and for the poetry:

> Quelli ch'anticamente poetaro
> l'età dell'oro e suo stato felice,
> forse in Parnaso esto loco sognaro.

Those who in old times sang of the age of gold and of its happy state perhaps dreamed on Parnassus of this place.[40]

The place, then, is the stuff dreams—poetic dreams—are made on, which is perhaps only possible on Parnassus, and in antiquity. Dante the pilgrim visits it in the other world, and Dante the poet, vying with his predecessors, evokes it in poetry. Then, with Christopher Columbus, the dream apparently comes true. Let us examine the two figural systems side by side. The prophet of Columbus is Isaiah, and his fulfilment that of an imminent and immanent Messiah; his descendants are all those Europeans who, in becoming Americans, founded not just Troys and Ithacas, but above all the many Salems, New Canaans, and New Salems; those who, through Thomas Jefferson, will later incorporate into the Declaration of Independence of the United States man's inalienable right to 'the pursuit of happiness'; and all those who, with Whitman, will exclaim: 'Ah Genoese, thy dream! Thy dream! |

---

[40] *Purgatorio*, xxviii. 139–41.

Centuries after thou art laid in thy grave, | The shore thou foundest *verifies* thy dream.' Columbus's typology leads to the 'American dream', possession, conquest, and the transformation of reality.

Tasso's *figura* is a mythic archetype, Ulysses, and his prophet, intertextually, Dante. Precisely when poetry meets history at another of its moments of crisis, the shipwreck disappears. Passing the Pillars of Hercules, venturing into infinite seas, and reaching the *Nova Terra* is no longer a transgression carrying the penalty of death. On the contrary, it becomes a paradigm for humanity's highest destiny, pursuing virtue and knowledge by the exclusive means of the human intellect, and on the planet earth. Dante's Ulysses is the *typos* of the pure Discoverer. This dream too, as marvellous as the first, has lasted, as we have seen, down to our own century. Yet this too, like all human undertaking, contains in its inception a core of shadow.

4. *From Land to Land, towards the Whirlpool: Obliquity, Impurity, and Restless Readings*

> Since then, at an uncertain hour,
> That agony returns:
> And till my ghastly tale is told,
> This heart within me burns.

It would be neither possible nor useful to propose a general, 'genealogical' reading of texts and events through time. It is of course useful to remember (cf. the previous chapter) that Western culture contains a number of significant typologies; but, to obey at least two of Calvino's six 'memos' for the next millennium, namely lightness and quickness, we must consider the sequence of works obliquely, laterally, taking side paths and paying attention to the 'sense of analogy',[1] and to the echo which poetry, narrative, and history send reverberating among themselves within time, which we can only catch if we listen with an open mind and ear.

To put it more directly: a complete genealogical reading of Ulysses would, at this point, mean the painstaking reconstruction of all references to him, direct and indirect, from the sixteenth to the twentieth century, and a discussion of the cause–effect relationship between them. What, for example, links Du Bellay with Ronsard, Ronsard to Bacon, and then Spenser, who in Book II of the *Faerie Queene* directs his Guyon towards the Bower of Bliss along the route mapped out in *Odyssey* XII, and so on.

A reading of the kind would produce two alternative results: either a simple but inevitably incomplete catalogue, the Library being by nature Babelic and infinite, as Borges realized; or a Plan like that followed by the protagonists of Umberto Eco's *Foucault's Pendulum* on the faint tracks of the Templars, constructing a parallel History in which everything is interdependent, meaning everything and nothing at the same time.

[1] I. Calvino, *Six Memos for the Next Millennium* (Cambridge, Mass., 1988). For the 'sense of analogy' see R. Calasso, *I quarantanove gradini* (Milan, 1991), 491 and *passim*.

Equally implausible is another kind of genealogical reading, similarly partial and collateral: taking the poems on Christopher Columbus in the various European languages, particularly Italian and Latin, from the sixteenth to the nineteenth century. From Giuliano Dati, who in 1493 produced an *ottava rima* version of Columbus's letter to the Spanish monarchs on his first journey, to Tassoni's aborted *Oceano*, to Tommaso Stigliani and Umbertino da Carrara, down to Bernardo Bellini and Lorenzo Costa, Italian culture, to limit ourselves to this alone, is bursting with Ulysses, Pillars of Hercules, and doves. These side roads are not without their diversions: in the Genoese writer Lorenzo Costa's *Cristoforo Colombo*, from 1846, the Admiral's son, Diego, falls in love with the beautiful native Azema, a descendant of the Dorias whose ancestors left with the Vivaldi brothers (the ones we met with Dante's Ulysses at the end of the second chapter) and were shipwrecked on the shores of the New World in 1292![2]

This sort of reading would meet with considerable obstacles. Against the advantages of an, as it were, archaeological, but still incomplete overview of the Italian or European *imaginaire*, the fact would remain that the interest of these works is substantially historical. They are without 'aura', they strike no chords in us, and project no shadows from their alterity which reach our modernity. The new episteme inspires only one great epic poem, Camões's *Lusiads*, celebrating Vasco da Gama's expedition to the *real* Indies. The Renaissance was obviously so struck by the sudden apparition of the 'false' Indies that its muse could only remain silent before the 'other'.

Having devoted some time to rhetoric in the preceding chapter, we shall once again be returning to poetry, after a moment of transition. It is here that readers are caught out in all their obliquity and impurity. Not only do they vault lightly and carelessly over the established canons of tradition, leaping from branch to branch of the family trees: they will also consciously undermine, with unpredictable aesthetic intuitions, the comfortable safety of historicist enquiry. They will sweep through time and space with restless, impatient desire, partly ignoring all philology's hard work and twisting and turning their heads to follow whatever shadow takes their fancy.

---

[2] For these, see the essays in *Columbeis*, 1 (1986) and 3 (1988).

An oblique and impure reading, an 'imperfect criticism',[3] is of course implied in the previous chapters, but is even more necessary in the present one, where it constitutes the minimum condition for an understanding of poetry in history. Let us begin from where we left off at the end of the third chapter. We left Ulysses in the light of the *nova terra*, suspended between events and texts, fulfilment and prefiguration, simultaneously inside poetry and rhetoric. We shall now start off, with thematic *ratio*, from America itself, from intertextuality and history, mid-way between rhetoric and poetry, but this time facing the shadow.

Let us begin with the account given in a Latin poem, perhaps the most famous and elegant of the Renaissance, Girolamo Fracastoro's *Syphilidis sive morbi Gallici libri tres* (1530),[4] in which Ulysses puts in an oblique appearance. The poem is dedicated to the terrible disease which spread (or became rife again) in Europe in the late fifteenth and early sixteenth century, and which the American Indians are blamed for transmitting to Columbus's sailors. This is how a cultured mind, considerably different, then, from that of Menocchio described in Carlo Ginzburg's *The Cheese and the Worms*,[5] reacts when faced with new facts.

In the third Book of his poem Fracastoro recounts Columbus's exploits, mixing bits and pieces from his various transatlantic voyages. Like Dante's Ulysses, he passes Gibraltar. Soon afterwards, he and his men are considered new Argonauts. On the night of 11 October the Moon announces to Columbus that on the following day he will sight the Island of Ophir. On landing the sailors meet, not the Indians, but a huge flock of parrots, which they proceed to shoot. A surviving parrot then prophesies that the wretched Spaniards will have to atone for the killing of the birds, sacred to the Sun, by undergoing terrible labours on land and sea, fighting many peoples, losing many ships, and encountering the Cyclops (i.e. the Cannibals), finally falling prey to a dreadful disease. Very few of them, the bird concludes, will ever return home.

The reader now expects to see Columbus's men meeting the natives—or rather, the nativesses—and catching syphilis. But

---

[3] A. Lombardo, *Per una critica imperfetta* (Rome, 1992).

[4] *Fracastoro's Syphilis*, ed. and trans. G. Eatough (Liverpool, 1984).

[5] C. Ginzburg, *The Cheese and the Worms: The Cosmos of a Sixteenth-Century Miller*, trans. J. and A. Tedeschi (Baltimore, 1980).

Fracastoro is much more subtle than that. The cacique of Haiti, Guacanagari (here, in classical fashion, called simply 'rex'), tells the European 'dux' that his people's ancestors, natives of Atlantis, were cursed with the pestilence 'for their offences against the Gods and the wrath of Apollo'. Syphilus, a shepherd who tried to replace Sun-worship with king-worship, was the first to catch it. As the Indian chief ends his story, the ships which had been sent back to the Old World return, bringing the astonishing news ('proh fata occulta Deorum', the poet comments) that the same pestilence is darkening the skies of Europe. At this point a more serious rumour runs through Columbus's ranks: his own men are in the grip of the illness, and only a tree from this strange world, the 'holy wood' of Hyacus ('guaiacum' or 'guaco'), can cure them.

In brief, we have in this proto-Felliniesque pastiche a splendid, indirect, and nuanced example of sixteenth-century mythologization of contemporary events. Potatoes, tomatoes, corn, and, less beneficently, tobacco all came from America. Syphilis too, probably. But whether it actually did or did not—so a mechanically historicistic and socio-psychoanalytical explanation would run—it was necessary and inevitable for the Old World to believe that all the New bestowed was not gold, or the Golden Fleece: that the shadow of death was hidden behind the light of Paradise.

In actual fact Fracastoro is a great humanist, a serious physician, and a brilliant writer. He never establishes a direct cause–effect relationship between the discovery of America and the outbreak of the disease in Europe, merely suggesting a complex and fatal parallelism ('proh fata occulta Deorum', precisely) between the two, obliquely reading the Spaniards' infection as 'fulfilment' of the parrot's prophecy. On the one hand, then, he practises a sort of mimesis which retains all the mystery and horror of syphilis, while elegantly sweetening the pill by creating a myth, giving the disease a name, and suggesting a cure for it. On the other hand, he is presupposing ('implying') a very special kind of reader (the book was actually dedicated to none other than Pietro Bembo), and putting him in a somewhat difficult position. Readers of Fracastoro's poem find themselves incapable of understanding his complicated syphilis mechanism unless they can make the connection between all the ingredients and interpret it: pastoral poetry, Dante's Ulysses, the Argonauts, Atlantis, the plague in the *Iliad* and in *Oedipus Rex*, the biblical Ophir, the Holy Rood, the general Virgilian frame, and, to come to our theme indirectly, as posited, the identification of Columbus's sailors with those of Odysseus' companions who had slain the Oxen of the Sun.

This oblique and impure 'invention' is the key to reality, and access to the key is through a spot of source- and allusion-hunting, one of the important 'pleasures of reading':[6] we need intertextual interpretation to understand the world. The 'implied' reader theorized by Wolfgang Iser will inevitably be oblique and impure.[7]

To come back to poetry now. Even the most strictly 'mythical' imagination realizes that all that glisters is not gold. After Fortune's prophecy, Carlo and Ubaldo, the knights of the *Gerusalemme Liberata* we followed in the third chapter, set their sail to the southwest, like Dante's Ulysses, and sight 'oscuro un monte', a dark mountain. In the 'real' world, this is Tenerife, in the Canary Islands. Tasso immediately compares it with a pyramid and at the same time Mount Aethna, identifying the archipelago with the Happy Isles where the 'prisca etate' situated the Elysian Fields. Fortune comments that they are 'fertile, beautiful, and happy', adding immediately, however, 'ma pur molto di falso al ver s'aggiunge' ('yet much that is false lies together with the true'). The 'oscuro monte' is a rereading of Dante's dark mountain, and its summit is soon afterwards revealed as a splendid garden which resembles the Earthly Paradise and is described through intertextual echoes of *Purgatorio* XXVIII. Furthermore, this is precisely the place where the beautiful enchantress Armida, whose appearance is preceded by that of a Siren, amorously holds Rinaldo prisoner in a gilded cage.

Dark mountain, Elysium, Eden, Siren: the 'unpurg'd images of [yester]day return'. But is this not the Renaissance, is this not Tenerife? Why should Tasso project a shadow on something which exists and is familiar to him? One answer might be, of course, that this is a literary game. Yet we only have to think of the historical context, and of Tasso's own psychological circumstances (the Counter-Reformation, now in full swing, bringing devastating doubts to an already precarious mental balance) to realize how unsatisfactory an answer this is. The process at work here, the interpreter is forced to conclude, is more complex.

[6] R. Alter, *The Pleasures of Reading in an Ideological Age* (New York, 1989).
[7] W. Iser, *The Implied Reader* (Baltimore and London, 1974).

Note, first, how the superimposing of literary past and present (Dante's ante-text beneath the Tasso text) produces a temporal short-circuit just when reality and invention make contact. When Carlo, bowled over by enthusiasm at the sight of the Blessed Isles, asks permission to set his foot on and see 'these unknown shores, the peoples and the cult of their faith'—i.e. to do now, at the time of the Crusades, what Ulysses could not do and what, by Tasso's time, Christopher Columbus and others had managed to do half a century before—Fortune replies (xv. 39–40):

> Ben degna invero
> la domanda è di te, ma che poss'io,
> s'egli osta inviolabile e severo
> il decreto de' Cieli al bel desio?
> ch'ancor vòlto non è lo spazio intero
> ch'al grande scoprimento ha fisso Dio,
> né lece a voi da l'ocean profondo
> recar vera notizia al vostro mondo.
>
> A voi per grazia e sovra l'arte e l'uso
> de' naviganti ir per quest'acque è dato,
> e scender là dove è il guerrier rinchiuso
> e ridurlo del mondo a l'altro lato.
> Tanto vi basti, e l'aspirar più suso
> superbir fòra e calcitrar co 'l fato.

The question is indeed worthy of you, but what can I do if the inviolable and severe decree of heaven is against the noble desire? The entire space of time has not yet passed which God has fixed for the great discovery, nor is it licit to you to bring true news from the deep ocean to your world.

To you it is given by grace and beyond the art and the custom of sailors to go through these waters and to land where the warrior is kept prisoner and take him back to the other side of the world. Let this suffice you; the aspiring higher would be pride and fighting against fate.

The prohibition thus reappears, but strangely. It is no longer eternal ('acciò che l'uom più oltre non si metta'), but limited in time (until the 'grande scoprimento'); it is also partial: Carlo and Ubaldo are now, at the time of the Crusades, allowed to sail these seas to free Rinaldo, though not to explore the *terra firma*. The fiction is exploded, in other words, but with a knock-on effect on the theology underlying the previous myth—no small matter, given that this is original sin. Lastly, by creating such an overtly fictional time parenthesis, and putting it on the same plane as his own present perfect, Tasso is indirectly undermining the 1492 of history.

The same displacement occurs at a spatial level. The island of Shakespeare's *The Tempest*, while implicitly referring to the New World, must geographically be somewhere in the Mediterranean. In the same way, Tasso's island, although representing America, is actually the archipelago of the Canaries. It is as if Tasso were forced to displace the sphere of the imaginary from outside-the-world, from the world of the imagination and the 'other world', to inside-the-world, but on the edge of it, on its *limen*.

And this displacement, this enforced 'liminality', is a covert indication that the enthusiasm for the refound 'pelago infinito', and the sense of wonder at the discovery of the new continent, have turned into an uncanny seduction. What terrors, what temptations may be hiding behind the pristine beauty of the New World? Could it be that the paradise apparently 'regained' on earth, out in the west, was actually 'lost' after all? With a single, subtle, merely intertextual brush-stroke, tormented Tasso sees the beautiful darkness ahead, detects the 'false' beneath the 'true', and deconstructs America.

Poetry reads its own forebears obliquely and impurely. Dante's Ulysses becomes Tasso's Columbus, and changes into a positive model. But Ulysses' adventure in *Inferno* XXVI—in its turn an impure medieval version of a classical myth—already established a literary model which undermined its century's episteme. In Tasso's hands, Dante's words and images become a torpedo launched against the culture and science of his own time, destroying Columbus's literal interpretation of the Bible and wiping out all the Renaissance's hope and faith. America is no longer Paradise (nor, admittedly, is it yet the place of a tragic shipwreck); it looks for all the world like an Eden where the serpent may at any moment slither out of the luxuriant vegetation—out of the shadow.

The poetic reading seeks out and widens the cracks already existing in the text it rewrites. Dante's Ulysses found a chink in the stony absoluteness of relations between Being and becoming, and his tongue of fire went licking into it. Now a piece of that stone has fallen. Metaphysical and, simultaneously, immanent value can no longer be attributed to the mythical prohibition of the supreme Other. The 'other' now shifts to the real world, within geography and culture: in America and its inhabitants, in the *nova* but now familiar *terra*, violated and possessed.[8]

Odysseus, however, was never a colonizer; nor was the Ulysses who succeeded him, founding Lisbon and Asberg, an Aeneas or a 'conquistador'. His descendant is not Robinson Crusoe but Magellan, whose flagship the *Victoria*'s coat-of-arms proclaimed 'sunt mi vela alae', proudly taking up with an ominous foreboding of disaster the Homeric and Dantean simile of the journey to Hades. The moment arrives, then, when division and alterity can no longer be projected outwards, on to a far-off world.

The problem, of course, has always been within ourselves: the Old English *Seafarer* was well aware of the torments and anxieties of winter sea-journeys, and felt it as an 'exile', but at the same time he yearned to be on the 'whale-paths', sighting far-off, foreign countries. Those who sail the oceans, he states, are possessed by perennial 'longunge': restlessness, weariness, and desire.

The awareness of how impossible it is for man, by his very nature, to unite the opposite banks of its inner division only becomes radical when the sea before him becomes infinite *within* him. Pascal (to skip obliquely among cultures and centuries) puts his finger on it in a famous passage which contains no explicit mention of Ulysses:

Voilà notre état veritable. C'est ce qui nous rend incapables de savoir certainement et d'ignorer absolument. Nous voguons sur un milieu vaste, toujours incertains et flottants, poussés d'un bout vers l'autre. Quelque terme où nous pensions nous attacher et nous affermir, il branle et nous quitte et si nous le suivons il échappe à nos prises, nous glisse et fuit d'une fuite éternelle. Rien ne s'arrête pour nous. C'est l'état qui nous est naturel, et toutefois le plus contraire à notre inclination; nous brulons de desir de trouver une assiette ferme, et une dernière base constante pour y édifier une tour qui s'éleve à l'infini; mais tout notre fondament craque, et la terre s'ouvre jusqu'aux abimes.

Such is our effective condition. It is this which renders us incapable both of full knowing or absolute ignorance. We row over a vast sea, forever uncertain and fluctuating, blown from one extreme to the other. Each end to which we intend to moor and fix ourselves eludes us; and, if we give it

---

[8] T. Todorov, *The Conquest of America: The Question of the Other*, trans. R. Howard (New York, 1984).

chase, evades us and escapes in eternal flight. Nothing will stand still for us. This is our natural state and yet that which is most contrary to our inclinations. We burn with the desire to find a firm footing and a final safe base on which to erect a tower rising up to infinity; but all our foundations flounder, and the earth opens up to the abyss.

An impure reader will meet old and new shadows within this passage, and more radical signs of disquietude. On the one hand, the sequence seems to be Dante's 'alto mare aperto', Tasso's 'pelago infinito', Pascal's 'milieu vaste'; humanity swept from one side to the other recalls the *Odyssey*, particularly the Scylla and Charybdis episode; and the Tower of Babel seems to rise up clearly. On the other hand there is the accent on fluctuating human uncertainty, the elusiveness of any 'end', and the flight of the object before the pursuing subject. The metaphorical language is chastened by a severe austerity; it is no longer *mythos* but implacable *logos*. At its centre lies the fundamental contradiction behind our knowledge: the 'natural state' on the one hand, and 'our inclinations' on the other. Thus the ardour of Dante's Ulysses becomes a burning Babelic desire and the shipwreck an apocalyptic catastrophe, the sinking of Atlantis, and the gaping open of Hell.

Nothing will stand still for us: there is no ultimate base, no *nova terra* to be reached, occupied, and constructed. 'Experience' as ultimate knowledge, of beginnings and ends, is ontologically impossible. Humanity, in the mass conferred on it by nature, is suspended between the two abysses, infinity and nothingness: a nothing compared with the infinite, but an everything compared with nothing—a middle way between everything and nothing. Infinitely far from understanding these extremes, humanity will find the end and beginning of things forever shrouded in impenetrable secrecy, and is as far from understanding the nothingness it comes from as it is the infinity which engulfs it. It only knows it must soon die; but, not knowing death, which in any case it cannot avoid, humanity is reduced to 'a *shadow* which lasts but for an instant without return'.

The darkness deepens within, and being itself is shadow. Whatever horizon Ulysses scans, this internal Hades, fully self-aware, will dog his steps. And if we avoid W. B. Stanford's[9] 'genealogical'

---

[9] W. B. Stanford, *The Ulysses Theme* (2nd edn., Ann Arbor, Mich., 1968).

route, continuing on our oblique way, we again meet Ulysses head on at the next 'dissociation of sensibility', when Romanticism is deliberately revolutionizing the traditional *imaginaire* and establishing a new one.

It is perhaps not incidental that the manifesto of English Romanticism, the *Lyrical Ballads* (1798), begins with Coleridge's *The Rime of the Ancient Mariner*, containing the first *nekyia* of the modern world. As 'ancient' as Odysseus and the flame apostrophized by Virgil in *Inferno* XXVI, and as old as Ulysses at the Pillars of Hercules, the Mariner returns to his homeland like Homer's hero and is shipwrecked like Dante's. He stops a wedding-guest, holds him with his 'glittering eye', and, with the obsessive rhythms of his words, transfixes his listener with his tale of the totally arbitrary shooting of the albatross, the ghastly stillness of the ship, the curse of his dying companions, the placing of the albatross like a cross around his neck, the encounter with the skeleton ship and its 'ghostly Crew'—Death and Life-in-Death—playing dice for the Mariner's life, his spontaneous blessing of the water-snakes, the albatross's dropping from his neck, the deep sleep during which he is driven towards his native country, and, when faced with the question 'What manner of man art thou?', the 'agony' which seizes him and forces him to tell his tale:

> Since then, at an uncertain hour,
> That agony returns:
> And till my ghastly tale is told,
> This heart within me burns.
>
> I pass, like night, from land to land;
> I have strange power of speech;
> That moment that his face I see,
> I know the man that must hear me
> To him my tale I teach.[10]

[10] The text of the *Rime* used here is that published by E. H. Coleridge, *The Poems of S. T. Coleridge* (London, 1961 reprint), 186–209. This substantially reproduces the 1834 edition in the *Poetical Works*, the last emended by Coleridge himself before his death. Between 1798 and 1834 the *Rime* underwent considerable textual changes, one of the most important being the addition of the prose gloss finally published in *Sibylline Leaves* (1817). For the significance of these changes, see the two classic studies by W. Empson, 'The Ancient Mariner', now in his *Argufying*, ed. J. Haffenden (London, 1987); and by P. Adair in her *The Waking Dream: A Study of Coleridge's Poetry* (London, 1967). For my purpose here it is essential to read the text(s) and gloss together, the latter supplying the first-hand commentary which inspires my own.

The Mariner enjoins the Wedding Guest to bless God's creatures, then disappears, while his stunned listener leaves the feast; the following day he awakes 'a sadder and a wiser man'.

To sail the seas, transgress, meet with all manner of wonders, encounter the Other, go beyond death, and tell his tale is Ulysses' destiny too, right from his appearance on the mythical and literary scene. The *Rime* takes up all these themes but bends them to its own poetic ends, superimposing symbols and allegories and blending different mythological and cultural elements taken variously from Platonism, Christianity, and the Romantic philosophy of nature, into a singular concretion. Above all, Coleridge's poem shifts the very centre of the Ulyssean imaginary.

Homer's Odysseus aims at return; Dante's at knowledge and the world behind the sun; Columbus at the discovery of a new route to the Indies and to Eden. The Ancient Mariner's journey has neither destination nor motivation. As in the real life of each one of us, and as in dream, everything *happens* to the Mariner. He is the object of events, of Nature, of the Spirits, and of Death-in-Life: an Odysseus frozen in the image projected through Books IX–XII of the *Odyssey*, when the gods are putting him to the severest tests, driving him from land to land in this world and the next, gradually killing off all his companions. Significantly, the two myths coincide on one point: both Odysseus and the Mariner are borne back to their homeland in their sleep, the ship manned by others.[11]

Under the influence of the unfathomable agents working on man from without, and the uncontrollable impulses of his own nature from within, in the end the Mariner becomes the object of his own story, which 'is told' whenever the agony returns and erupts from his burning heart.[12] He acts as subject, that is, on only four occasions: when he kills the Albatross; when he bites his arm and sucks the blood to announce the apparition of the ghost ship; when he blesses the sea-snakes; and when he asks the Hermit for confession.

The first gesture is clearly fundamental, the whole of the rest of the action springing from it, as we and the protagonist soon learn. Now, whether or not we want to interpret the Albatross as a Christian symbol (as the sailors themselves do, greeting it 'in God's

[11] J. L. Lowes, *The Road to Xanadu* (Boston, 1927), 286–8.
[12] The impersonal emphasis is a later change. In 1798 the lines read: 'That anguish comes and makes *me* tell | My ghastly aventure'.

name' 'as if it were a Christian soul'), it is first and foremost a manifestation of being. Appearing through the mist, the bird suddenly passes, and 'crosses' the sky, an immanent and incarnate presence. The Albatross appears as *that which is*: all that is other and Other than man, independent and different from him but open to contact and communion. A silent trace of being in human space and time, it is surrounded by a halo of beauty; when, for nine nights, it stays on the mast or the sails, a white luminescence gleams.

But 'humankind cannot bear too much' numen, and it provokes irresistible, congenital evil. Just as a child puts out the light of the glow-worm by squashing it in his palm, so the Ancient Mariner, in an act of unmotivated *hamartia*—an error which is blameable only in the context of general human fallibility—destroys being and crucifies beauty with his cross-bow.

His punishment will thus be a precise and terrible retaliation, in Dantean terms a *contrapasso*: to experience the dread of non-being, to be immobilized and burn in a putrefying hell; and to die while living. It is at this point, significantly, that the Mariner acts for the second time, biting his arm. At the first apparition of the mysterious sail, ready for the *nekyia*, he drinks the blood like the souls of Hades before Odysseus. He confronts the Other, accepts and evokes death, acquires the word which only death can give, and succumbs to the Life-in-Death towards which Dante's Ulysses rushes, desirous: becoming a being full of non-being, a shadow.

This experience, which marks him and changes him for ever, is, however, vital. Having outstared death—in the sea, in the sky, in his companions, and, through their dead eyes, in himself—the Mariner is now able to look at the world around him quite differently. In the shadow cast on the water by the ship in the moonlight, being no longer appears full of horror, but of light:

> Beyond the shadow of the ship,
> I watched the water-snakes:
> They moved in tracks of shining white,
> And when they reared, an elfish light
> Fell off in hoary flakes.

> Within the shadow of the ship
> I watched their rich attire:
> Blue, glossy green, and velvet black,
> They coiled and swam; and every track
> Was a flash of golden fire.

To be contemplated in the happiness and splendour of living things, beings have to return to the shadow. Humans never meet their vision of beauty face to face. Its blaze is reflected in the wake it leaves behind it, and remains ineffable ('no tongue | their beauty might declare'): it can only be blessed in a sudden rush of love, unconsciously, accepting the trace it offers gratuitously. The Mariner is able to pray. The dead Albatross his companions hung around his neck like a cross falls off into the sea.

The journey is resumed in sleep, in oblivion, and, more prosaically, in rain. His soul is now light, the dead bodies have been transformed into angelic choirs, and harmony resounds throughout the whole of Nature. The second phase of expiation can thus be shorter than the first. Meanwhile, in a trance, the Mariner is directly accused of killing the Albatross, and the chain of love between the Spirit, the bird, and man is fully revealed to him. It is this man, the Mariner, who broke the chain (the Spirit 'loved the bird that loved the man | Who shot him with his bow'). Recognizing the demon voices within his soul, he also recognizes his own fault. The unmotivated error, man's unconscious, original *hamartia*, is thus subsumed under his personal sin. This is the moment Oedipus realizes he has killed his father and fathered his children with his own mother.

Once taken back to his homeland, the Mariner turns to the Hermit for confession, and probably for Christian absolution and penitence. Both are denied him. Even earlier, when the second spell had been broken, he was able once again to contemplate the green sea and far-off horizon, but could see only a minimum part of what had previously been visible. He proceeds, like Dante, terrified of the devil at his back: 'Like one, that on a lonesome road | Doth walk in fear and dread, | And having once turn'd round, walks on, | And turns no more his head; | Because he knows, a frightful fiend | Doth close behind him tread.' The 'alto passo che non lasciò già mai persona viva', which the *Inferno* XXI quotation intertextually glances at, was, then, even at that point, a burden in the soul, the enemy breathing down and at his neck. The lacerating agony which seizes the Mariner and forces him to speak leaves him free at the end of his narration, only to return constantly 'at an uncertain hour' until the story has again been told. Pain produces poetry, but poetry without salvation, and poetry which is always the same.

Homer's Odysseus is moved by Alcinous' poet to tell of his own adventures; he then repeats them to Penelope, and lastly returns with himself, his affections, his house, and his kingdom intact. Dante's Ulysses labours atrociously to eject a voice, but, by the end of his tragedy, the flame is straight and still 'and speaks no more', unburdened of the need to transform the fire into a tongue although it is condemned to burn for ever.

The Ancient Mariner's destiny is a concentration of the two sentences. Although he knows it would be pleasanter even than joining the marriage feast to go with other human beings to the church to pray, his fate is to remain outside the church and the place of the wedding-feast (and therefore outside the Kingdom of Heaven, according to Matthew 22), to walk the earth with a tongue of fire which can never be extinguished. His journey and narration are endlessly recurrent, like the circles of Hell.[13]

To expiate, accept and bless beauty, pray, and confess—nothing will be sufficient for the man who, in common with the rest of humanity, has (even once) annihilated that which is. Human poetry can only retell its own genesis: not its creation, but how it is engendered by humanity's intrinsic fallibility and unattainable redemption. Poetry sings the pain of a creature which forever stands on a threshold.

Whoever is touched by the white and leprous skin of Death-in-Life remains suspended in it, beyond the reach of Pascal's mankind, between infinity and nothingness. At the moment humanity is closest to the beauty-which-is, it desires an all which lies forever beyond its reach. As the Ancient Mariner in the prose gloss Coleridge later adds to his *Rime*:

In his loneliness and fixedness he yearneth towards the journeying Moon, and the stars that still sojourn, yet still move onward; and every where the blue sky belongs to them, and is their appointed rest, and their native country and their natural homes, which they enter unannounced, as lords that are certainly expected and yet there is a silent joy at their arrival.

Alone and immobile, humanity yearns for an impossible Odyssey through the whole cosmos: movement which is also fixity, a somewhere and an everywhere which will always belong to it, and a journey over the great sea of being towards its destined port, but also the return of the long-awaited master. Wracked by this desire for eternal motion and eternal rest within silence, humanity's

---

[13] See A. Serpieri, *Retorica e immaginario* (Parma, 1986), 301–31.

destiny is however to wander, like the night, from land to land with a 'strange power of speech', become a shadow among shadows, and become, as the Ancient Mariner appears to the Wedding Guest, 'long, and lank, and brown, | As is the ribbed sea-sand': just a thin, dark, barely perceptible line on the shore, made and erased by each whisper of the waves, the slenderest of threads between being and non-being.

Such is Ulysses' Romantic fulfilment: beyond return, beyond shipwreck into the vortex, towards the fate of the Wandering Jew, he seems embarked on Odysseus' final journey as prophesied by Tiresias—a journey now, literally, without end. Far behind the sun, beyond the sunset in which Life-in-Death claims him for her own, he himself becomes the disquieting 'other'.

But where, then, is the *nova terra*, readers may ask at this point? We know that the Ancient Mariner's route was based on Magellan's circumnavigation, and even more closely on Captain Cook's second expedition. Here, however, in the metamorphosis of sixteenth-century history into Romantic poetry, the same Magellan Tasso had proclaimed emulator and conqueror of the sun now becomes night moving from land to land. James Cook, who had penetrated the emerald ice of the South barely thirty years before the writing of the *Lyrical Ballads*, had concluded with near certainty that the 'Terra Australis Incognita', the great antarctic continent theorized by geographers, either did not exist or lay so near the Pole as to be unreachable by sea. Coleridge's tale would be very different without this vanishing of the *nova terra* at the 'other pole', into the nothingness or unreachable distances.

The epigraph to the *Lyrical Ballads*, taken from the seventeenth-century Thomas Burnet's *Archaeologia-Philosophica* and added by Coleridge in 1817, states that in the universe invisible presences are more numerous than visible ones, and that human intelligence has always tried to learn about them in vain:

It is therefore useful to contemplate the image of this better and greater world from time to time in the soul as if it were in a picture, so that the mind, accustomed as it is to the minutiae of present life, restrict not itself too much and be not completely reduced to small thoughts.

Cook's experience wipes out or makes irremediably remote the scientific hypothesis of a *nova terra* in the south, circumscribing with great precision the bounds of ascertainable reality. Coleridge uses these bounds as dividing lines between the real and the imaginary, as poetry's inner shores. The latter would be impossible without the former. Science is necessary to poetry, offering it the margins on which to construct myth.

The myth of the character we can now rightly call the *Ancient Mariner* is, in a figural sense, the shadow which geographical explorations project on to a 'greater' world, that which in the human soul reflects, as in the artist's canvases, the unfathomable mystery of things. This world has no use for a *nova terra*: everything it contains is new and old and unchanging. For this reason the myth of the Ancient Mariner is, in an existential sense, the shadow of living-dying which we all experience and out of which poetry is produced before our eyes, telling the same tale over and over again.

We, oblique and impure readers, are now profoundly restless. Like the Wedding Guest listening to the Ancient Mariner, we stand stunned and senseless, as if reeling from a blow. Sadder and wiser men—and women—tomorrow, without doubt, we too turn our backs on the wedding-feast. Touched by poetry, we remain outside human company and outside the kingdom of heaven.

As we have already seen, Christopher Columbus and several others after him, down to Walt Whitman, believe this kingdom can be brought about, on this earth and within human time, in the New World. Let us now return, then, quickly and obliquely, to the continent which marked our departure-point at the beginning of this chapter. The Ancient Mariner's suspended state could not last long: it is anathema to humanity, which prefers death to living-and-permanently-dying. The Mariner's most direct descendant, the ghostly Flying Dutchman, perpetrates Ulysses' transgression by trying to double the Cape of Good Hope. He is therefore condemned to wander the seas endlessly until the Day of Judgement, when the dead are reborn and he will be absorbed into the nothingness he so desires. The second wave of Romanticism gives an alternative, however: his agony will end if he finds a woman who will be faithful to him unto death.

In Wagner's *Der Fliegende Holländer* (performed for the first time in 1843), the Dutchman finds her: he is saved by Senta who at the end of the opera dives into the sea out of love for him. The ship immediately sinks into a vortex which is that of both Dante's

Ulysses and Coleridge's Mariner: 'Das Meer schwillt hoch auf und sinkt dann in einem Wirbel wieder zurück'—the sea swells up and falls back into a whirlpool. The scene, however, is now dominated by the light of the rising sun, in which Senta and the Dutchman are seen to emerge, transfigured, from the wreck of the ship and ascend to the sky.

The New World is meanwhile producing whirlpools which are second to none. The imagination of an Edgar Allan Poe, for example, presents itself as a spiral which whirls deep into the abyss. In three of his best-known works, the *Manuscript Found in a Bottle* (1833), the *Narrative of A. Gordon Pym* (1838), and *A Descent into the Maelstrom* (1841), the scene returns obsessively, tied to the Earth's farthest extremes and accompanied by the shadows of the Dutchman and the Ancient Mariner.

The narrator of the *Manuscript* sets out from Java as a passenger on a ship bound for the Sunda archipelago. The crew is then swept overboard by a hurricane which lasts for five days, taking the ship further and further southwards until it is immersed in an 'eternal night'. A giant vessel suddenly looms up out of the darkness, rams the ship, and sinks it. Thrown on to this ship by the force of the collision, the protagonist gradually discovers all its terrifying weirdness. This crew sweep over the decks like ghosts, unseeing: decrepit sailors, the residue of foreign chronicles and days long gone, their voices low and broken, their skin shrivelled, their eyes full of anxiety and disquietude. The passenger at this point decides to keep a ship's log and then entrust the manuscript to the sea, in a bottle. The ship is driven by the current towards monstrous ramparts of ice, 'walls of the universe', at the South Pole, clearly directed at 'some exciting knowledge—some never-to-be-imparted secret, whose attainment is destruction'. The ice splits and the ship begins to turn in immense concentric circles, around the borders of a gigantic amphitheatre, the walls of which disappear upwards into darkness and distance. The circles narrow, the ship vibrates with the ocean's roar, and then hurtles into the neck of the vortex.

The adventures of Gordon Pym, although often a paraphrase of actual journeys, similarly feel the tug of the final whirlpool. Mutiny, the near-destruction of the ship in a storm, an encounter with a Dutch vessel piled high with a cargo of corpses, hunger, cannibalism, rescue by a schooner, savages—nothing can stop the protagonist's 'foolish flight' towards the southern limits. In the tracks of Captain Cook and the explorers who followed him, Pym is hell-bent on solving the great problem of the antarctic. He ends up in a tiny canoe driven by the currents to the threshold of the South Pole itself, but beyond the glaciers, in darkness and surrounded by ever hotter water the colour of milk. A curtain of vapour stretches before him over the whole horizon; like a never-ending cataract which silently drops from a mountain-top, a sheer and remote 'wall' in the seething ocean, slicing open an abyss. In the final moment, as his canoe rushes forwards, out of the vortex there appears a shrouded human figure, gigantic, its skin 'the perfect whiteness of the snow'.

In the third tale we descend into the maelstrom, this time near the North Pole. The Norwegian sailor who tells the story is sucked with his brother and their fishing-boat into the great Moskoe-ström; he spirals downwards on the inside edge of the enormous funnel, overcome by the desire to explore it even at the price of death. By the golden moonlight he sees deep within the abyss the spray of the waters hurtling down, and over it a wonderful rainbow, 'like that narrow and tottering bridge which Musselmen say is the only pathway between Time and Eternity'. From the bottommost mists an inhuman cry is raised. Clutching a barrel, the sailor throws himself into the sea, leaving brother and boat to their fate; they circle round two or three times before descending prow-forwards into a chaos of spray. When the whirlpool has subsided, the barrel and sailor float to the top. Rescued by fishermen, friends of his, the protagonist is neither believed nor recognized, such is the change and ageing he has undergone.

The journeys to Hades Poe describes in these stories are inserted one within the other like the arms of a spiral. First, there is the penetrating of the I within the depths of self, the wrapping of the psyche round itself in a constant confrontation of unconscious impulses and *a posteriori* attempts to rationalize. The narrative is dominated by plausible details, fragments of reality, and cause and effect; in the *Manuscript*, for example, the protagonist rushes sternwards when the great bulk of the ghost ship crashes on to the prow, so that he is almost levered on to its rigging. The story's seemingly total logical cohesion proves, however, to be like the surface up to which the Norwegian sailor's barrel finally floats. It carries the clinging human figure who has experienced the underwater spirals: the fantasies, horrors, and transgressions; the obsessive and disquieting repetition of ontogenetic and philogenetic scenes such as the desired and displaced encounter with the 'other'; the impulse towards annihilation and death; and the barriers, the void, and the pulverization of the I into spray.

This deliberate and inexorable psychic descent holds out no salvation even in analysis, in the narration which opens out before our eyes like a second, tortuous ascent from hell. The sailor who tells of his descent into the maelstrom ages in one short day: he is neither recognized nor believed, and expects no credence from his listener, the narrating I of the story, and of course the reader. Between experience and narration the gulf of death has opened. The narrative comes, like that of the tongue of fire, from the beyond, bearing arcane traces of it: inscriptions in undecipherable characters precede it, as in *Gordon Pym*, like mute signs pre-announcing the writing to follow; casual pen-strokes, as in the *Manuscript*, trace the word 'Discovery'. The account is presented as an accidentally surviving posthumous residue—a manuscript in a bottle. Writing and reading have become a living dying.[14]

One thing the Norwegian sailor does not dare to describe: the cry rising from the bottom of the abyss. This cannot and must not be repeated by human tongue, since it contains the cry of the soul reaching its own innards, and the deafening rumble of being crashing against the nothingness.

The journey towards the maelstrom also has its metaphysical dimension. Over the appearing void is thrown the shining and delicate bridge joining the two banks of Time and Eternity. Below this wavery bound, in the jaws of nothingness, there should lie the *sub-stantia*, the very substratum of being: hence the gigantic walls, and the never-ending cataracts. But in reality both are simply curtains of spray. Should we then look for being in the funnel itself, in its solid, ebony-hard walls? But these are formed by the whirlwind motion of water, of becoming. The only conclusion this vain circling around interpretation can possibly lead to is thoroughly paradoxical: being exists only within the absurd vortex of becoming towards nothingness. All we can do is contemplate the sphinx in which all contradiction is exposed and transcended: the white Titan, wrapped in a shroud, which rises up from the bottom of the earth.

[14] See J. G. Kennedy, *Poe, Death, and the Life of Writing* (New Haven, Conn., 1987).

The psychic, artistic, and metaphysical journey has all the trappings of a scientific expedition: if the protagonist of the *Manuscript* feels he is rushing at the cost of his life towards the discovery of an inviolable secret, the Norwegian sailor is desperate to poke his nose into the abyss and worm out its secrets. Like a new, more attentive Columbus, he observes with pleasure and almost pedantry every particular of this natural phenomenon, and quotes Archimedes to explain how a barrel will survive a maelstrom better than any other object. Gordon Pym is anxious to experience the other pole and find the solution to the enigma of the Antarctic, succeeding where Cook and his successors failed. What he finds, however, as he gets nearer and nearer to his goal is an unexpected and populated new world, from which the ice has melted, where the climate is mild, and where there is no continental mass, but a warm, milky ocean plunged in darkness. The Pole is there, but as a 'void', looking the exact opposite of that described by traditional geography. This is a 'negative' Pole, a hole on which everything converges and by which everything is swallowed, according to Captain Symmes's rather quaint theories, defended before the Congress of the United States by the Reynolds Pym quotes so frequently. The exploratory expedition follows very real historical routes, uses the actual accounts of modern navigators, and celebrates with an excess of pedantry the triumphs of the rational-experimental *logos*. Once beyond the Pillars of Hercules, however—beyond the 'walls of the universe' which the ice raises to mark the edge of the world—the log-book records a growing sluggishness of body and spirit, and makes its oneiric entrance into the dimension of *mythos*. At this point the science on which the Western world, and America in particular, intends to found the kingdom of heaven on earth is once again forced into silence. Within sight of the mountain, Ulysses once more plunges into the abyss.

Moby Dick (1851), the apex of the 'American Renaissance',[15] is final proof that nineteenth-century American culture felt its own Mariner-like compulsion to repeat a scene of this kind. Here, too, the narration ends with shipwreck into the abyss, and again it acts as a 'marker' of a journey of transgression, beyond the limits imposed by God and nature, undertaken by an old man who

---

[15] F. O. Matthiessen, *American Renaissance* (New York, 1941).

abandons his wife and child. Like Dante's Ulysses, Ahab persuades his men (who, significantly, never become his 'companions') to follow him in his desperate undertaking, in an 'orazion' which quickly turns into an initiation ceremony and act of diabolic communion. The motivation is now to all appearances sheer revenge against the monster which has taken off the captain's leg, and no longer 'virtue' and 'knowledge'.

Dante's Ulysses is certainly one of Ahab's relatives, one of his 'figures' several times removed. Other shadows come between them, separating but also uniting them: within history, Columbus, who, Melville informs us, comparing his voyages to whaling expeditions, 'sailed over numberless unknown worlds to discover his one superficial western one'; and Magellan, whose circumnavigation of the globe the *Pequod* repeats, but which Ishmael, *Moby Dick*'s narrator, considers aimless wandering towards 'barren mazes' or the inevitable shipwreck:

Were this world an endless plain, and by sailing eastward we could forever reach new distances, and discover sights more sweet and strange than any Cyclades or Islands of King Solomon, then there were promise in the voyage. But in pursuit of those far mysteries we dream of, or in tormented chase of that demon phantom that, some time or other, swims before all human hearts; while chasing such over this round globe, they either lead us on in barren mazes or midway leave us whelmed.

In myth and literature, Ahab is preceded by the Prometheus who so obsessed the Romantic imagination (Ishmael compares them explicitly); by Faust, whom he obliquely but most clearly incarnates; and above all by the Ancient Mariner—as the evocation of the albatross and the skeleton, ghost-like whaler *Albatross* prove.

Dante's Ulysses wishes to experience the other world and reaches the threshold of the new one, the mountain of the earthly Paradise forbidden to humanity after the Fall: hence his sinking by the Christian God. Ulysses' audacious final journey is undertaken out of a desire for exclusively human knowledge: without, but not against, a God whom in any case he does not know. Ahab, an 'ungodly, god-like old man', is in obsessed pursuit of what his chief mate Starbuck considers a mere 'dumb brute', but which Ahab himself sees as the 'wall' keeping humanity prisoner, the 'mask' behind which 'some unknown but still reasoning thing puts forth the mouldings of its features'. 'Sometimes I think,' Ahab confides to Starbuck, 'there's naught beyond. But 'tis enough. He tasks me, he heaps me; I see in him outrageous strength, with an inscrutable malice sinewing it.' This 'inscrutable thing' is precisely what Ahab loathes; the White Whale can be its 'agent' or prime cause, demiurge or Creator: either way, it is the divinity Ahab is pitching himself against.

At the roots of being Ahab sees an eternal cancer, devouring its own creatures. Ahab's God is a Satan who has condemned humanity to a life of physical, mental, and moral torment; Moby Dick is the 'monomaniac incarnation of all those malicious agencies which some deep men feel eating in them', the 'intangible malignity which has been from the beginning':

All that most maddens and torments; all that stirs up the lees of things; all truth with malice in it; all that cracks the sinews and cakes the brain; all the subtle demonisms of life and thought; all evil, to crazy Ahab, were visibly personified, and made practically assailable in Moby Dick.

Ahab's is a limitless anger, a radical, ontological rage which is the 'sum of all . . . hate felt by his whole race from Adam down', towards fate and all the evils flesh has forever been heir to, and which humanity cradles within itself, as if it were a self-generated disease. Job-like, Ahab indicts God himself. Rejecting all idea of original sin in humanity ('Talk not to me of blasphemy, man' he hurls back at Starbuck's reproof), he turns the accusation against humanity's Creator: 'damned, damned most subtly and most malignantly! damned in the midst of Paradise!' Rarely has literature voiced our inevitable protest at being 'flies to wanton boys' with more vehemence.

Ulysses trespasses beyond the Pillars of Hercules and is killed by the Other, which his tongue of fire then challenges, *sottovoce*, from the depths of Hades. Ahab is then Ulysses' unhired killer, attempting intertextual vengeance against this Other. Driven by an inner fire and an irresistible, 'nameless, inscrutable, unearthly' power, he is a living tongue of fire, a 'darkness leaping out of light' who calls to the bar the supreme Fire, the 'unbegotten', 'unborn', 'omnipotent' Spirit himself. He 'fulfils' Ulysses by trying to take the ultimate rebellion of his *typos* to its extreme conclusion, actively contesting the 'Other' who 'willed'.

In Moby Dick's 'whiteness'—a neutral sign, or empty symbol waiting for meaning to rush in—neither Ahab nor Melville now read the basic stuff of being, as Coleridge and the Mariner had in the *Rime*'s albatross. This whiteness now stands for 'indefiniteness', which 'shadows forth' (that shadow again . . .) 'the heartless voids and immensities of the universe', and thus 'stabs us from behind with the thought of annihilation'. Being has been replaced by 'visible absence', 'dumb blankness'—by the nothing of non-being, in itself empty, but full of bewildering, terrifying meaning.

Stabbed by this nothing, Ahab becomes timelessly old, 'feeling deadly faint, bowed, and humped, as though [he] were Adam, staggering beneath the piled centuries since Paradise'; an Adam who sees, not the dark mountain of the *Purgatorio* but 'a hump like a snow-hill', Poe's white giant. Moby Dick, the ubiquitous, eternal White Whale, the 'grand god', surprisingly reveals himself in 'gentle joyousness—a mighty mildness of repose in swiftness', like a serene mask of unperturbed Being. To be allowed to contemplate this placid and almost benign theophany from afar is in itself sufficient: to desire to kill it and 'strike through the mask' is irresistible, but fatal. The sublime Whale is transformed by man into a horrifying 'other'.

The circumnavigation of the seas, the obsessive search, the Faustian *hybris*, and the merciless hunt all founder against this insuppressible manifestation of being. At the end of one of the greatest and most subversive Odysseys ever written, Melville has Ahab and his men perish at the very moment they encounter and engage with the Whale. In three meagre days Leviathan destroys a crew which, coming from every region of the earth, represents the whole of humanity. Ahab, the obsession-ridden leader of the expedition, is strangled by the line of his harpoon rammed into the monster's flank, and hurtles with it through the air in a flight towards the void. The ship is then struck, and the 'Descartian vortices' observed months before from the mainmast—the 'scientific' images whereby humanity attempts to reduce the cosmos to mechanical laws[16]—are revealed in all their foolishness when confronted with the concentric circles of the universe which truly *is*:

[16] H. Beaver in H. Melville, *Moby Dick* (Harmondsworth, 1972), 764–5, 965. See also W. H. Auden, *The Enchafed Flood: or The Romantic Iconography of the Sea* (New York, 1951); H. Bruce Franklin, *The Wake of the Gods: Melville's Mythology* (Stanford, Calif., 1963); Z. Zoellner, *The Saltsea Mastodon* (Berkeley, 1973).

And now, concentric circles seized the lone boat itself, and all its crew, and each floating oar, and every lance-pole, and spinning, animate and inanimate, all round and round in one vortex, carried the smallest chip of the *Pequod* out of sight . . .

The ship sinks with a sky-hawk caught inside Ahab's flag: 'like Satan' the *Pequod* 'would not sink to hell till she had dragged a living part of heaven along with her'. And 'now small fowls flew screaming over the yet yawning gulf; a sullen white surf beat against its steep sides; then all collapsed, and the great shroud of the sea rolled on as it rolled five thousand years ago'.

Melville so perfectly understood the tragic message Dante's Ulysses had bequeathed to the modern age that he superimposed the Fall of Milton's Satan and the time of the Flood on the Dantean shipwreck: hence his comparison, in *White Jacket*, of the first navigator's doubling of 'terrible' Cape Horn with the 'descent of Orpheus, Ulysses, or Dante into Hell'. Ishmael, *Moby Dick*'s narrator, is himself sucked towards the vortex, rotating 'like another Ixion', and rises again attached to a 'coffin life-buoy', to be rescued by the *Rachel* and thus ready to tell his tale: a *nekyia*, another circular *mythos*. The myth is a Genesis narrating the entry of the New World into History with the shadow of a transgression and the 'great shroud' of death. Now, through Whitman's poetry, America is celebrating itself and Christopher Columbus. With Melville that same America is paying for its original sin by repeating, as if in ritual sacrifice, the shipwreck of the Ulysses who had discovered it.

5. In Breve Carta: *Science and the Poetry of Knowledge*

e il naufragar m'è dolce in questo mare

and shipwreck sweetly comes in such an ocean.

IN Book Three of Wordsworth's *Prelude*, the first *epos* of the self, the protagonist recounts his experiences during his student years in Cambridge. On moonlit nights, from his room in college Wordsworth could see the entrance to Trinity College Chapel and the statue of Isaac Newton. In memory he appears 'with his prism and silent face': an image in which the instrument used to develop Newton's theory on light-refraction seems to throw a mysterious, polyhedric glow over the marble face of silence.

More than thirty years after this version of the poem, Wordsworth, inspired by Thomson's elegy 'sacred to the Memory of Sir Isaac Newton' (1727), added two verses which were to become famous. The statue, with its mute prism face, now appears as 'The marble index of a mind for ever | Voyaging through strange seas of Thought, alone'.

The Odyssey of Wordsworth's Newton is solitary and unending, like that of Coleridge's Ancient Mariner, but there is no circularity, nor any idea of suspension or damnation. The static marble indicates a possibly labyrinthine route, through unknown and astonishing seas, and among the green islands of the blessed which, as Thomson wrote in the elegy, shine in 'vast eternity's unbounded sea'; but the line dictated by the 'index' is unending. Leaving aside, then, the Romantics' objections to science in general and Newton in particular, guilty of 'destroying all the poetry of the rainbow by reducing it to the colours of a prism',[1] what emerges here in Wordsworth's lines could be considered a poetic icon of scientific thought in its progess through space and time. Modern science has moved, in Alexandre Koyré's words,

---

[1] M. H. Abrams, *The Mirror and the Lamp* (London, (1953), 309, paraphrasing Keats. And see M. Nicolson, *Newton Demands the Muse* (London, 1946).

from a 'closed world' to an 'infinite universe'.[2] Newton's statue is a portrait of the past and a present symbol conceived, however, for the future. In this *imago* the light of the moon (and, in the corrected version, of the stars too) is refracted by the mind which will make its solitary and perennial voyage through the infinite cosmos.

Poetry gives voice to the silent face, launching science, too, on to the 'alto mare' first opened up by Ulysses, and the infinite seas of Tasso and Columbus. Wordsworth's Newton has no need of a mythological *typos*; he himself, in the statue, has become—in death, in memory, and in the imagination—a myth. The same fate had already befallen Galileo, called a new Tiphys by Campanella and Marino; in 1807, in his *Sepolcri*, Foscolo honours his tomb, defining him simply as he who 'to the Englishman of wide-spreading wing | First cleared the wide route to the firmament'.

Considerably different is the poetic Odyssey Wordsworth traces in *The Prelude* itself, an account of the development of a 'transitory Being' and his mental growth. This Odyssey, like Dante's *Commedia*, is circular in structure but with a linearity stretching unswervingly towards the *telos* of the supreme Vision.[3] The poem opens with a walk which brings the protagonist, at twilight, to the Valley chosen for his seclusion, and ends at the moment when, settled finally into his Grasmere Valley home, he reminds his interlocutor, Coleridge, of the spirit in which the poem was begun.

The *Prelude*, then, is the account of an ideal *nostos*, a return through memory. It records the genesis of poetry as a series of waves of powerful illumination, and, like all poetic Odysseys, a repetition of scenes of recognition: *anagnorisis*. The journey itself is the main thread of the narrative. This is a factual account (Wordsworth's journey through the English and Welsh countryside, through Revolutionary France, through the Alps, and into Italy) which, in the remembrance of things past, takes on a symbolic, mythic, and historical value: the Christian's pilgrimage throughout the world; an Odysseic voyaging over 'the barren sea' towards 'other coasts'; a Dantean itinerary through the hereafter;

---

[2] A. Koyré, *From the Closed World to the Infinite Universe* (Baltimore and London, 1967), and P. Zellini, *Breve storia dell'infinito* (Milan, 1990).

[3] M. H. Abrams, *Natural Supernaturalism: Tradition and Revolution in Romantic Literature* (New York, 1971), ii, i; v, ii; G. Hartmann, 'A Poet's Progress: Wordsworth and the *Via Naturaliter Negativa*', *Modern Philology*, 69 (1962), 214–24.

the return of Milton's Muse from hell to paradise; and the sentimental and educational journey of the Romantic and the Englishman on the Grand Tour.

The culmination of the journey is the ascent of Mount Snowdon. Here, in moonlit contemplation of the silent ocean of mist which, pierced only by the mountain-peaks, covers the whole countryside down to the sea separating Wales from Ireland, the poet suddenly notices a clearing in the haze, through which emerges the rumble of numerous streams. In this deep, dark cleft Nature has deposited 'the soul and imagination of all'. In this meditation on the mountain, the new Moses receives the revelation of

> The perfect image of a mighty mind,
> Of one that feeds upon infinity,
> That is exalted by an under-presence,
> The sense of God, or whatsoe'er is dim
> Or vast in its own being—[4]

Nature has become transcendent in the poetic imagination. From the beginning poetry was perceived as a 'mild creative breeze', a 'prophecy' which becomes a 'tempest, redundant energy'; the mind which, through its meditation, makes the world begin, like the dove-like Spirit brooding over the abyss a second before Creation in Milton's *Paradise Lost*.

Its task will be to discern 'something unseen before', to sing the world of suffering beings and common things, thus transforming it into a *new world*, to experience with ineffable joy and above all to recognize and give utterance to 'the sentiment of diffused being' over organic and inorganic material; over everything which, lost to human thought and consciousness, and invisible to the human eye, the heart recognizes as alive:

> the sentiment of Being spread
> O'er all that moves and all that seemeth still;
> O'er all that, lost beyond the reach of thought
> And human knowledge, to the human eye
> Invisible, yet liveth to the heart;
> O'er all that leaps and runs, and shouts and sings,

---

[4] Wordsworth, *The Prelude* (1805), xiii. 69–73; ed. J. Wordsworth, M. H. Abrams, S. Gill (New York and London, 1979).

> Or beats the gladsome air; o'er all that glides
> Beneath the wave, yea, in the wave itself,
> And mighty depth of waters.[5]

While science sails over the strange seas of Thought, poetry journeys towards a knowledge of being, beyond the limits of thought and human learning, towards a new world: for the Romantics, the poet is the true Ulysses.

Keats spent one evening 'looking into Chapman's Homer', and transfigured the idea in one of his most memorable sonnets. Here his travels through 'the realms of gold', his visits to the 'many goodly states and kingdoms', and his wanderings 'round many western islands' constitute oblique readings of Ulysses' own peregrinations. But it is the poets who 'in fealty to Apollo hold' the very archipelagos, the Happy Isles beyond the setting sun; and Homer himself now rules the 'wide expanse' of the new world. An Eldorado of poetry, a paradisal Parnassus rising from the depths of the Ocean (as Keats's echo of Cary's *Paradiso* XIX suggests) glitters with its 'pure serene' through the aura of Chapman's translation. The encounter with Homer's text produces the shock of excitement and wonder which comes to scientists, discoverers, and conquerors alike. Keats feels like 'some new watcher of the skies | When some new planet swims into his ken'—the same awe the astronomer Herschel must have felt when he discovered Uranus. In a similar stupor Balboa stared at the Pacific, and Cortez at Mexico City (Keats superimposes the two images). There, 'upon a peak in Darien', the Ulyssean reader contemplates the ancient *nova terra* of poetry among men who mirror his dazed wonder by looking at each other 'with a wild surmise'. Like Odysseus standing before the Sirens, he is surrounded by total silence.

If the aim of poetry is to speak Wordsworth's knowledge with joy, and to provoke Keats's astonished silence, then Ulysses can reach the new world without being shipwrecked; humanity—or at least the poet and his reader—will be without sin for all its tasting of the fruit of the tree of Eden: indeed, precisely because it is still tasting it. In the previous chapters we saw the New World's two totally

---

[5] *The Prelude* (1805), ii. 420–8; and see G. Hartmann, *Wordsworth's Poetry 1787–1814* (2nd edn., Cambridge, Mass. and London, 1971).

divergent reactions to this positive scenario, through Whitman and Melville respectively. Meanwhile, back in the Old World, things are more complex; at this point in the nineteenth century, its explorers are combing the globe and conquering at least three continents.

Tennyson, the poet-symbol of the Victorian age, writing in the most romantic and simultaneously most imperial of nations, England, wrote his 'Ulysses' in 1833, although it was published in 1842, when Wordsworth was revising *The Prelude*. No better platform, then, from which to review the poetry of knowledge at another crucial moment in history: the age of faith in scientific progress, of the triumph of technology and industry, of imperial expansionism, and of the affirmation of capitalism.

'Ulysses' is a dramatic monologue based, at Tennyson's own admission, on Tiresias' prophecy in *Odyssey* XI, and *Inferno* XXVI: the two shadows, the two 'figures' whose reincarnations we have been following—whom we have been shadowing—throughout the present work. After long years back in his homeland, Tennyson's Ulysses, 'tardy with age', wishes to set out again on one last great journey westwards.

At the beginning of the monologue he is at the point between abdicating and departing. Seemingly weary of reigning, Lear-like, he feels listless, idle, and redundant. The island he governs is 'barren', its inhabitants 'savage', 'that hoard, and eat, and sleep', and its laws, which he himself 'mete[s] and dole[s]', are far from even-handed. It is with this ruthless diagnosis of *petit-bourgeois* materialism and the arbitrary nature of power that Ulysses begins to speak. Contrasting impulses war within him: curiously, in the very first line he states that to reign over such a state is useless and 'profitless', immediately adding that his hearth is 'still'; his now elderly wife Penelope is a burden to him, and above all else he resents the fact that his people do not 'know' him. In short, this is a Ulysses who speaks the same economic language as his subjects, but behind it, bursting with *amour propre* and almost limitless egoism, he displays an irrepressible disgust for the tedious normality of family and administrative life.

Gone is the Dantean Ulysses' 'duty to an aged father', and withered his love for Penelope; even his 'fondness for a son' is transformed. Tennyson's Ulysses loves Telemachus, and mid-way through his monologue appoints him his successor ('This is my son, mine own Telemachus ... Well-loved of me') with the words of the Father ('This is my beloved Son, in whom I am well pleased'); he praises his discerning and steady prudence, and proclaims him 'most blameless'. He considers him both too much his own flesh, and at the same time too much his own man: 'He works his work, I mine.' It is difficult not to read ambiguity in his praise of Telemachus, with hints of high-handed irritation and superiority. The son's task will be to complete the work of the father: to civilize a 'rugged people' with prudence, and subjugate it gently, by degrees, to the 'useful and the good'. His sphere of action is to be that of 'common duties': 'decency', the sense of what is right and proper; the 'offices of tenderness' and sensitivity, and 'meet adoration' of the 'household gods'. Ulysses sees in Telemachus the model of political wisdom, fairness, and conservative but reasonable and enlightened administration—the 'pious Aeneas' of the Roman tradition, and the fair-minded and scrupulous progressive of the British Empire.

Against the figure of his heir (who within the poem is granted no right of reply), the old man sets himself: a hero of ancient times, an untiring seeker of knowledge, a Ulysses who is truly 'impious' and satanic and at the same time uncertain, contradictory, Hamlet-like, with premonitions of death: ready to depart, but not yet into the 'alto mare aperto'. From the beginning, after his confession that he is weary of reigning, he announces that he 'cannot rest from travel', which is for him a 'drink[ing] life to the lees'. It is his past life which he considers: his memories of great joy and great suffering, alone and in company, on land (although significantly the word he uses is 'shore', as if life within sight of the ocean were the only conceivable one), and when 'the rainy Hyades | Vext the dim sea'.

This line, with its echoes of Virgil, Horace, Shelley, Shakespeare, and Milton, is Ulysses' utterly serious presentation of himself: intrepid sailor and man of endless experience. 'I am become a name', the line ends: he is conscious of being a myth: the myth of a man who, endlessly journeying 'with a hungry heart', has, like the hero of the *Odyssey*, 'seen and known ... cities of men | And manners' but also himself, and, like the hero of the *Iliad*, has 'drunk the delight of battle with [his] peers, | Far on the ringing plains of windy Troy'. Ulysses has reconstructed his identity as man and literary character. Introducing Virgil to Byron, Classicism to Romanticism, he now declares himself 'a part of all that [he has] met', like Aeneas and Childe Harold. Like Dante's Ulysses possessing 'experience of the world', he has become a living portion of that world, and has experienced life in its totality.

Transporting Dante's Ulysses on to a Romantic stage implies, however, charging him with tensions which will reproduce and intensify the tragic division of *Inferno* XXVI. The yearning for universal participation which rules Tennyson's Ulysses is in sharp contrast with experience, in that it is Dante's 'esperienza' transformed by Romantic yearning—primarily a personal aware-ness which strives to become universal knowledge of what experience itself actually is. And experience is 'immobilized' because radically divided. On the one hand it appears as 'an arch wherethrough | Gleams that untravelled world', a vision through a glass, darkly, as it were, of a luminescent 'mondo sanza gente', of the undiscovered country of death from whose bourn, as Hamlet reminds us, no traveller returns; on the other, it seems the surfacing awareness of that world's unattainable 'liminality', and humanity's absolute marginality, the knowledge that the threshold 'fades | For ever and for ever' 'when [man] moves':

> I am a part of all that I have met;
> Yet all experience is an arch wherethrough
> Gleams that untravelled world, whose margin fades
> For ever and for ever when I move.

Basically, this is again the tragic consciousness of modern civilization so vibrantly described by Pascal: the unattainable mooring-place, the eternal flight of things, the objects of know-ledge, from humanity's grasp. Here, however, there is no Pascalian God hidden away, but only 'that eternal silence', Pascal's 'silence éternel de ces espaces infinis', but above all *that* silence, like *that* untravelled world—the suppressed but strenuous breath of imminent death, which 'closes all'.

Halting is senseless, Tennyson's Ulysses insists; it is merely idle to establish a definitive *telos* in life, and wearisome and foolish, as Hamlet and Shakespeare's Ulysses, in *Troilus*, also maintained, to 'rust unburnished, not to shine in use!'. As if breathing were living! 'Life piled on life | Were all too little'; and in any case this Ulysses too, like Dante's, knows he has come to 'this so brief vigil of the senses that remains to us': 'of one to me | Little remains'.

Yet just as, some lines earlier, Ulysses had set his awareness of being part of the entire experience of things against the awareness of a diminishing of experience itself by the remote light of death, in the same way he now feels that although little of life remains, each hour is still saving 'something more' 'from that eternal silence'. Ulysses' monologue, like his life, is all contradiction: the 'but's and 'yet's undermine the 'for's which attempt explanation of his psyche and his world. Every element of his speech is in a state of suspension and development, re-enacting our lives and our thought processes. Everything, in his perception and experience as in ours, is vague or unclear: a gleam of light, 'something more', 'something ere the end'.

There is a good dose here of that Romantic indeterminacy which likes to suggest mysterious depths, the arcane echo between things and the human mind: like the flashes of semi-extinct thought, the 'sense sublime | Of something far more deeply interfused, | Whose dwelling is the light of setting suns' which Wordsworth speaks of in *Tintern Abbey*. But this vagueness is also a fulfilment of the laboured murmuring of Dante's tongue of fire. The 'something more', the excess which saves us from the eternal silence, is the announcement of the new gospel (the 'bringer of new things'), whose prophet was Dante's Ulysses:

> and vile it were
> For some three suns to store and hoard myself,
> And this grey spirit yearning in desire
> To follow knowledge like a sinking star,
> Beyond the utmost bound of human thought.

At an existential level Tennyson's Ulysses rejects the grossly material *ethos*, the acquisitive frenzy of his subjects. Life will be spent and extinguished by death, and must, with urgency, be spent and not saved by living mortals: 'choose not to deny experience', as Dante's Ulysses urges his companions. In re-creating the Dantean 'ardour', however, Tennyson makes a series of decisive transformations, not least that of actually doubling this ardour into a desire turned in on itself, a 'yearning in desire' which feeds off itself: the Gospel's first announcement is the *cupido cupiendi*. From the second and most important object of this desire, Dante's 'virtute' has disappeared, leaving only 'conoscenza': hence the unexpected image 'like a sinking star'. In the ambiguous convolution of the lines, the clearly luciferine charge of the simile hangs over both subject and object, both man and his knowledge, both classified as sinking stars, suns which are setting. Lastly, the knowledge Ulysses pursues is without a goal, aiming 'beyond the utmost bound of human thought'.

These are most certainly not the seas Wordsworth's Newton sailed over which, however strange, are still the seas of Thought. Nor is this the aim of Wordsworth's poet, which was to perceive 'all that is lost beyond the reach of thought | And human knowledge' but merely in so far as it was the recipient of the sentiment of being.

The question, then, is: what knowledge is possible beyond the bounds of the thought which should produce it, in the absence of any kind of poetic imagination? The only conceivable answer seems to be in terms of literary and cultural prediction and fulfilment. Tennyson's Ulysses fulfils that of Homer's Tiresias and of Dante's *Inferno*, but in so doing creates a short-circuit between experience and marginality, desire and knowledge, learning and thought, prophecy and rhetoric. With no way out for himself, he can predict only one, of which we become personal and impure witnesses: the crucial moment in European culture when Nietzsche's Zarathustra will announce that he must 'go down' and set like the evening sun, when it goes behind the sea carrying light to the nether world—in short, that he must follow knowledge like a sinking star. When Zarathustra descends from the mountain with the knowledge that God is dead, enters the city, and speaks in the market-place, he informs the crowd that:

Man is a rope, fastened between animal and Superman—a rope over an abyss.

A dangerous going across, a dangerous wayfaring, a dangerous looking-back, a dangerous shuddering and staying-still.

What is great in man is that he is a bridge and not a goal; what can be loved in man is that he is a *going-across* and a *down-going*.

I love those who do not know how to live except their lives be a down-going, for they are those who are going across . . .

I love those who do not first seek beyond the stars for reasons to go down and to be sacrifices: but who sacrifice themselves to the earth, that the earth may one day belong to the Superman.

I love him who lives for knowledge and who wants knowledge, that one day the Superman may live. And thus he wills his own downfall.

A new Ulysses, Zarathustra indicates the journey awaiting us, and which we are loath to undertake:

There stands the boat—over there is perhaps the way to the great Nothingness. But who wants to step into this 'perhaps'? None of you wants to step into the death-boat.[6]

But this is precisely what Tennyson's Ulysses does:

> There lies the port; the vessel puffs her sail:
> There gloom the dark broad seas.

In the *orazion picciola*, when he finally addresses his 'old and slow' sailors after speaking at such length to himself, this Ulysses shows he is fully aware that 'death closes all'. Yet—a further contradiction—he believes that something worthy of fame, 'something ere the end', can still be achieved. The lights begin to twinkle on the cliffs, the long day closes, the moon slowly rises, and the abyss groans with many voices. This is the moment to turn the prow towards morning, to make wings of oars for the foolish flight, and to encourage those who only now become 'friends', the only 'others' he acknowledges outside himself in that they are his own appendages:

> Come, my friends,
> 'Tis not too late to seek a newer world.

This is his aim: not a *nova terra*, but a new*er* world, a place which is doubly 'other'. Ulysses' explicit purpose is:

> To sail beyond the sunset, and the baths
> Of all the western stars, until I die.

'Di retro al sol'—'beyond the sunset': the scriptures are fulfilled. Tennyson's Ulysses follows Dante's; he undertakes the long journey prophesied by Tiresias; he resolves to go beyond the sunset which, for Wordsworth, contains the sublime essence of things; he decides, like Zarathustra, to *set*. That 'something ere the end' now moves towards its end: 'until I die'. There, in that 'meantime', in

---

[6] F. Nietzsche, *Thus Spoke Zarathustra*, trans. R. J. Hollingdale (2nd edn., Harmondsworth, 1971), 43–4, and 224. 'To follow knowledge like a sinking star . . .' was also the young Tiresias' aim in Tennyson's first draft of 'Tiresias'. A very different choice is announced by some of Odysseus' sailors in Tennyson's 'The Lotos-Eaters': 'Oh rest ye, brother mariners, we will not wander more.'

the Nietzschean 'perhaps', the newer world opens up. There, in that fore-seen, much-desired, and unrecounted moment, we die.

But even now Tennyson's Ulysses is positing an alternative: shipwreck or arrival at the Happy Isles, where, he declares, he may 'see the great Achilles'. This is the supreme illusion, the greatest repression, like Dante's Ulysses on sighting the dark mountain, and a hope shared by Tennyson himself, writing 'Ulysses' immediately after the death of Hallam, and desperately creating for him an afterlife among the blessed. A similar reading is macroscopically 'impure', however, for both Ulysses and Tennyson know quite well that Homer's Achilles is spending eternity, not in the Elysian Fields, nor in Tasso's Happy Isles, but in darkest Hades.

Poetry cannot solve problems of life and death; rather, it increases them, making its reader even more restless. The tiniest chink, a moment's *lapsus*, or an intertextual discordancy is sufficient to reveal what Montale calls 'la piccola stortura | d'una leva che arresta | l'ordegno universale' ('the slight distortion | of a lever, arresting | the mechanism of the universe').[7] If Tennyson was trying, as he stated, to express in 'Ulysses' the need to 'go on' and 'face life's battle' after the loss of Hallam, what he describes is not progress, but motionless, Hamlet-like suspension, ending with Hamlet's own question, which we put when looking at *Inferno* XXVI: where does Ulysses think he is going; where is knowledge, or, for that, life itself, going?

It is, of course, possible to see the alternative Tennyson's Ulysses posits for himself as only apparent, and, reading 'Greek' consistency in a text which barely glances at it, consider the two ends as sequential: first death-by-water, then, obviously (Hades or Elysium), the world of the dead. The fact remains, however, that in Tennyson's monologue Ulysses' last journey, the one prophesied by Tiresias and which Dante has him narrate, neither begins nor ends. The voyage, the shipwreck, and the immortality of Tennyson's Ulysses are potential, not actual. He is, as he is keen to inform us, a name. But which: Odysseus, Ulysses, or Nobody? His marginality, his need for knowledge without an object, his being-for-death, are

---

[7] E. Montale, 'Avrei voluto sentirmi', in *Ossi di seppia: L'Opera in versi*, ed. R. Bettarini and G. Contini (Turin, 1980), 57.

reflected in this mere potentiality, this anonymity of a myth with which the reader is all too familiar.

From the beginning of the monologue, Ulysses' journey is projected towards the shadow of an *arkhe* and a *telos*, a beginning and an end, a Genesis and a Revelation, which intertextually drag him back towards ancient, Homeric and Dantean myth. Typologically, i.e. figurally, this hero fulfils Ulysses' destiny now, in Victorian England, in what has been called the Doom of Romanticism,[8] but opens up a gap devoid of content and full of questions. He becomes a name in his turn, a sign devoid of a potentially embodied signifier: a myth open to the future.

Ulysses appears as a sort of scales in which the 'much which is taken' and the 'much which abides', as he puts it in the final verses of the monologue, weigh equally, human destiny being to live between privation and permanence, yesterday and tomorrow, today belonging to words and desire: to the rhetoric of prophecy and poetry.

He can accept this weight, which runs the permanent risk of suddenly becoming unbearable lightness (of non-being) in the eternal silence, in that he and his companions, 'made weak by time and fate, but strong in will', are at his own recognition individual components of being, in the Pauline formulation of God's *ho on*: 'I am That I am' in Exodus, 'I am what I am' in Paul, and 'That which we are, we are' in Tennyson.

The 'being' intended here is open to our choice as readers: divine, if we opt for the Old Testament; prophetic and apostolic, if we opt for the New; heroic, if we accept Ulysses' definition of himself and his fellow-sailors as 'One equal temper of heroic hearts'; satanic, if we heed the echo which Milton's great Fallen Angel, reiterating the cry of his forerunner in Tasso, sends resounding across the whole ending of Ulysses' fraudulent speech to emerge in the last line of the poem:

> To strive, to seek, to find, and not to yield.

As a last solution we could find being in becoming. It is impossible to resist historicist temptations when considering the tensions in

---

[8] H. F. Tucker, *Tennyson and the Doom of Romanticism* (Cambridge, Mass. and London, 1988), to which I am greatly indebted.

Tennyson's 'Ulysses', and not to detect in its composition a ruling class, a bourgeoisie becoming dangerously petty in its aspiration to go beyond 'common duties', decency, and traditional religion in escapist pursuit of adventurous knowledge beyond the common good and even beyond utilitarianism (and we might be tempted to add, reading Nietzsche in the sinister light of twentieth-century totalitarianism, 'beyond any sense of good and evil').

It is not impossible to see in this figure, in post-Hegelian fashion, the anticipated antithesis between, as it were, progress and its guilty self-consciousness, which would basically produce a short-circuit paralysing the hero. We should ask ourselves why Tennyson, the poet-laureate of the Victorian age, creates a Ulysses not content to rule over 'a rugged people'—nominally Ithacan, but British under the surface and European or Western in general—which has filled the earth with its wonders and inventions; which hardly recognizes any more Pillars-of-Hercules limits, and which believes in figuralism (for example, Ulysses' predicting Columbus—and Tennyson has a poem on the theme which is significant in this context) only inasmuch as this coincides with consecration of self, self-satisfaction, and imperial self-fulfilment.

Lastly, it may seem inevitable to consider Ulysses as the prototype of the 'padre padrone', the domineering domestic male, who, in his old age, becomes a despotic Lear disclaiming all responsibility towards the kingdom and above all towards his wife. 'That which we are, we are' might, after all, simply mean that, with a shrug of the shoulders, we each tend our own garden without over-worrying about the world, our fellow-beings, and being itself: a metaphorically couched 'I'm all right Jack'.

Tennyson's 'Ulysses' bears a message which is complex, delicate, and dramatic, and which ultimately touches on Hamlet's dilemma: to be or not to be. 'Ulysses' is not principally, as an eminent contemporary critic sees it, a 'misreading' of Keats, Shelley, Wordsworth, and Milton perpetrated by a poet who has fallen victim to the 'anxiety of influence'.[9] Misreading apart, it represents at a given moment in history, within the contemporary episteme it subverts, the tragic fulfilment of the literature of

---

[9] H. Bloom, *A Map of Misreading* (Oxford, 1975), 156–9; *Poetry and Repression* (New Haven, Conn. and London, 1976), 157–60; and in general *The Anxiety of Influence* (Oxford, 1973).

knowledge[10] which European culture has built up from Homer to Dante, Columbus to Tasso, Pascal to Coleridge, and Milton to Wordsworth. At the same time 'Ulysses' constitutes a prediction of the poetry and tragedy of knowledge which the imminent crisis within the social, the political, and the imaginary will write into European literature. Both fulfilment and prefiguration have historical and social but also existential functions: the escaping, striving, seeking, finding, and not yielding depends on each one of us.

Let me now set against this English Ulysses, with all his Hamlet-like wavering, seemingly resolute but deeply divided, an Italian anti-Ulysses who considers being a nothingness, and shipwreck the only hope. In 1820 Leopardi composed the *canzone* 'Ad Angelo Mai', in which he celebrates the great Italians of the past. After Dante and Petrarch, he lights on Columbus, devoting two whole stanzas to him. In the first, the echo of Parini's ode 'Innesto del vaiuolo' refers us clearly back to Tasso's verses on Columbus, and to Dante's Ulysses:

> Ma tua vita era allor con gli astri e il mare,
> ligure ardita prole,
> quand'oltre alle colonne, ed oltre ai liti
> cui strider l'onde all'attuffar del sole
> parve udir su la sera, agl'infiniti
> flutti commesso, ritrovasti il raggio
> del Sol caduto, e il giorno
> che nasce allor ch'ai nostri è giunto al fondo;
> e rotto di natura ogni contrasto,
> ignota immensa terra al tuo viaggio
> fu gloria, e del ritorno
> ai rischi.

But your life was then with the stars and with the sea, | intrepid son of Liguria, | When beyond the Pillars, and beyond the shores | upon which, it seemed, the waves could be heard hissing at the headlong plunge of the sun; | committed to the infinite billows, you discovered the ray | of the fallen Sun, and the day | which is born when on our shores it has reached its end; | and broken down all contrasts in nature, | that unknown, immense land of your journey | was the glory, and [glory too] to the risks of return.

---

[10] See J. J. McGann, *Towards a Literature of Knowledge* (Oxford, 1989).

Yet Leopardi cannot simply accept the glory Columbus receives from sailing infinite seas and discovering the 'unknown, immense land' of America. He immediately adds almost twenty lines of comment on this Renaissance-Enlightenment-like encomium:

> Ahi ahi, ma conosciuto il mondo
> non cresce, anzi si scema, e assai più vasto
> l'etra sonante e l'alma terra e il mare
> al fanciullin, che non al saggio, appare.
>
> Nostri sogni leggiadri ove son giti
> dell'ignoto ricetto
> d'ignoti abitatori, o del diurno
> degli astri albergo, e del rimoto letto
> della giovane Aurora, e del notturno
> occulto sonno del maggior pianeta?
> Ecco svaniro a un punto,
> e figurato è il mondo in breve carta;
> ecco tutto è simìle, e discoprendo,
> solo il nulla s'accresce. A noi ti vieta
> il vero appena è giunto,
> o caro immaginar; da te s'apparta
> nostra mente in eterno; allo stupendo
> poter tuo primo ne sottraggon gli anni;
> e il conforto perì de' nostri affanni.

Alas, alas, but the world, once known, | ceases to grow, and shrinks, and far more vast | the resounding ether and the maternal earth and the sea | to the child appear, than to the sage.
  Whence are sped our fleeting dreams | of the unknown refuge | of unknown inhabitants, or of the daytime | dwelling of the stars, and of the far-off bed | of young Aurora, and of the secret night-time | slumbers of the largest planet? | Gone, all gone in one moment, | and the world is represented in a small map; | everything is similar, and, through discovering, | only the nothingness increases. You are forbidden us | the moment truth reaches us, | oh dear imagining; for eternity | our mind separates from you; years take from us your first stupendous power; | and this comfort of our sufferings perishes.

After his fourth and last transatlantic crossing, Columbus had written: 'El mundo es poco.' 'Il mondo non è una piccola cosa, anzi vastissima e massimamente rispetto all'uomo' ('the world is no small thing, but is most vast, especially with regard to man's measure'), Leopardi rejoins in the *Zibaldone*. In place of Columbus's (mistaken) considerations of geography, Leopardi supplies a meditation which goes to the heart of things, and contemplates the infinite variety of nature on this earth and on 'infiniti altri mondi'. No, the world is not small; it is knowledge which reduces it and shrinks it within human consciousness. Columbus, the new Ulysses, flattens the earth by making it uniform and transforming it into a small map, a *breve carta*. The modern explorer uproots Leopardi's 'caro immaginar', the 'dear imagining' of the child and of humanity in its infancy, kills off the wonderful primitive power of the imagination, replacing it with the merely real, and wipes out the dream of another world, the *nova terra* beyond the sunset, by fixing it in one precise geographical spot. By 'dis-covering', Columbus simply increases the nothing. The world, Leopardi repeats in the *Zibaldone*, is far from small; the world is huge:

Ma basta che l'uomo abbia veduto la misura di una cosa ancorché smisurata, basta che sia giunto a conoscerne le parti, o a congetturarle secondo le regole della ragione; quella cosa immediatamente gli par piccolissima, gli diviene insufficiente, ed egli ne rimane scontentissimo. Quando il Petrarca poteva dire degli antipodi, *e che 'l dì nostro vola A gente che di là* FORSE *l'aspetta*, quel *forse* bastava per lasciarci concepir quella gente e quei paesi come cosa immensa, e dilettosissima all'immaginazione. Trovati che si sono, certamente non sono impiccioliti, né quei paesi son piccola cosa, ma appena gli antipodi si son veduti sul mappamondo, è sparita ogni grandezza ogni bellezza ogni prestigio dell'idea che se ne aveva.

Once man has seen the measure of a thing that is measureless; once he is able to know some parts of it, or to surmise them within the rules of reason, then that thing immediately appears to him as immeasurably small; it no longer suffices him, and he is dissatisfied with it. When Petrarch could say of the Antipodes, 'and our day flies To other people PERHAPS waiting there', that 'perhaps' sufficed for us to imagine that people and those countries as immense and delightful to the imagination. Now that they are found, although clearly they have not diminished in size, nor are those countries a small matter, yet now that the Antipodes are to be seen on the map of the world, vanished is all greatness all beauty all prestige of the idea we once had of them.

Science is 'an enemy to the greatness of ideas, though it has enormously extended our natural knowledge'. It has enlarged them as 'clear ideas', but 'the smallest confused idea' is greater than 'a great one which is totally clear'. The uncertainty as to a thing's existence supplies it with a greatness which is destroyed by the certainty of that existence. Humanity is satisfied only by limitless greatness: thus ignorance, 'which alone can hide the limits of things, is the main source of indefinite ideas', while experience inevitably reveals those limits to us.

Columbus and Vespucci negate the value Dante's Ulysses attributed to experience and knowledge. Vasco da Gama and James Cook remove for ever Petrarch's Antipodean 'perhaps'. The imagination of the first men, Leopardi writes in his *Discorso intorno alla poesia romantica*, 'roamed freely over vast lands'. By 'widening the empire of the intellect, namely, increasing practical knowledge and knowing', that imagination has been 'driven from its ancient domains', only to find itself in the present age, 'cramped and imprisoned and near-immobile'. Gone are the countries of the Cyclops, and of the lotus-eaters, the Isles of Aeolus, the Sirens, Calypso, and the Phaeacians. Odysseus can no longer sail the seas of the imagination.

An inexorable antagonism separates science from poetry, and reason from the imitation of nature, the poet's task. Science circumscribes, dissects, looks for causes, and knows every part of 'the innermost forces and mechanisms, the relations and connections and correspondences of the great universal compound'; it enters within the human soul, 'sure, *quasi*-mathematical and resolutely "analytical" ', to expose it almost in angles and circles (Oh Enlightenment and Romantic psychology! Oh psychoanalysis of the future!). Poetry, on the other hand, responds to humanity's basic impulse towards pleasure, and must therefore imitate nature 'virgin and intact', constituting her 'near-ultimate refuge'. Its task is to take us back, following our natural 'incontrovertible leaning to the primitive', to the original *arkhe*, the lost paradise of our being-with-nature; to the golden age which, to quote Leopardi's own 'Inno ai Patriarchi', today reigns only 'among the vast Californian forests' threatened by civilization.

Through the imagination, poetry has to adapt to nature, and open up for us 'a fount of celestial delights which pass belief', revealing the 'immortal power' which unchanged and incorrupt nature has over the human mind. Through their art, the poets must

quasi trasportarci in quei primi tempi, e quella natura che ci è sparita dagli occhi, ricondurcela avanti, o più tosto svelarcela ancora presente e bella come in principio, e farcela vedere e sentire, e cagionarci quei diletti soprumani di cui pressoché tutto, salvo il desiderio, abbiamo perduto.

near-transport us to those times, and bring back before us that nature which has vanished from our eyes; rather, reveal her to us as present and beautiful as hitherto, and allow us to see and to feel her, and cause in us those superhuman delights of which we have lost almost everything except desire.

The conflict is actually considerably more radical than it appears as stated here in the *Discorso*. It is not exactly reason which is the enemy of nature, but, as Leopardi writes in the *Zibaldone*, 'science and cognition: that experience which is their very mother'. 'In the beginning', in that same *arkhe* humanity feels drastically drawn towards, lie the seeds of division. Both the account of original sin in Genesis and the classical fable of Psyche show humanity's decline into corruption from a state of former happiness to have been caused by knowledge and the need to know, and that 'la scienza di se stesso e del mondo, e il troppo uso della ragione' ('the science of ourselves and of the world, and too great a use of reason') was the origin of human unhappiness.

The degeneration of humanity was certainly not due to the 'obfuscation of the intellect'. 'Anzi dopo il peccato, e *mediante* il peccato l'uomo ebbe l'intelletto rischiaratissimo, acquistò la scienza del bene e del male, e divenne effettivamente per questa, *quasi unus ex nobis*' ('Indeed, after sinning, and *through* sin, man's intellect was greatly sharpened; he acquired the knowledge of good and evil, hereby becoming effectively *quasi unus ex nobis*'), as God himself recognizes in Genesis. Rather, it was caused by the clash and growing imbalance between two 'qualities' which were to become incompatible, nature and reason, and the latter's ascendancy over the former. 'L'uomo non è fatto per sapere, la cognizione del vero è nemica della felicità' ('Man was not made to know; the awareness of truth is the enemy of happiness'): truth can only reveal the nothingness.[11]

Ulysses, then, is challenged on all fronts: as a gnoseological paradigm extolled by antiquity, and as a modern epistemic model proposed by Dante's poetic message. His *saviezza*, Leopardi writes in the *Pensieri*, almost generates hatred. This takes us well beyond

---

[11] See E. Severino, *Il nulla e la poesia: Alla fine dell'età della tecnica: Leopardi* (Milan, 1990).

Erasmus's ironic judgement in his *In Praise of Folly*, where he recounts that Plutarch's Gryllus, one of Ulysses' companions turned into swine, opted to remain in his brute state, grunting around the pig-sty, rather than expose himself once more to Ulysses' adventures and misfortunes. Homer himself, the 'father of fables', was clearly in agreement with Gryllus, as Erasmus points out, since Ulysses alone, of all the heroes in the *Iliad* and the *Odyssey*, is described as 'unhappy'. The cause of this unhappiness was precisely his following Pallas' advice in applying his 'truly excessive intelligence'; for this search for knowledge, Erasmus ironically concludes, 'was far removed from the guidance of nature'.[12]

Leopardi, as we have seen, is altogether more savage and relentless in his criticism of the hero of the *Inferno*'s search for experience. And if Tennyson's Romantic-Victorian Ulysses burns with an infinite desire for knowledge, Leopardi recognizes that this is necessarily innate, inherent, and inseparable from humanity's very nature in being an inevitable consequence of *amour propre* ('which is a consequence of living'). He maintains, however, that its ineradicable existence in the human being does not prove the faculty of human knowledge to be infinite: it merely proves that this *amour propre* is. 'E se noi avessimo delle facoltà precisamente infinite, la nostra essenza si confonderebbe con quella di Dio' ('And were we to have precisely infinite faculties, our essence would merge with God's'). Ulysses is the Adam who wishes to be the Other and discovers he is Nobody.

Columbus, the fulfilment of Ulysses in history, who breaks all the laws of nature, who finds the 'fallen sun's ray' beyond the sunset, and overcomes the risks of return, of the *nostos*, is responsible for revealing to humanity, however, that everything is 'similar', the world almost dull in its monotonous equality, and flat for all its acclaimed roundness. While he was discovering America, 'Angelo Mai' recounts, Ariosto was growing up, and filling life with his knights and ladies, with 'felici errori', 'vanità' and 'strani pensieri'. Now that we, his heirs, enlightened progressives, have put away all 'fantastical beauties' (*belle fole*)—'or poi che il verde | è spogliato delle cose' ('now that green | Has been stripped from

---

[12] Erasmus, *In Praise of Folly*, xxxv; Plutarch, *Moralia*, 985–92, 'Gryllus, or Beasts are Rational'.

things'), there remains 'il certo e solo | veder che tutto è vano oltre che il duolo' ('that all is vain | is the one true knowledge, excepting pain'). To that same Tasso who extolled Ulysses and Columbus despite the dark mountain he saw rearing up on the horizon from the infinite ocean, *this* world seemed, states Leopardi in 'Angelo Mai', 'sanza gente': 'ombra reale e salda | ti parve il nulla, e il mondo | inabitata piaggia' ('a real and solid shadow | appeared to you the nothingness, and the world | an unpeopled shore').

Here, then, we have Columbus sailing towards his New World. Leopardi's *Operette Morali* show him conversing with Pedro Gutierrez one enchanted night, when Columbus frankly confesses to his friend that he may have been wrong: that perhaps there was no world beyond the sea. His conjecture grew out of a 'speculation' based on foundations which, if proved false, would lead to the inevitable conclusion that the human intellect is unable to form a plausible 'judgement' by working from hypotheses and predictions deduced from 'signs', thus moving towards knowledge by analogy and induction. In brief, science would be simply a matter of seeing 'presently' and physically touching things themselves.

On the other hand, 'practice is frequently, indeed principally, at variance with speculation'. It cannot be presumed that one part of the world resembles another; if the eastern hemisphere is made up partly of land and partly of sea, it does not follow that so, therefore, is the western part. It could be entirely covered by an immense sea, or by elements which are neither sea nor land. It could be uninhabited or uninhabitable; and if inhabited, possibly by other 'animals with intellect', or by men who are 'bodily larger', more intelligent and more civilized than ourselves. For nature is so potent, her effects so 'varied and multiple', that it is impossible to proceed logically from the unknown to the known. 'Thus we see with our own eyes', exclaims an amazed Columbus, unable to take in quite what is happening, 'that the needle declines from the star for no inconsiderable space westwards: a new and unheard-of phenomenon for all mariners'.

Before the Admiral's gaze, as before a boy's, a poet's, or primitive humanity's, the unknown universe opens up its infinite possibilities. Over the abyss, however, far beyond that 'Naiveté der Wissenschaft' which Hölderlin speaks of in his *Kolomb*, is suspended discourse, the very *logos* of science: 'many conclusions drawn from excellent discourse cannot pass the test of experience'.

Why continue to journey, then, Gutierrez asks, why continually risk one's own life and that of others 'on the basis of a merely speculative opinion'? Columbus, always aware of that solitary and insecure journey towards the unknown which is life itself, and restive before the boredom which threatens to annihilate humanity, replies:

Se al presente tu, ed io, e tutti i nostri compagni, non fossimo su queste navi, in mezzo di questo mare, in questa solitudine incognita, in istato incerto e rischioso quanto si voglia; in quale altra condizione di vita ci troveremmo essere? in che saremmo occupati? in che modo passeremmo questi giorni? Forse più lietamente? o non saremmo anzi in qualche maggior travaglio o sollecitudine, ovvero pieni di noia?

If at this moment you, and I, and all these our companions, were not upon this ship, in the middle of this ocean, in this unplumbed solitude, in a condition which is, granted, incalculably uncertain and hazardous: in what other condition of life should we then find ourselves? with what should we be occupied? how then should we pass our days? More contentedly, perhaps? or should we not be in yet greater torment or solitude, or brimful of boredom?

The journey undertaken may well yield no fruits, but at least it keeps Columbus off the streets, so to speak; it keeps boredom temporarily at bay, gives life value, and makes precious things which would otherwise go unconsidered. America was discovered out of boredom, *taedium vitae*, ennui, and a desperate awareness of the nothingness.

The ancients write that unhappy lovers throw themselves into the sea from the cliffs of Leucas, Columbus says in Leopardi's *Dialogo*; if they survive, Apollo frees them from the chains of love. 'Each voyage, then, is in some wise a leap from the cliffs of Leucas.' Running the constant risk of death, sailors are better able to value life. Constantly far from land, they are more attached to every nook and cranny of it. The participants of the voyage under discussion are no exception: uncertain of the journey, they fall asleep and wake up again with the idea of land; 'and if even once a *mountain*-peak or forest or some such object is discovered, we are beside ourselves with *happiness*'.

And land there was. Columbus reveals that the sounding-line has been touching the bottom for days; the clouds have gone, the air is sweeter, and the wind uncertain and variable. Flights of birds appear; a piece of freshly cut bamboo floats on the water, followed by a twig with 'fresh red berries'. The circle closes with the announcement of these signs of land, mysterious epiphanies of rebirth. Although still diffident, Columbus is aware of a 'great and good expectation'.

Rejecting science, Ulysses has become a boy who finds surfacing before his eyes things which reason has no way of proving. The wonder and fascination of humanity's original being are only revealed when the *logos* has ended. The long-dreamt-of happiness of Dante's Ulysses before the mountain now returns, and, hazy to the intellect but clearly visible in the sky and sea—i.e. within nature—all Columbus's hopes appear: the aura and the colours of paradise, lost in the Old World and now rediscovered in the New.

For this to happen, it has to be recognized that every voyage is a leap from the cliffs of Leucas: that the passionate, desperate bound towards death is vital to ensure that life, even at the cost of pain, is something more than ennui and the sense of suffocation which comes from the 'too, too solid' nothingness lying behind and before all human action. This is indeed an unexpected 'fulfilment' of Dante's Ulysses: a Columbus who puts Wordsworth's Newton behind him and syllogizes like Hamlet, questioning and challenging the use of reason; a Ulysses who sails past the Pillars of Hercules in search of a world *sanza gente*, throwing himself off the cliffs of Leucas to cure that illness which is life.

Leopardi's poetry had already sailed in the direction of this particular sea, taking his revenge on science and staging a shipwreck which is at the opposite pole from that of *Inferno* XXVI. I refer, of course, to 'L'infinito'. I propose to give only a brief analysis of this 'idyll', which in my opinion contains one of the most oblique Ulysses figures poetry ever created.[13]

> Sempre caro mi fu quest'ermo colle,
> e questa siepe che da tanta parte
> dell'ultimo orizzonte il guardo esclude.
> Ma sedendo e mirando, interminati
> spazi di là da quella, e sovrumani

---

[13] See M. Picone, 'L'Infinito di Leopardi e il mito di Ulisse', *Lettere Italiane* (1989), 73–89.

silenzi, e profondissima quiete
io nel pensier mi fingo; ove per poco
il cor non si spaura. E come il vento
odo stormir tra queste piante, io quello
infinito silenzio a questa voce
vo comparando: e mi sovvien l'eterno,
e le morte stagioni, e la presente
e viva e il suon di lei. Così tra questa
immensità s'annega il pensier mio:
e il naufragar m'è dolce in questo mare.

Always dear to me was this solitary hill, and this hedge, excluding the gaze from so vast a part of the final horizon. But sitting and surveying, endless space beyond it, more-than-human silence, and deepest quiet I fashion in the mind; at which the heart is near afraid. And when I hear the wind rustling through these plants, I that infinite silence and this voice compare: and I recall the eternal, and the dead seasons, and the living present one, and its sound. In such immensity the mind can drown: and shipwreck sweetly comes in such an ocean.

We find ourselves, then, on the solitary hill (although the *Argomenti di idilli* speaks of 'beach', 'shore', and 'bank'), staring into space. The presence of the hedge, the counterpart of the 'foce stretta' of Gibraltar, excludes the gaze from so vast a part of the final horizon, Leopardi informs us, making it the equivalent of the infinitely reduced 'wake' of the senses which is left to us: the threshold beyond which stretches the world behind the sun. The final line is drawn behind this fragile and deceptive barrier. As the 'final' horizon, it creates in us pain and melancholy, the *Zibaldone* glosses, but at the same time a sensation of pleasure, 'e piacevole nel medesimo dolore'—pleasurable in its pain—because of the infinity of ideas evoked by the word 'ultimo'. We begin to realize what a terrible, divided *Sehnsucht* this vigil and the west, the extreme horizons of sentient life, represent. Leopardi's gloss continues: 'La cagione di questi sentimenti è quell'*infinito* che contiene in se stesso l'idea di una cosa *terminata*, cioè al di là di cui non v'è più nulla; di una cosa terminata *per sempre*, e che non tornerà *mai più*' ('The cause of these feelings is that *infinity*, containing in itself the idea of something which has ended, and beyond which there lies *nothing*; something which has ended *for ever*, and which can never return'). The reason for the division we feel, and the contradiction which pleasure and pain generate in us, lies in the feeling of dying to life when we see the end and desire it as a prologue to the nothingness.

The fragility of the threshold stimulates our imagination; 'sitting and surveying' we leave the 'bank' mentioned in the *Argomenti* and with the imagination enter the endless oceans, the eternal silence of an unexplored country, and the bottomless quiet of death. In thought we have gone beyond the permitted bounds, into the 'alto passo che non lasciò già mai persona viva'. There, in the infinite space which the indefinite creates in the mind, 'there lies *nothing*', and before this void we are lost, and reel back, appalled.

When the breeze rustles among the leaves, the 'here' and 'there' are projected in time, and the voice of life replies to the infinite silence of death. But the echo between the two evokes the memory of eternity, the infinite nothingness of time, beyond the threshold between the living, palpable present and the 'dead seasons' of the past; between our today and the buried history of each one of us, and of the whole of humanity—between Odysseus' being and non-being, or the 'being of having been' of the souls in Hades.

In this 'alto mare aperto' our 'mind' or 'thought' ('pensiero') founders, and shipwreck in such an ocean can indeed seem 'sweet': not like Ulysses, but like Glaucus, the fisherman in Ovid and Dante who, eating the magic grass and suddenly feeling the desire to leave the earth, jumps into the waves where the gods welcome him as one of themselves. We are now off the cliffs of Leucas and are squarely landed in Zarathustra's 'perhaps', in the condition described by Ariel in the *Tempest*:

> Nothing of him that doth fade,
> But doth suffer a sea-change
> Into something rich and strange.

We have to stop and ask, though, who pushed us, and why this shipwreck should be 'sweet'. Leopardi himself, from the top of his solitary hill on the sea-shore, without actually pushing, certainly pressed us, in just five words—'hedge', 'horizon', 'wind', 'plants', and 'ocean'—evoking the beginnings of the world, when nature was virgin and intact. It is poetry which is 'fashioning' (*fingo*) infinity behind this static (*sedendo*, 'sitting') adventure of a second, the destination of which is always and never. In contemplation and in astonishment at the sheer wonder of things (suggested by *mirando*, here given its primary meaning of 'looking' or 'gazing', 'surveying'), it creates the 'shore' and the 'infinite silence', the 'here' and 'there', the *arkhe* and the *telos*: the *fictio* of human imagination, it gives life to shadows, and evokes being, nothingness, and the dying which interconnects them.

The wind which rustles among the leaves is hardly that which 'wearies' Ulysses' flame when it labours to produce words, far less the Other's implacable 'whirlwind' which sets the seal of the sea on humanity's narrative. It is the 'impetuous wind' and 'tumultuous roar' (*Argomenti*) which reaches us from primitive nature and from the imagination which identifies itself with nature: the wind which blows from the 'more-than-human silence', making the listener shiver, and, meeting the 'sound' of the world, becomes *this voice*. And like he who, following Dante in *Inferno* I, 'fatigued, | having reached the shore from the ocean, | turns and looks back at the perilous waters', in the same way, as readers, survivors of the wreck after our leap from the cliffs of Leucas, we hold 'L'infinito' in our hands with gratitude and 'dolcezza', sweetness, in that:

lo stesso conoscere l'irreparabile vanità e falsità di ogni bello e di ogni grande è una certa bellezza e grandezza che riempie l'anima, quando questa conoscenza si trova nelle opere di genio. E lo stesso spettacolo della nullità, è una cosa in queste opere, che par che ingrandisca l'anima del lettore, la innalzi, e la soddisfaccia di se stessa e della propria disperazione.

even to recognize the irreparable vanity and falsity of all that is beautiful and great is a certain beauty and greatness which fills the soul when this recognition is found in works of genius. And this spectacle of nothingess is, however, something in works of this kind; seeming to enlarge the soul of the reader, to elevate it and make it satisfied with itself and its own desperation.

The *dulcedo naufragii* was never so much as a speck on Ulysses' horizon. As poetry advances into the nineteenth century, however, the 'sweetness' of shipwreck is increasingly often the answer to an epistemic model which pretends to find all the answers to humanity's problems in technical progress, the all-embracing philosophical 'system' (for example, that of Hegel, of the Positivists and the Materialists) and the 'scientific' politico-social utopia. Alexander von Humboldt's *Voyage aux régions équinoctiales*, the monumental account of a journey which set the foundation of modern physical geography in its painstaking enquiry into phenomena and their distribution in space, was published in 1807, and his popular *Examen critique de l'histoire de la géographie du Nouveau Continent* in 1834. All the poems on the Ulysses theme mentioned so far in this chapter, from Wordsworth to Tennyson, and Hölderlin to Leopardi, were written in the interval between.

In 1839 Darwin published his Diary of a *Voyage of the Beagle*, modelled on Humboldt's and which in turn forms the basis of his *Origin of the Species* (1859) where he presents his complete version of the evolutionary theory which once again subverts the whole modern episteme. The most fascinating aspect of the *Voyage* consists in the simultaneous presence of two perfectly blended voices: the poetic and Romantic voice in which, recalling Coleridge, Wordsworth, Shelley, and Byron, the narrator records his emotions at the sublime spectacles of the natural world; and the voice of science in which the naturalist catalogues, lists, compares, and analyses natural phenomena.

On finally returning to England after five long years' odyssey on board the Beagle, Darwin takes stock of his journey. He lists the negative points, offset by the positive: the lack of home and friends versus the excited anticipation of homecoming; the lack of space, privacy, and rest, the impression of constant pressure, and privation of general comforts, but the substantial improvement in travel conditions on board a modern ship; seasickness versus the pleasures of sailing. The 'boasted glories of the illimitable ocean' consist in no more than a 'tedious waste, a desert of water'. Nature would stage marvel after marvel: full-blooded storms, or clear moonlit skies over dark and sparkling seas, but it is 'incomparably finer' to watch storms from the shore (as 'spectators', to use Blumenberg's term).[14]

Finally, the greatest joy: stunned awe at the landscape: the sublimity of the primordial forests in Brazil, where the life force almost audibly hums, or those of the Tierra del Fuego, dominated by 'Death and Decay'; the endless, unknown, unpopulated plains of Patagonia, which, if one believed with the ancients in a flat land surrounded by water or by blazing deserts, would be considered, 'with deep but ill-defined sensations', as the 'last boundaries to man's knowledge'. Then the amazement on the first encounter with the 'other', the savage 'barbarian' who, however, is possibly the likeness of our own ancestors, and whose difference from

---

[14] H. Blumenberg, *Schiffbruch mit Zuschauer* (Frankfurt, 1979), 28–46.

'civilized' man it is impossible to define; the 'love of the chase', the instinctive passion for life in the open air, and for 'the savage returning' to mankind's 'wild and native habits'; the warm sense of happiness felt when taking the first breath in a foreign country, or when walking on earth never before trodden by human foot: in short, all the joy felt by Odysseus, Ulysses, and Columbus.

There also existed sources of equally profound pleasure 'of a more reasonable nature'. While, as Leopardi's Columbus admitted to Pedro Gutierrez, the traveller inevitably tends to fill in the wide gaps of knowledge with imprecise or superficial hypotheses, for the scientist:

The map of the world ceases to be a blank; it becomes a picture full of the most varied and animated figures. Each part assumes its true dimensions: continents are not looked at in the light of islands, or those islands considered as mere specks, which are, in truth, larger than many kingdoms of Europe. Africa, or North and South America, are well-sounding names and easily pronounced; but it is not till having sailed for some weeks along small portions of their coasts that one is thoroughly convinced how large a portion of our immense world these names imply.[15]

Darwin, who shares and experiences at a concrete level all Leopardi's nostalgia for the uncontaminated *arkhe* of nature, keeps his mental distance, however, from the man-child, the savage barbarian who deserves *pietas* but whose radical alterity must be recognized, unless we are to return to the very beginnings of the entire human race. Above all, Darwin delights in what Leopardi deplores as a reduction of the world within *breve carta*. The 'map of the world' holds for Darwin no flat uniformity concealing the inexorable inching forwards of nothingness, but a vital and varied fullness in which every detail dwelt on by the observer fleshes out the bare names into their appropriate dimensions, left to the imagination by Petrarch's and Leopardi's 'perhaps'. Geographical discoveries made all their antipodean dreams vanish into so many dots: the very dots which, Darwin insists, become immense after weeks and weeks along tiny stretches of their coasts. For him, it is the 'experience' so despised by Leopardi, the 'truth' which revealed the nothing, which confers greatness on things; only by measuring, circumscribing, and giving them 'real' confines can their 'true' immensity be appreciated.

[15] *Voyage of the Beagle*, ed. J. Browne and M. Neve (Harmondsworth, 1989), 376.

This particular episode is the clearest demonstration of the tragic rift between poetry and science in the nineteenth century. Further confirmation comes from Baudelaire, who, in 'Le Voyage', the next-to-last poem in his *Les Fleurs du mal* (1857), returns to Odysseus-Ulysses taking precisely this image of the map as his starting-point:

> Pour l'enfant, amoureux de cartes et d'estampes,
> L'univers est égal à son vaste appétit.
> Ah! que le monde est grand à la clarté des lampes!
> Aux yeux du souvenir que le monde est petit!

To the child, with its passion for maps and prints, | the universe is equal to his vast desire. | How big the world is in the light of a lamp! | How small in the eyes of memory!

So his 'Le Voyage' begins by recalling Leopardi's child and Tennyson's infinite desire, but also by turning the atlas on its head, as it were. The world is vast before the experience of it, while the endless yearning is still projected on to it in the 'clarté' of the imagination. At the end of the journey, in memory, the same world has infinitely shrunk.

Between the two, modern humanity's Odyssey unfolds, a tragic mockery of fulfilment of its Homeric and Dantean counterpart. Some, like Tennyson's Ulysses, depart in bitterness, escaping from the horror of their homeland; others, to slip the grasp of tyrannical Circes, become drunk on light, space, and flaming skies. The true travellers, of course, are those who 'leave for the sake of leaving', without knowing why they say 'Allons!', and with a light heart 'never leave their destiny far behind'. They are possessed by desires in the form of clouds, immense, mutable, and unknown joys the human spirit has never been able to name. These are the Ulysses of today: like Dante's, full of 'Curiosité', these 'old wanderers' set out on the 'sea of Shadows'; they sail before the 'charmantes et funèbres' voices of the Sirens who invite them to the perfumed Lotus of an unending afternoon; they observe cities in the splendour of the setting sun; they visit enchanted palaces; they learn of customs 'which to the eye are pure inebriation'; they everywhere find the 'wearisome spectacle of eternal sin': woman in love with herself, man hard, lascivious, 'a stream in a cess-pool'—talkative humanity, drunk with its own genius, as crazed as ever, 'who to God in its mad | agony cries 'O my equal, O master, | I curse thee!'

The new apostles, the Wandering Jews, set their sails to escape from this 'abominable retiarius'. Columbus, on the other hand, is today merely a drunken sailor who *invents* America. Every island he sights is 'an Eldorado promised by Fate' which then, in the light of day, is revealed as no more than rocks, a mirage 'which makes the abyss more bitter'. The shining paradises he dreams of with his nose in the air turn into illusory lands which only an 'orgy' of the imagination could construct. The great 'descubrimiento' has come to this: an invention without substance or poetry: pure, alcohol-inspired nothingness.

What 'nobles histoires' can we then read in the sea-deep eyes of these 'étonnants voyageurs'? No more than a 'bitter science':

> Le monde, monotone et petit, aujourd'hui,
> Hier, demain, toujours, nous fait voir notre image:
> Une oasis d'horreur dans un désert d'ennui!

The world, small, monotonous, today, | yesterday, tomorrow, and always shows us our own image: | an oasis of horror in a sea of tedium!

The world is once again small and 'similar', reflecting our condition: an oasis of horror in a desert of boredom. Behind the boundless desire which makes this Ulysses carry his cargo of infinity over the finite of the sea there lies a terrified disgust, a horror of present and future alike. Time appears like a spectre, in continual flight. In the soothing voices of the Sirens he hears what Circe had prophesied to Odysseus: death. At their song our dearest friends, 'our Pylades', stretch their arms towards us from the underworld; our beloved, Electra, beckons us to swim towards her, so that our hearts can be 'refreshed' in the icy sea.

With devastating irony, Baudelaire openly invokes the supreme shadow we have been stalking across these chapters. Death is here the captain of this final journey, the only one which can take us away from tedium and nothingness. Ulysses now invokes Charon:

> O Mort, vieux capitaine, il est temps! levons l'ancre!
> Ce pays nous ennuie, ô Mort! Appareillons!

Oh Death, old captain, it is time! Weigh anchor! | This land wearies us, Oh Death! Let us set sail!

Dante's Ulysses, reduced to a spirit enveloped in flames, spoke of his ardour 'to gain experience of the world'. Now fire inflames the brain of his satanic descendant, who declares his desire to 'plonger au fond du gouffre' (throw himself into the abyss), because only by going through the ultimate vortex can he experience Hell or Heaven. Which of the two hardly matters, as long as the descent into the Unknown leads to the 'new':

Au fond de l'Inconnu pour trouver du *nouveau!*

Baudelaire's anonymous Ulysses, then, reads in his Dantean prototype the desire for life-in-death, and consciously fulfils his destiny.[16] But Death is no mere shadow. The whole of the last section of *Les Fleurs du mal* is dedicated to him; this immense creature 'for whom an infernal desire wells up into a sob' is the true poetic Muse. Far from lying behind the sun, beyond the sunset, Death is suspended above the earth, he writes in 'La Mort des artistes', 'like a new sun', making the flowers of poetry blossom.

Putrefying flowers of the sickness eating away at us—what a distance we have come from the wild broom ('La Ginestra') in Leopardi's desert! And how many light years are these flowers from the ferns and mimosas Darwin makes his way through in the 'selva oscura' of the harsh Brazilian forests! He describes with immense care the way the ribs of the fronds bend back, producing a large, visible track when trodden on; adding that, while it is easy to describe the single parts, the whole communicates an infinitely greater sense of wonder, and 'elevating' devotion.

Here, in the mid-nineteenth century, our Ulysses embodies the divergence which gradually wedges itself between poetry and science, both of which, as a model of the 'literature of knowledge',[17] he has always carried about within himself. It begins to be expressed in a substantial difference in rhetoric which scientific and poetic discourse self-consciously develop in a spirit of increasing mutual hostility. Wordsworth's Newton can still 'voyage through strange seas of thought'; Leopardi's Columbus must destroy the *logos* to evoke the *mythos* of the cliffs of Leucas; Baudelaire's Ulysses chooses a language *maudit* to deconstruct his journey. Finally, Rimbaud will embark on his 'bateau ivre', on the

[16] See L. Pertile, 'Baudelaire, Dante e il mito di Ulisse', in *Rivista di letterature moderne e comparate*, 36 (1983), 109–22.

[17] See McGann, *Towards a Literature of Knowledge*.

'foolish bark' to which 'ineffable winds' give wings, to sail, with and beyond Dante's Ulysses, towards a 'saison en enfer'.

These two languages, the precise embodiment of C. P. Snow's 'two cultures',[18] correspond to two increasingly opposed impulses. Nineteenth-century science is keen to circumscribe and divide in order to 'possess' objects, the world, and knowledge more easily. Romantic poetry extends and reunites because, dispossessed of things although possessing words and knowledge, it yearns to imitate and re-create the voice of the universe.

Like philosophy, both are born, as Aristotle would say, out of wonder, because humanity, in the beginning and from then on, has marvelled at natural phenomena and been in love with *mythos*. Like philosophy, both pursue truth. Science, however, analyses the existent and the apparent—the *phenomenon*, which it seeks to understand and on to which it tries to impose a series of 'laws'. Poetry, with all the freedom of mimesis and imagination, tries to represent all that humanity has felt and thought, the *noumenon*. Lastly, poetry attempts to grasp the shadow of *that which is*, being and non-being, and in so doing continually moves towards and withdraws from the threshold separating living and dying, the infinite and the nothingness. It is only in the next century, our own, that the 'new spirit of science'[19] will again concern itself, in its own language, with thresholds of this kind.

---

[18] C. P. Snow, *The Two Cultures*, and *A Second Look* (Cambridge 1969). For further debate cf. V. Gentili, 'Le due culture in Inghilterra fra Illuminismo e fine Ottocento: intersezioni e opposizioni', in V. Gentili and P. Boitani (eds.), *L'età vittoriana: l'immagine dell'uomo fra letteratura e scienza* (Rome, 1982), 31–72; W. Schatzberg (ed.), *Literature and Science* (New York, 1985); J. Christie and S. Shuttleworth (eds.), *Nature Transfigured: Science and Literature, 1700 to 1900* (Manchester, 1989).

[19] G. Bachelard, *Le Nouvel Esprit scientifique* (Paris, 1934); and J. D. Barrow, *The World within the World* (Oxford, 1988).

6. The Final Journey and an End to All Journeying: The Functions of Irony

O mito è o nada que è tudo.

Myth is the nothing which is everything.

If, on the threshold of the twenty-first century, we look back over the 'alto passo' of the last one hundred years, we see Ulysses virtually jet-setting across the planet and beyond, towards the 'Space Odyssey' of 2001. Even confining ourselves to Western literature, and citing those examples which come immediately to mind, we could produce a list of 'pure' and 'direct' sightings of our hero which would rival Mozart's catalogue of Don Giovanni's exploits. 'In Italia', then, in Leporello's words, if not 'seicento-quaranta', a good handful: Pascoli, D'Annunzio, Gozzano, Saba, Savinio, Quasimodo, Pavese, Primo Levi, Moravia, and Luigi Dallapiccola;[1] in Greece, Cavafy, Seferis, and Katzanzakis; in Portugal, Pessoa; in France, Giraudoux, Gide, Giono, Valéry, and René Char; and Borges can speak for the Spanish language in general. In English (covering Great Britain, Ireland, and North America) Ulysses has travelled with Conrad, Joyce, Pound, and Eliot down to Robert Graves, Wallace Stevens, Robert Lowell, Thom Gunn, and Eiléan Ní Chuilleanáin; the writers of the former British Empire take him to Africa, Australia, the Caribbean, and the Indies discovered by Columbus.[2] In Germany, where Ulysses has for the most part been absent from the mainstream literature of past centuries, the twentieth has produced at least eleven rewritings of the myth, from Gerhart Hauptmann's *The Bow of Ulysses* (1914) to Walter Jens's *Das Testament des Odysseus* (1957). In Sweden Eyvind Johnson, in Prague Kafka, in Russia Osip Mandelstam and Joseph Brodsky, and in Romania (and France)

[1] And see P. Petrobelli, 'On Dante and Italian Music: Three Moments', *Cambridge Opera Journal*, 2/3 (1991), 219–49.

[2] Poets and works such as, for example, Wilson Harris, *Eternity to Season*; Edward Brathwaite, *The Arrivants: A New World Trilogy*; Derek Walcott, *Omeros*; and David Dabydeen, *Coolie Odyssey*, all complex texts with very different slants, which would require more space than is here possible. The myth has clearly lost none of its potency.

Benjamin Fundoianu all treat some aspect of it; Elias Canetti—born in Bulgaria of a Jewish, Spanish-speaking family, who has lived in Austria, England, and Switzerland, and writes in German—confesses that from the age of 10 Ulysses has been the prime model, 'complete and composite', who has taught him more than any person living. Towards the 'metamorphosis' Ulysses undergoes in his continual attempts to 'diminish himself', which constitutes the supreme ideal every poet should covet, and towards the 'irrepressible curiosity' Ulysses evinces about the Sirens, Canetti acknowledges a 'profound and absolutely complete' interior dependence.[3] His most famous work, *Auto da fé* (in which Ulysses has a chapter to himself), is, at Canetti's admission, a testimony to the enormous power Ulysses has over him.

His appearances, alive and well, in twentieth-century literature are, in short, proportional to the number of times modern writers and critics have proclaimed the death of literature and the end of myth. Indeed, it could be argued that our age's 'disinherited mind'[4] is continually returning to ancient myth for explanations of the foundations of history and poetry, using it almost as a touchstone between the everything and the nothing.

In *Mensagem*, an occultist poem published in 1934, Fernando Pessoa,[5] the greatest twentieth-century Portuguese writer, uses Ulysses to open a very complex celebration of his country's history, from Viriatus to Henry the Navigator, from Bartholomeu Diaz to Vasco da Gama, Columbus, and Magellan, while simultaneously ridiculing the mythologizing traditionalism of Portugal and Europe in general. Ulysses is, of course, the legendary founder of Lisbon (Ulixabona). In 'Ulisses' he represents for Pessoa precisely that 'nothing' which is everything: his never having been is true being, the beginning of creation. It is myth which fertilizes the imagination, as we have seen throughout the present study; whereas life 'below', the poet notes with scorn tinged with bitterness, is dying:

> O mito è o nada que è tudo.
> O mesmo sol que abre os céus
> E um mito brilhante e mudo—
> O corpo morto de Deus,
> Vivo e desnudo.

[3] See n. 5 to Introduction.
[4] E. Heller, *The Disinherited Mind* (London, 1952).
[5] *Mensagem de Fernando Pessoa*, ed. S. R. Lopes (Lisbon, 1986).

Este, que aqui aportou,
Foi por nao ser existindo.
Sem existir nos bastou.
Por nao ter vindo foi vindo
E nos criou.

Assim a lenda se escorre
A entrar na realidade
E a fecundá-la decorre.
Em baixo, a vida, metade
De nada, morre.

Myth is the nothing which is everything. | That same sun which opens the heavens | is a brilliant and mute myth— | The dead body of God, | living and naked.

He who took harbour here, | was through his non-existing. | Without existing he sufficed for us. | Through not coming, he came | and created us.

Thus the legend unravels | entering reality, | and begins to fertilize it. | Below, life, half | of nothing, dies.

In this spirit of semi-enchantment, semi-irony I propose to read the adventures of the twentieth-century Ulysses in these last three chapters. Here, too, it would be impossible and implausible to follow him on every single excursion, and the censuring of texts will once more lead inevitably to the obliquity, impurity, and restless-ness pre-empted above.

I shall divide the material into three parts, so as to offer more than one possible conclusion to the account. In this chapter we shall concentrate on Ulysses' last journey as a model of oscillation between the all and the nothing, working our way gradually towards the parodic versions which predict the end of travelling. In the following chapter we shall be looking for the point of contact between history and literature. In the last we come to three of the conclusions a twentieth-century Ulysses leads to: Word, Enigma, and Silence.

For Pessoa Ulysses is an *arkhe* of reality within the fiction: a beginning in myth and poetry which foreshadows a slender hope of the imminent rebirth of life and culture. The Odysseus of the Greek poets is similarly seen as embodying the roots of their personal and national history. In 'Ithaka' (1911) Cavafy extols the bare, poverty-stricken island as a symbol of life itself shining out at the end of a long journey—a journey mankind should undertake at leisure, learning from the various figures of wisdom encountered and amassing wealth in the Phoenician emporia or among the inebriating perfumes of the cities of Egypt. 'Fortunate he who's made the voyage of Odysseus', Seferis sings, through Du Bellay's voice, in *Reflections on a Foreign Line of Verse* (1932). The hero appears before him like a giant ghost, 'whispering through his whitened beard words | in our language spoken as it was three thousand years ago'. This is a father teaching his son how to build a wooden horse to conquer Troy; who articulates 'the harsh pain you feel when the ship's sails | swell with memory and your soul becomes a rudder'; who brings with knowing hands 'the waveless blue sea in the heart of winter'—Odysseus as, first and foremost, a *maestro* of life and truth.[6] In Kazantzakis's long *Odyssey* (1938) the protagonist again sets sail from Ithaca and experiences the All: after building a utopic city in the desert, becoming an expert in esoteric sciences, and a hermit in search of being, he finally dies on an iceberg in the Antarctic.[7]

In Italy the Homeric paradigm is inextricably linked to Dante. Italian poets look for the beginning in the end. Ulysses' final journey is what counts for them, the one prophesied by Tiresias in the *Odyssey* and ideally fulfilled partly by the *Inferno* and partly by Columbus in 1492. We have seen above how in 1897 Arturo Graf writes an 'Ultimo viaggio di Ulisse' in which he is shipwrecked on the coasts of America, the tragic shadow sublimating itself in a heroic version. This theme, and the figure of Odysseus in general (five poems are dedicated to him), is a near-obsession for Giovanni Pascoli.

He oscillates, significantly, between precisely the two typological poles of the final journey, the Dantean and the Columbian. In his 'Inno degli emigrati italiani a Dante', composed in 1911 for the inauguration of the Dante monument erected in New York, the Renaissance interpretation of *Inferno* XXVI is taken up and read in a Romantico-heroic light. Dante is now the prototype of the emigrant whom the cruel fatherland has driven into exile and on to the seas like a 'legno senza vela', a ship without sails. This

---

[6] G. Seferis, *Collected Poems*, ed. and trans. E. Keeley and P. Sherrard (3rd edn., London, 1982), 82–7.

[7] See W. B. Stanford, *The Ulysses Theme* (2nd edn., Ann Arbor, Mich., 1968), 222–40. Stanford's account is so exhaustive as to make further exposition superfluous.

expression, which Dante had coined for his own exile in the *Convivio*, is the precipitating factor in Pascoli's celebratory 'hymn'. Dante descended into hell, Pascoli writes, to question the 'molto errante', the much-journeying Ulysses, and brought the message back for the whole of humanity:

> Uomini, non credete all'occidente:
> ciò ch'è a voi sera è prima aurora altrui.
> Seguite me nel mondo senza gente:
> dire, anche morti, gioverà: Vi fui!

Men, never believe in the west: | that which to you is evening is first dawn elsewhere. | Follow me into the unpeopled world: | it will be worth it to say, even if dead: I was there!

Sitting, sleepless, beside the ocean, Dante announces his prophecy: 'There are no Pillars!', and it is Columbus who hears and fulfils it. It was Dante in command of the *Santa Maria* 'quando sul limitare | del nuovo Mondo, ella attendea l'aurora' ('when on the threshold | of the New World, she awaited the dawn'), which makes him the true 'eternal helmsman of Italy'. Poetry meets history with a vengeance! Poetic rhetoric takes on a cathartic value, transforming the national tragedy of emigration (which Pascoli's *pietas* cannot totally cancel out) into a nationalistic *epos*. Ulysses–Dante–Columbus: such is the figural sequence going back to the ancient roots of the present: the beginning of the end.

It is in this light that Ulysses' last voyage enters the canon of the Italian turn-of-the-century educational establishment, to be transmitted by various generations of teachers as a model of the heroic destiny of the race. It will shortly afterwards be celebrated in marble on the façade of the Palazzo della Civiltà del Lavoro, known to Romans for its tiers of arched terraces as the 'Square Colosseum' (in Rome's EUR district, planned for the World Fair of 1942), taking its place among a 'people of saints, poets, navigators, and transmigrators', and Renaissance figuralism will find its *telos*—irony of ironies—in the collective, Mussolini-led exaltation of Fascism.

Pascoli, however, was too sensitive not to be receiving signals not only of an Italy anxious to assert itself but also of a world which was aware it was nearing its end. As far back as 1904, in the *Poemi Conviviali*, he had published a twenty-four-part poem (as many as the Cantos in the *Odyssey*) recounting the famous last journey,

'Ultimo viaggio'. This time the end of Odysseus' wanderings is not America but again, as in the *Inferno*, death. Like Tennyson's Ulysses, 'old' but 'tired' of hearth and home, our restless hero departs from Ithaca with Phemius the poet, Irus the beggar, and all his earlier companions, to retrace the steps of their original, fabulous journey. There is now no Circe in the Isle of Aeea, however, because the storm of passion subsides in old age; and Phemius dies in the enchantress's palace, leaving his lyre hanging from the branches of a tree. The Cyclops have gone from the Island of Goats; in their place are good-natured and hospitable shepherds who only know of Polyphemus from tales told by their ancestors. Odysseus is thus denied the glory of once more pronouncing his real name before the giant, and Irus stays behind as house-boy in one of the new settlers' comfortable homesteads. Odysseus, however, is still eager for the only good ('bello') left to humanity, the knowledge of things ('saper le cose'), and sets off in search of the Sirens and truth. The ship sails by Hades (and in vain the life-sated dead invite the elderly to share their eternal rest), by the Islands of the Lotus, of the Sun, and of Aeolus, between the Wandering Rocks, and through Scylla and Charybdis. Finally, in a calm, quiet sea, the flowering meadow of the Sirens appears, surrounded by a pile of bones. No longer tied to the mast, nor by Circe's warnings, Odysseus wants to stop, and calls them, asking them to say who he was and now is. They stare ahead fixedly, without singing or pronouncing a syllable. Again he implores them:

> Ma voi due, parlate!
> Ma dite un vero, un solo a me, tra il tutto,
> prima ch'io muoia, a ciò ch'io sia vissuto!

Speak, the two of you! | Speak one sole truth to me, among all things, | before I die, so that my life may have had a purpose.

But there is no answer. The foreheads of the Enchantresses rise up over the sea as the ship splinters between the two rocks. The current drags Odysseus' body on to the deserted island of Ogygia 'which waves its fronds in the navel of the eternal sea'. Calypso, 'she who hides', mourns over the sterile waves for the man who refused her offer of immortality:

> Non esser mai! non esser mai! più nulla,
> ma meno morte, che non esser più!

Never to be! never to be! nothing at all, | but less dead than no longer to be![8]

For the first time since Plato we see Odysseus dead. But while, in the *Republic*, he was on the point of reincarnation, here he is simply a corpse. Life, love, adventure, glory, and knowledge are all over. As in Tennyson, the small wake of old age leads inexorably to death, and the ensuing silence is only broken by the final cry, desperately rejecting being, and yearning for non-being.

Against this void poetry is defenceless: like the psalmist's harp, the poet's lyre hangs sadly from the branches, the sound of its strings distant and confused with the thin tinkling of the wind. The Sirens remain obstinately silent, like Kafka's thirteen years later (we shall meet them later, in the last chapter): dead are the enchanting voices of beauty, knowledge, and death itself. In the shattering of consciousness which takes place between the nineteenth century and our own, Ulysses finds himself among 'cork-oak seaweed asteriae', 'useless wreckage', as Montale calls them a few years on,[9] dredged from the abyss and strewn over silent and deserted shores at the centre—the dead centre—of the sea and of the world. For Pascoli myth is not, as for Pessoa, the nothingness which is everything, but quite the reverse; in his search for a truth which can make sense of life his Odysseus proclaims 'ciò che non è tutto, è nulla' ('that which is not everything is nothing'). But the germ of remorseless annihilation lies precisely in this desire for absoluteness and totality. Nineteenth-century man wanted to possess the entire universe. At the end of the journey he is left clutching a few grains of sand.

Pascoli's Odysseus answers D'Annunzio's. In *Maia*, the first of the *Laudi*, published in 1903, the Greek hero explicitly states that he desires everything:

> Sol una è la palma ch'io voglio
> da te, o vergine Nike:
> l'Universo! Non altra.

---

[8] The meaning of the last line is controversial, and the translation given is itself an interpretation.

[9] E. Montale, 'Antico, sono ubriacato dalla voce', in *Ossi di seppia: L'Opera in versi*, ed. R. Bettarini and G. Contini (Turin, 1980), 52.

Sol quella ricever potrebbe
da te Odisseo
che a sé prega la morte nell'atto.

One only is the palm I want | from you, Oh virgin Nike: | the Universe!
Naught else. | Only that could Ulysses receive from you,| he who prays for
death in action.

Odysseus is the role model for the man D'Annunzio wants to be. In
the invocation to the Pleiads and the Fates which opens the *Laudi*,
he announces his desire to burn the rudder and figurehead from
the ship wrecked in the last storm. To those who ask what god is
concealed in the fire, he replies: 'Not a god, but Laertes' son' who,
seen in Dante's fire, is worth more than the 'Galilean' Christ. The
latter's word is 'feeble', while the former's 'eccita i forti' ('excites
the strong').

Ulysses—Dante's Ulysses, that is—sets sail towards unknown
lands, an unsleeping spirit whose heart is quelled only by the
'virtute' which is his one anchor. From 'Latin blood' comes the
only word 'worthy of the Pelasgian King'. Dante has fulfiled
Homer by giving his hero 'greater wings'. Well beyond Christian
Scripture, Ulysses was from the start the modern prophet, the
inspiring muse, and Siren of poetry:

> Re del Mediterraneo, parlante
> nel maggior corno della fiamma antica,
> parlami in questo rogo fiammeggiante!
>
> .   .   .   .
>
> o tu che col tuo cor la tua carena
> contra i perigli spignere fosti uso
> dietro l'anima tua fatta Sirena,
>
> infin che il Mar fu sopra te richiuso!

Mediterranean king, speaking | in the greater horn of the ancient flame, |
speak to me in this flame-tossed pyre! | . . . | Oh you who with your heart
your keel | against all dangers were wont to turn | following your Siren
spirit, | until the Sea was closed over you!

The last journey of Dante's Ulysses will thus be a literary and
existential paradigm. Reread in the light of Nietzsche, *Inferno* XXVI
and the *Odyssey* trace the new man's path towards 'Holy Hellas' 'as
an exile returns | to the cradle of his fathers | on a light ship'.

Having loved, desired, tried, aspired, and longed for everything,

the poetic 'I' is in fact in search of the Life beyond life. The
'experience' of Dante's and Tennyson's Ulysses has found its
extreme form: 'Ah perché non è infinito | come il desiderio, il
potere | umano?' ('Why is human power not as infinite as longing?')
'Laus Vitae', at the beginning of *Maia*, yearns with irresistible
fascination. The principle behind the art of poetry and the art of
living is once more the 'sempiternal wonder', the 'terrestrial siren':
the diversity of creation which gives the soul the strength of ten
thousand spirits. Every resting-place, every reawakening, every vital
aspect of nature, every woman possessed, all comfort enjoyed and
melancholy endured is recalled and sublimated in *Maia* during the
summer night when the unquiet, Titanic heart becomes a
concordant force which struggles with the tallest shadow, touches
the galaxy, disturbs the sleep of Aurora, and reanimates all the
strings of Nature and of the human heart.

Transhumanized, the poet now possesses the world, and invokes
the daughters of Atlas (Maia, Electra, Halcyon, and the other
sisters). He receives the gift of Dionysus—the grape (*vite*) which is
inebriating Life (*vita*)—and of Aphrodite, the boundless joy of the
body. In the summer night, the flesh performs the 'fleeting act'
'sotto la specie dell'Eterno' ('under the guise of the Eternal'), and
life itself seems subsumed within the violent myth, 'a sacred sign
over the ways of the Earth'.

This, then, is the new *arkhe*, the shore from which we depart for
the final journey. The symbol of the new Ulysses is no longer the
oar, but the Odysseus of antiquity himself, shining out from
Dante's fire: he is the first person the poet-hero meets as he sails
towards Greece, towards 'the image | which makes visible to man |
the laws of perfect strength'. Under the white cliffs of Leucas (from
which desperate lovers threw themselves into the sea, readers will
remember: the paradigm, according to Leopardi's Columbus, of
the end of all sea voyages), Ulysses rises up in the hollow ship, his
fist grasping the sheet-anchor. He sails on, armed with his bow,
continuing 'his necessary labour | against the implacable Sea'. The
poet and his companions vainly apostrophize Odysseus, the 'King
of storms', begging to be taken along. When the narrator asks to try
his strength with the bow, Odysseus turns to him 'less disdainfully'
and the force of his gaze strikes his forehead; he then continues on
his endless journey. The poet finds himself alone for ever, and
believes in no virtue beyond that of a powerful heart, his own. His

thoughts have become 'scintille dell'Atto', sparks from the Act. Dante's Other has definitively disappeared. Superman, the modern 'Ulisside', can do without God and humanity alike, and leaves Penelope and Telemachus to fling himself

> Contra i nembi, contra i fati,
> contra gli iddii sempiterni,
> contra tutte le Forze
> che hanno e non hanno pupilla,
> che hanno e non hanno parola.

Against the storm-clouds, against the Fates, | against the sempiternal gods, | against all the Forces | which have and have not pupils, | which have and have not words.

His companions include another of Ulysses' descendants, the explorer Guido Boggiani, an expert of 'new stars in an arched heaven', destined to fall 'beneath the club of a plundering savage'; but the message the protagonist receives forces him to journey on, alone on the 'ultima altura', the final heights, which are both 'alto passo' and 'montagna bruna'. In the moment of greatest weakness he again sees Ulysses, the symbol of the supreme teacher, in the waters of Leucas:

> Odi il vento. Su! Sciogli! Allarga!
> Riprendi il timone e la scotta;
> ché necessario è navigare,
> vivere non è necessario.

Hearken to the wind. Come! Weigh anchor! Sheer off! | Take up the rudder and the sheet-sail; | a necessity it is to sail, | to live is no necessity.

Myth is everything: the 'figure' of life which fulfils itself in myth and purifies itself through the human, all too human suffering of existence and history: the wars, diseases, infernal cities, starvation, revolts, and death which D'Annunzio describes in the second half of *Maia*. Between Homer and Dante, poetry becomes the 'canto novello' of the foolish flight towards this radiant fullness, forever poised for further flight. Beyond 'perhaps' and nothingness, Ulysses and his poet have the face of Zarathustra.

Any uncertainty seems to have been thrown to the winds and waves. This early twentieth-century Ulysses is seized by an irrepressible energy and endless desire to possess the whole of reality. At the moment in which Western civilization feels itself omnipotent (ignoring the first rumblings of crisis, which the poem registers with furious anguish), poetry reads the hero of the shadows as a Titan of light. If the nihilistic howl of Pascoli's Calypso is the lament of a whole epoch for its own fate, the 'selection of words',[10] in D'Annunzio's triumph of rhetoric and life, has produced the same era's sustained and high-pitched tenor note.

How long will it be possible to hold this note? Not even four years. By 1907 Guido Gozzano was already working on 'L'ipotesi'[11] which he completed the following year, and which was to have been the prelude to the 'idyll' 'La signorina Felicita'. With 'L'ipotesi' a slight shadow returns to envelope Ulysses—that of the 'Signora vestita di nulla', the Lady dressed in nothing: death. She opens and closes the poem:

> Io penso talvolta che vita, che vita sarebbe la mia,
> se già la Signora vestita di nulla non fosse per via ...

What life, what life would be mine, I sometimes consider, | if the nothing-clad Lady were not fast posting hither ...

Imagine a man, the poet suggests, who, in the place of this 'imminent' Lady, has married a girl of good family, sensible, no-nonsense, and smelling of camphor, soap, and lavender, who lives with her father in an old villa in the Canavese region of Piedmont and is called after the earthly beatitude, Felìcita-Felicità. Imagine him, the poet's *alter ego*, in what to Gozzano might have seemed the far-off, rosy future in the summer of 1940. Mature, staid, and greying, all dreams, anxieties, and youthful pride long-forgotten, he lives peaceably with his lady wife in his house in the Canavese countryside. Letters come from children in far-off cities with news of a six-month pregnancy, or job successes. Destiny seems fulfilled, but life, 'in well-to-do simplicity', still has its pleasures. In the evening, the mayor and other notables go round for a hand of cards, often joined by the curate (as the years go by, the 70-year-old protagonist again enters the fold of the 'gioventù clericale', the clerical youth movement),

[10] H. Blumenberg, *Work on Myth*, trans. R. M. Wallace (Cambridge, Mass. and London, 1985), 164–72.
[11] G. Gozzano, *Poesie*, ed. E. Sanguineti (3rd edn., Turin, 1980), 330–40.

poi che la ragione sospesa a lungo sul nero Infinito
non trova migliore partito che ritornare alla Chiesa.

since reason, so long suspended over black Infinity | finds no better course
than to return to the Church.

Bald, or their little remaining hair grey or dyed, his surviving
friends are also visitors in his modest, hospitable home. They
undoubtedly find a somewhat changed person, in whom 'who
knows how many myselves have died within myself', but the dining-
room still hums with beeswax, quince, and cigar-smoke. Then with
Foscolo, Petrarch, and Dante's Guido da Montefeltro, *Inferno*
XXVI suddenly steps from between the lines:

Che importa! Perita gran parte di noi, calate le vele,
raccoglieremmo le sarte intorno alla mensa fedele.

Però che compita la favola umana, la Vita concilia
la breve tanto vigilia dei nostri sensi alla tavola.

No matter! A large part of us now perished, and, folded the sails, | we
would gather the shrouds around the faithful table. | Since the human tale
is told, Life reconciles | the so brief vigil of our senses to the festive board.

In summer, under a clear sky, they would be eating in the open to
the sound of crickets, the wheeling of the last swallows, and the first
twitchings of bats. They would be talking of this and that, their
hostess popping in and out of the kitchen to oversee the fate of a
recalcitrant sweet ('Sono così malaccorte le cuoche': clearly 'you
can't get the staff these days' was a refrain in Gozzano's time, too),
and the farm-hand comes with freshly picked fruit. The sharp
perfume of the muscat grapes, plums, the rosy peaches and apples
tasting of roses ('non è poeta chi non è ghiotto dei frutti!', 'He who
loves not fruit is no poet!' Gozzano proclaims, parodying the fruit-
fetishes of D'Annunzio in 'O rus!', from the *Poema paradisiaco*) is
strong enough to resuscitate lost time.

They would go on to dead friends, once-beautiful women, love,
and destiny, before the conversation turned to literature, the poetry
of the previous century, the inevitable brevity of poetic fashions,
and the silence of their dearest heroes:

Mah! Come sembra lontano quel tempo e il coro febeo
con tutto l'arredo pagano, col Re-di-Tempeste Odisseo

How distant that time seems, and Phoebus' choir | with all the pagan
trappings, with King-of-the-Storms Odysseus . . .

The hostess, who possesses a brain despite her gender-stereotyped 'ignorance', would then, intrigued, ask about the exploits of this (D'Annunzian) King of Storms, the 'navigator-hero' of Pascoli's 'Ultimo Viaggio' who is evoked in 'La signorina Felicita'. The ancient 'tale' would then be told, 'con pace d'Omero e di Dante', to 'confused laughter', for the benefit of his 'ignorant wife' ('ad uso della consorte ignorante').

And so begins the new tale of Ulysses, the almost limerick-like rhythm and rhyme constituting an integral part of the poetic message. The King of Storms was a man

> che diede col vivere scempio
> un bel deplorevole esempio
> d'infedeltà maritale.

who gave, in a life of some foolishness | a deplorable example of unruliness | and marital infidelity.

After years on board a yacht, he and a few of the boys draw up on the beaches most frequented by famous 'cocottes'. Now old, he returns home, and is pardoned by his faithful wife. But instead of living out a peaceful old age, 'come si vive tra noi', as people of our sort do, he decides to leave once more, and, like the adventurers of the past and the Italians of his present, sets off to seek his fortune in America. The American Dream, the Ulysses–Columbus typology and all the thirst for knowledge—everything which has dominated Western culture for centuries—is swept away at one fell and derisive swoop:

> Ma né dolcezza di figlio,
> né lagrime, né la pietà
> del padre, né il debito amore
> per la sua dolce metà
> gli spensero dentro l'ardore
> della speranza chimerica
> e volse coi tardi compagni
> cercando fortuna in America . . .
> —Non si può vivere senza
> danari, molti danari . . .
> Considerate, miei cari
> compagni, la vostra semenza!

But not fondness for a son, | nor tears, nor duty | to an aged father, nor the love | he owed his better half | could quell within him the ardour | of the hope he did importune | and with his slow companions | in America went seeking his fortune . . . |—Without money, a lot of money | A man can't do a thing . . . | Take thought, my dear companions, | of the seed from which you spring!

'America' now rhymes with 'chimerica' (or, *pace* Gozzano and modern pronunciation, 'importune' with 'fortune'); 'semenza', seed (which for Dante's Ulysses marked the beginning and end of man within a scheme of knowledge), with 'senza' (without); and 'cari' (in all senses, 'dear'), with 'danari' (money).

And so the last fatal journey begins. The fairy-tale aspect both undermines and sustains the story's ancient *Sehnsucht*. The shiver provoked by sailing through the darkness towards the other world now returns from the opposite side—not from the mystery and tension of unknown space as against the measured time of moon and stars, but from the sheer indeterminacy which mocks all co-ordinates. Hercules' 'foce stretta', the west, and the unpeopled world behind the sun have all disappeared. The 'foolish flight', the stars of the southern pole, the open sea, and the high mountain remain, however; framed in rhyme by the mesmerizing repetition of 'viaggia', they lead towards the tragic shadow with the comic force of the distance between Dante's text and Gozzano's:

> Viaggia viaggia viaggia
> viaggia nel folle volo,
> vedevano già scintillare
> le stelle dell'altro polo . . .
> viaggia viaggia viaggia
> viaggia per l'alto mare:
> si videro innanzi levare
> un'alta montagna selvaggia . . .

Journey journey journey | journey in the foolish flight, | they saw already twinkling | the stars of the opposite pole . . . | journey journey journey | journey through the open sea: | they saw before them rear | a mountain of savage height . . .

There are no readerly surprises in Gozzano's plot: everyone follows the script. We are, however, continually wrong-footed by single expressions. When Dante's 'montagna bruna', Tasso's 'oscuro monte' and D'Annunzio's 'ultima altura' change before our eyes into an 'alta montagna selvaggia', all oblique and impure readers will remember the wood, the 'selva selvaggia', which opens the

Divine Comedy, and will then think, immediately before or after, of the 'savage' by definition in our culture: the wilderness of the New World and Leopardi's 'vaste californie selve'. Gozzano immediately comes up with another mocking negation, wiping America off the centuries-long Ulysses map and going back to Dante's tragic end for the hero, and with a further ultra-Dantean twist in that it is not California at all, but Purgatory; not a port, but the sea; and not Purgatory, but the Inferno:

> Non era quel porto illusorio
> la California o il Perù,
> ma il monte del Purgatorio
> che trasse la nave all'in giù.
> E il mare sovra la prora
> si fu rinchiuso in eterno.
> E Ulisse piombò nell'Inferno
> dove ci resta tuttora . . .

It was not that illusory port | California or Peru, | but the mountain of Purgatory | which down the great ship drew. | And the sea over the prow | was closed *in eterno*. | And Ulysses went to the Inferno | and has stayed there to this day.

The shadow returns and wraps the whole 'hypothesis' in the gossamer veil of nothingness which life wears, transforming it into death and the 'if', *se*, which disturbs our comforting bourgeois illusions of a peaceful old age:

> Io penso talvolta che vita, che vita sarebbe la mia,
> se già la Signora vestita di nulla non fosse per via.
> Io penso talvolta . . .

A precarious balance has been reached in the short space of the Ulysses story. The fable falls somewhere between the Homeric-Dantesque-D'Annunzian myth and parody, between the 'Signora Felicita' and the 'Signora vestita di niente'—between all and nothing. Suspended on its spider-thread, the poem evokes the astonished moment of existence. 'Ma dunque esisto! O strano! | vive tra il Tutto e il Niente | questa cosa vivente | detta guidogozzano!'; 'I exist, then! How strange! | it lives between All and Nothing | this living thing called guidogozzano!', the poet exclaims in 'La via del rifugio'.

The prime function of irony is to provoke this delicate comic astonishment.[12] The Ulysses story is veiled with a general air of false credulity: recited 'for the benefit of an ignorant wife', it pretends to presuppose an equally ignorant reader while presuming on that same reader's intertextual dexterity. By ridiculing myth and putting literature in its place among the things considered obsolete,[13] the story confuses its listeners with all their remembered snatches of poetry; they then find themselves in a stupid, astonished stupor and a healthy, 'confused laughter'.

Another step along the road to this purifying idiocy is taken by Alberto Savinio in his play *Capitano Ulisse*[14] ('Captain Ulysses'), written in 1925 but published in 1934 and performed in 1938. Here the trick is quite openly Pirandellian, and the mythical hero undergoes radical treatment when he goes on stage, passing as it were 'through theatre'. In the long introductive *Giustificazione*, significantly entitled 'The Truth about the Last Journey', Savinio explains the causes and effects of the metamorphosis he imposes on Ulysses. 'I'd suspected for some time that an overwhelming desire to *have done with it* was tormenting Ulysses', he states. This is then confirmed by the character's own confession, his heart-breaking lament haunting the playwright's sleep. In search of an author, Ulysses is 'condemned to an endless night'.

If Homer's heroes were 'a cross between the *Commendatore* and the *Chevalier de la Légion d'Honneur*', it was necessary to remove the Navigator's cardboard nose and carnival costume. Having regained his natural stature, the unhappy, misunderstood man of thought and of pure intellect is presented as essentially 'futile'. No longer either the 'heart of bronze' nor a 'purely spiritual' intelligence, Ulysses is now the man of 'radical good humour', totally given over to a 'metaphysics of foolishness' which makes him nickname Calypso 'Dea Clisopompo'—basically 'Goddess Enema'—and Penelope 'orinale', 'chamber-pot'. He is as acquainted with the modern Greece of the Venizelos as with that of the Atrides; a sarcastic populace now lumps under the one word 'the most domestic of household objects with the most domestic of women'. Ground down by earthly tedium, it would have been unjust to

---

[12] See N. Borsellino, 'Il comico', and G. Gorni and S. Longhi, 'La parodia', in *Letteratura italiana*, gen. ed. A. Asor Rosa, vol. v (Turin, 1986), 419–87.

[13] See E. Sanguineti, *Guido Gozzano* (Turin, 1966).

[14] A. Savinio, *Capitano Ulisse*, ed. A. Tinterri (Milan, 1989).

expose Ulysses to the 'celestial tedium without end' of a Christian conversion.

He had, then, to be made man, and given a human face while conserving his mythical features. He had to be taught to live: hence his appearance in the 'drama' as a Captain straight from the pages of Jules Verne. Hence, too, his abandoning of the D'Annunzian *femme fatale*, Circe, and his shaking off the motherly attentions of Calypso, the eternal Maman Colibrì, the ambiguous Goddess of Hide and Seek, with skin the colour of yoghurt, the 'poltrona Frau dell'amore', an amorous armchair of domestic passions. The whole of the *Odyssey*—the court of the Phaeacians, the journey through deep sleep, the return to Ithaca, the murder of the suitors, and the reunion with Penelope—is dramatized with great psychological and philosophical attention, in a dream atmosphere and *crescendo* of crazed horror and dazed languor in which Ulysses sheds all hope and illusions and refuses to recognize his now elderly wife.

Spurred on by the 'voracious old maid' Minerva to fulfil his supreme destiny, he embarks for his final journey, but immediately turns back to change into civilian clothes. With overcoat, hat, and stick, still sick at heart but free and proud in spirit, Ulysses takes the Spectator confidentially by the arm, descends into the pit, and walks out of the theatre. As the *Giustificazione* preannounces, the supreme cultural 'fiction' of the last journey is thus exploded:

Fermo davanti a un mare di pece, a una nave egualmente nera e sempre pronta a salpare: quella nave sulla quale Ulisse non voleva imbarcarsi più, perché sapeva che appena iniziato, l'*ultimo viaggio* si converte in *penultimo*. Era necessario dare un porto a questo navigatore senza porto, un termine al suo viaggio, una morte alla sua vita. La sorte di Ulisse è rimasta in sospeso. La fama un giorno lo consacrò *uomo dell'ultimo viaggio* . . . Aveva creduto per molto tempo alla sincerità dell'*ultimo viaggio*. Sfinito da quel continuo girare a folle, gli fu giocoforza convincersi che l'ultimo viaggio era come i capelli di Eleonora, che quando non ce n'è più ce n'è ancora. 'E quasi non bastasse' mi confidò una volta Ulisse 'questo trucco dell'*ultimo viaggio* me lo vollero abbellire, inzuccherare. Me lo chiamarono il folle volo!'. Fumava di rabbia 'Che ingenuità! che mancanza di riguardo! Eppure, Dante lo credevo una persona seria . . .'. Tacque un momento poi aggiunse: 'Forse per questo appunto. Gli uomini *seri* sono stati i miei peggiori nemici'.

Standing before a sea of pitch, before an equally black ship always ready to set sail: the ship on which Ulysses no longer wished to set foot, knowing that once undertaken, the *last journey* would become the *last-but-one*. It was necessary to find a harbour for this harbour-less navigator, to find an end for his travels and a death for his life. Ulysses' fate has remained pending. Fame was one day to consecrate him *the man of the last journey*, and for a long time he had believed in that *last journey*. But, exhausted by idle wanderings, he had had to convince himself that the *final journey* was like Eleonora's hair: the less there appears to be, the more there is. 'And as if that weren't enough,' Ulysses once confided, 'they tried to pretty it up, this "last journey" business. They decided to call it a "mad flight".' He was fuming. 'The naïvety! The tactlessness! And I'd always considered Dante a person to be taken seriously . . .' He was silent for a moment, then added, 'Perhaps that's why. Serious men have always been my worst enemies.'

'True,' the narrator of the introductory essay wryly remarks, 'an idiotic destiny, an addle-headed fate have invariably pushed Ulysses into the *serious* areas of life.' While still alive he was forced to become a ghost suspended in a state of half-life, half-death.

This has indeed been the story so far, as it were. Savinio now enters like a breath of fresh air to dismiss Ulysses' destiny as 'idiotic', adding that, having learnt to live and reject the idea of a final exploit, he will, when he so decides, be able to die. Humanity returns to life and literature from the ashes of reductive irony. To rise again we have to recognize the comic element of the mythical tradition while fanning the flame of the literary and human element. The 'metaphysics of idiocy' are vital survival-tools in a world obsessed with tragic exaggeration: laughter is necessary for wonder and new beginnings. 'History', Savinio semi-Aristotelically writes, 'tells things as they are, Theatre as they should be.' There is no other way of untying the 'knots of life so neatly, so aseptically, and so painlessly'. Irony is the catharsis of the real: the one point of balance between everything and nothing.[15]

The drift towards laughter extends beyond Italian culture. In *Hugh Selwyn Mauberley* (1920) Pound, who, as we commented at the beginning of the present study, will open his *Cantos* with Odysseus' journey to Hades, ironically celebrates 'l'election de son sepulchre' *à la* Ronsard. The 'new' artist, who has vainly tried to 'resuscitate the dead art of poetry' and 'maintain "the sublime" in the old sense', realizes that he was born 'in a half-savage country',

---

[15] See G. Guglielmi, 'L'ironia', in *Letteratura italiana*, v. 489–512; G. Highet, *The Anatomy of Satire* (Princeton, NJ, 1962).

America, and that the modern age asks of poetry not the 'alabaster of rhyme' but 'an image of its own accelerated grimace'. In his Odyssey as man and poet, Mauberley is storm-bound for a year; he declares Flaubert to be his true Penelope, and says he has 'fished among obstinate isles' observing the 'elegance of Circe's hair | Rather than the mottoes on sundials'. He pulls up in a Pacific Ogygia, in the 'scattered Moluccas' where the Lotus reigns, and where on the oar, the ancient symbol for Ulysses, the ironic inscription runs:

> I was
> And I no more exist;
> Here drifted
> An hedonist.

In Jean Giono's *Naissance de l'Odyssée* (1938), satire and parody dress Ulysses as a loose-living sailor who wanders from port to Greek port for ten years, sampling a woman in every one of them. The 'hero' now decides to return home, but fears Penelope's tongue (although she herself has taken Antinous as her lover) given his long, unjustified absence. One evening, while crossing the Peloponnese in the direction of Ithaca, he invents for a spell-bound audience a whole series of fantastic tales. A poet among the by-standers transforms them into a saga. It quickly becomes famous and reaches Penelope's ear, whereupon the 'faithful' wife kicks out her lover and prepares a hero's welcome for the great impostor. From the 'false stories' Homer's hero was so prodigal of, the Odyssey itself is now born (hence Giono's title).

The fictional motivation is still substantially the same in 1957, when Walter Jens publishes his *Das Testament des Odysseus*, the 'autobiography' Ulysses writes for his grandson once back in Ithaca where he lives anonymously as an outside observer of his much-changed family (Penelope has remarried) and in a kingdom no longer his. He now confesses that the stories he made up to cheer Priam through the long winter nights, at the end of the Trojan War, were converted into the legend of his own exploits by some slave or the court doctor.

Having managed to rid himself of Dante's last journey by means of thematic and structural irony—irony as the narrative principle of what T. S. Eliot called the modern 'mythical method'[16]—Ulysses

[16] T. S. Eliot, 'Ulysses, Order and Myth', in S. Givens (ed.), *James Joyce: Two Decades of Criticism* (New York, 1963).

now wants to be rid of Homer. The same mechanism is at work in Robert Lowell's 'Ulysses and Circe' (published in the collection of poems entitled *Day by Day*). Here the hero 'dislikes everything | in his impoverished life of myth': both life with Circe and the *nostos* towards a still personable Penelope, both the fraudulently won war and the journey 'seeking the unpeopled world beyond the sun' and the shipwreck 'in an uncharted ocean'.[17] Joseph Brodsky uses a similar device in 'Odysseus to Telemachus' (1972), imagining Ulysses writing to his son, years after a war the outcome of which he no longer remembers, of a dirty, overbuilt, overgrown island with 'great grunting pigs' and 'some queen or other'. The way home is too long, Poseidon having evidently 'stretched and extended space': Odysseus sinks into oblivion, forgets and is forgotten.[18]

The irony slowly becomes existential and ontological, Valéry's *Cahiers* marking the process most explicitly and eloquently:

Ulysse— —
Les enchantements, les obstacles, les charmes contraires, les périls, tout enfin lui apparaît sous les espèces de la niaiserie de l'univers et des dieux.
L'incident, le malheur jeté sous les pieds— —Surmonter, surmonter—
Pas de but.
—Je retrouve ce matin un thème qui fut le mien: *Celui de la bêtise des dieux*.
— — —Et au fond de la détresse et de l'enfer même, un *rire*. Les catastrophes amoncelées font rire enfin—Elles perdent tout sérieux. La sensibilité craque et se renverse.
Et puis tout cela a déjà été fait cent mille fois—assez—assez—n'abusez pas de mes *facultés*.

Ulysses— —
The incantations, the obstacles, the bad spells, the dangers: all appeared to him under the guise of the foolishness of gods and the universe.
The accident, ill-luck thrown at his feet— —Overcome, overcome—
No aim.
  —This morning I rediscovered a theme which interested me greatly : *that of the stupidity of the gods*.
— — —And in the depths of misery and hell itself, *laughter* ...
Accumulated one after the other, in the end catastrophes make us laugh— they lose their seriousness. Our sensitivity is ruined, and is inverted.

---

[17] R. Lowell, *Day by Day* (London and Boston, 1978), 3–10.
[18] J. Brodsky, *A Part of Speech* (Oxford, 1987), 58.

And then all this has already been done one hundred thousand times—enough—enough—do not abuse my *faculties*.

The enchantment of adventure and all that is marvellous and monstrous in myth appear, as Savinio would say, idiotic. The continual mishaps, Chance which never happens by chance but which the gods 'chance' to throw our way, and the need to overcome and conquer at all costs—the *Odyssey* is not a metaphysics of foolishness, but the stupidity of metaphysics: ontological and divine imbecility. In substance, the story of Ulysses—Homer's hero, with his horrific misfortunes, Dante's in hell, and the Ulysses of all those to have written about him—is profoundly comic, because the sense of the tragic implodes on itself after the litany of disasters, and explodes into a burst of laughter without shadow which threatens everything in its range: 'sensitivity' is inverted. The serious, *spoudaion*, becomes risible, *geloion*. The *déjà vu* is no longer pleasant, as it appeared in the pseudo-Aristotelian *Problemata*, where music reheard confers the additional delight of recognition without being defamiliarized or perturbing as it would be for Freud. It is simply intellectual and literary abuse. Valéry rejects our shadow.

The limit has been reached: the twentieth-century readers and writers, after their eternal return to Ulysses, are now sick of him and his endless wanderings. Joyce seems well aware of this; in his *Ulysses*,[19] arriving from the Platonic beyond, where he sought the form of his reincarnation in the life of a common man, the Irish Jew Leopold Bloom 'fulfils' his own Odyssey.

An idle urban wanderer who lives totally within the Mediterranean of his unconscious consciousness and in the Dublin Ogygia of the senses and of the intellect, he travels across the entire cosmos, within his own imagination and his apparently insignificant, even sordid, daily routine. At the end of *Ulysses* Bloom lies in the maternal and marital bed, betrayed but not abandoned by his earth-like wife, who sleeps beside him. He surfaces in her passionate memories, at the point where the rhododendrons of Howth Head, on Dublin Bay, are grafted on to the roses, jessamine, geraniums, and cactuses of Gibraltar: in a circumscribed world,

[19] All quotations are from James Joyce, *Ulysses* (Harmondsworth, 1969).

then, and totally unable to go beyond the Pillars of Hercules in a final voyage.[20]

Bloom is not allowed to reach the shore of Hades, nor experience the other, or the new, world. The nearest he gets is when, in the sixth section of *Ulysses*, he goes to Paddy Dignam's funeral, where death appears mere bodily decomposition, the extreme metamorphosis of the flesh, the eternal life ('practically'!) of the cells alone:

I daresay the soil would be quite fat with corpse manure, bones, flesh, nails, charnelhouses. Dreadful. Turning green and pink, decomposing. Rot quick in damp earth. The lean old ones tougher. Then a kind of a tallowy kind of a cheesy. Then begin to get black, treacle oozing out of them. Then dried up. Deathmoths. Of course the cells or whatever they are go on living. Changing about. Live for ever practically. Nothing to feed on feed on themselves.

This is the brutal non-being of brute matter, not the being-of-having-been. It is true that in the next-to-last section of *Ulysses* ('Ithaca'), Bloom, now finally home, his *nostos* accomplished, feels such disgust at his own 'senescence' and the indifference or contempt with which he is looked at by men, women, children, and dogs, that he is possessed by a sudden desire to leave, to travel around Ireland, go to Jerusalem, Athens, the Straits of Gibraltar, and on towards the shadow, and exotic countries which can hide for him the nothingness of death—'the forbidden country of Thibet (from which no traveller returns), the bay of Naples (to see which was to die), the Dead Sea'. He dreams of cosmic, Ancient Mariner wanderings, but with a Ulysses and Count of Montecristo return:

Would the departed never nowhere nohow reappear?

Ever would he wander, selfcompelled, to the extreme limit of his cometary orbit, beyond the fixed stars and variable suns and telescopic planets, astronomical waifs and strays, to the extreme boundary of space,

---

[20] It will be evident from the following account that I do not agree with R. Ellmann, *Ulysses on the Liffey* (2nd edn., London, 1974), 171–2, and *The Consciousness of Joyce* (London, 1977), 29–39, 48–9, nor with the critical current which follows Ellmann. If *Ulysses* is, as Umberto Eco theorized, a model of 'opera aperta', this is because of its formal rhetorical devices: see U. Eco, *Le poetiche di Joyce* (2nd end., Milan, 1966), 59–111. The cosmos of *Ulysses* is actually a closed one, in a sense 'infinite' but 'limited' like the universe postulated by modern physics. *Ulysses* itself is, Hugh Kenner writes in his *Ulysses* (London, 1980), 173, 'proteiform yet bounded'. See Blumenberg, *Work on Myth*, 80–5.

passing from land to land, among peoples, amid events. Somewhere imperceptibly he would hear and somehow reluctantly, suncompelled, obey the summons of recall. Whence, disappearing from the constellation of the Northern Crown he would somehow reappear reborn above delta in the constellation of Cassiopeia and after incalculable eons of peregrination return an estranged avenger, a wreaker of justice on malefactors, a dark crusader, a sleeper awakened, with financial resources (by supposition) surpassing those of Rothschild or of the silver king.

The sheer irrationality of such a return immediately strikes him, however: the irreversible passage of time no longer permits 'an exodus and return in time through reversible space' (whereas Dante's Ulysses threw himself into his 'folle volo' despite his old age). More significantly, the departure itself seems to Bloom definitely 'undesirable'. It is late, the night dark, and the thoroughfares uncertain and 'perilous': hardly the moment to face the 'alto passo'. Rest seems a far better bet. Nearby lies 'an occupied bed, obviating research'; it emanates human warmth, and cool linen. His mind tingles with the irresistible awakening of 'self-desiring desire', and, no longer Ulysses, Leopold Bloom seems on the verge of turning into 'the statue of Narcissus, sound without echo, desired desire'.

Finally, we may be tempted to see him for a moment as Sinbad the Sailor, but Joyce immediately deconstructs the suggestion in parodying phonic variations—'Tinbad the Tailor and Jinbad the Jailer and Whinbad the Whaler and Ninbad the Nailer . . .'. The last 'figure' of Leopold Bloom is a mere name—in Frege's acception, he has a sense, but no meaning.[21]

On the very same page we are told that Bloom 'has travelled'. Now 'he rests'. And this seems to me Joyce's definitive word on his Ulysses. Further journeys are neither rational nor desirable. Indeed, they are impossible: Gibraltar and Howth Head shut humanity inside the jail it has built for itself in its own brain by making the whole world (and only this world) its home.

This reaction towards tradition and revolt against Dante's Ulysses is not, however, only literary, nor is it exclusively metaphysical. The tragicomic death of the poetry of the Eternal Return and of the Final Journey seems to pre-empt a complex and ongoing social and

---

[21] See n. 8 to Introduction.

historical phenomenon: the absurd increase and the inevitable end of travel. In *Tristes Tropiques*, from 1955 (i.e. nearly half a century ago!), Claude Lévi-Strauss deplored both aspects in memorable pages entitled precisely 'An End to Journeying'. On the one hand there was (in the 1950s!) what we call mass tourism:

The end of one civilization, the beginning of another, and the sudden discovery by our present-day world that it is perhaps beginning to grow too small for the people inhabiting it—these truisms are brought home to me less tangibly by figures, statistics and revolutions than by the fact that when, a few weeks ago, after a lapse of fifteen years I was toying with the idea of recapturing my youth by revisiting Brazil in the same way, I was told on the telephone that I would have to book a cabin four months in advance.[22]

On the other hand, there is the concomitant littering of the entire globe by Western civilization, transforming it into 'breve carta' in only the most ironic sense: the global rubbish-tip, indiscriminately strewn with scraps of paper. Wonder quickly vanishes or is feigned, in an update of Odysseus' deceit, in conventional travellers' tales in which increasing numbers of 'explorers' have increasingly less to explore and to tell:

Journeys, those magic caskets full of dreamlike promises, will never again yield up their treasures untarnished. A proliferating and overexcited civilization has broken the silence of the seas once and for all. The perfumes of the tropics and the pristine freshness of human beings have been corrupted by a busyness with dubious implications, which mortifies our desires and dooms us to acquire only contaminated memories.

Now that the Polynesian islands have been smothered in concrete and turned into aircraft carriers solidly anchored in the southern seas, when the whole of Asia is beginning to look like a dingy suburb, when shanty towns are spreading across Africa, when civil and military aircraft blight the primeval innocence of the American or Melanesian forests even before destroying their virginity, what else can the so-called escapism of travelling do than confront us with the more unfortunate aspects of our history? . . . The first thing we see as we travel round the world is our own filth, thrown into the face of mankind.[23]

---

[22] C. Lévi-Strauss, *Tristes Tropiques*, trans. J. and D. Weightman (Harmondsworth, 1976), 23.
[23] Ibid. 43.

The end to journeying prefigured by literary irony towards the Ulysses myth coincides with only one 'overwhelming conclusion'— that the 'other' is vanishing and 'the history of the past twenty thousand years is irrevocable'. But if we want to rediscover the freshness of forgotten wonder beneath the horror of our civilization, it is precisely to history that we must turn.

7. The Mirror of the Sea: A Hope for Literature within History

And shippes by the brynke comen and gon,
And in swich forme enduren a wowke or two.

THERE is an emblematic moment for Ulysses' entry on to the twentieth-century European stage. It is that in which Joseph Conrad, a Ukraine-born Pole who lived in Russia, was brought up in Cracow, emigrated to France, under whose flag he sailed before moving to the Merchant Navy and taking British citizenship, published a book of impressions dedicated to the sea, the Muse inspiring almost all his fiction. A collection of sketches and articles, most of them previously published in newspapers and magazines, it appeared in English (in which he was already well-established as a major writer) in 1906 (and thus considerably before Joyce's *Ulysses* and Pound's 'Ulyssean' poems), under the title *The Mirror of the Sea*. In the Note introducing the 1919 edition, Conrad states that he has tried 'to lay bare with the unreserve of a last hour's confession the terms of [his] relation with the sea, which beginning mysteriously, like any great passion the inscrutable Gods send to mortals, went on unreasoning and invincible'.[1]

The passionate relationship Conrad describes is of some complexity, and the 'mirror' many-faceted. We can best approach them and their implied polysemia through the two epigraphs from Chaucer which open the book, one from his translation of Boethius, the other from the *Franklin's Tale*. In the first, Boethius questions Philosophy about a 'miracle' or 'wonder': 'For this miracle or wonder troubleth me right gretly.' In the second, one of the characters from the *Franklin's Tale* wonders whether an expert in 'natural magic'

---

[1] J. Conrad, *The Mirror of the Sea* and *A Personal Record*, ed. Z. Najder (Oxford, 1988), pp. xxxiii–xxxiv. All quotations from this edition.

> may make,
> To mannes sighte, that alle the rokkes blake
> Of Britaigne weren yvoyded everichon,
> And shippes by the brynke comen and gon,
> And in swich forme enduren a wowke or two.
>
> (ll. 1157–1161)

Boethius' wonder takes us back to the origin of the love of true knowledge and myth which Aristotle speaks of at the beginning of the *Metaphysics*, and which was mentioned in the Introduction to the present essay. In the *Consolation*, this wonder regards the singleness of providence, the course of fate, the suddenness of chance, the knowledge and predestination of God, and the freedom of the will. In other words, the sea is the 'mirror' of man's fundamental problems: the living image of a metaphysical mirror ('mirror' and 'miracle' both deriving, it will be remembered, from the Latin *miraculum*) clouded by a mass of gnoseological and ethical problems.

The 'apparence' talked of in the *Franklin's Tale* reflects the illusory aspect of the mirror. On the 'brynke'—the horizon, edge, limit, or margin—of the sea, the ships seem to appear and disappear, and remain suspended in this 'forme' for a week or two: all human things continually oscillate between movement to and movement from, between presence and absence; they permanently hover, in a mere illusion which totally convinces the human eye, on the final threshold between appearance and disappearance. The book is in one sense not only a call to traditional order, a return to the mainstream of English literature begun by Chaucer with his *Tales*, but also a reminder that this mainstream is based on a translation, Chaucer's of Boethius, which is a rewriting of a philosophical and poetic text and simultaneously a cultural transcription: a mirror, then, of a vision of a world and language in another culture and another language.

The act of writing *The Mirror of the Sea* is itself a 'speculum' of the double tragedy of humanity and the insolubly problematic nature of the world and of existence: its transience and marginality. 'Wonder' and 'brink': the beginning of English literature gives the European Conrad the two shores of poetico-philosophical awe and the ontologico-existential margin between which to enact his own journey in life and fiction.

It will come as no surprise at this point to discover that Conrad's

voyage in his 'paper boats' launched upon 'that terrible sea that . . .
lies within the circle of an Eternal Shadow'[2] deliberately retraces
the historical, cultural, and poetic itinerary of the Ulysses who at
the end of the *Mirror* comes to stand as the symbol for humanity,
the representative of the autobiographical 'I', and the *typos* of the
writer. In the evocation of departures and landings, the description
of hopes and fears, the meticulous account of nautical techniques,
and the discussion of the winds and whirlwinds which rule the seas
and make them seem immemorially ancient, the early sections of
the book bring about the phase of 'initiation', when, with echoes
from the Psalms, the final, 'most amazing' 'wonder of the deep' is
revealed to the protagonist: its 'unfathomable cruelty'.

Then, in a sequence which mirrors the succession of human
civilizations as well as personal and artistic experience, we reach the
'nursery of the craft' (chapters 37–9), an image which significantly
retains the idea of 'vessel' within 'craftsmanship'. 'Happy he who,
like Ulysses, has made an adventurous voyage', Conrad exclaims
after Du Bellay at the beginning of chapter 38. This is undoubtedly
Homer's Odysseus, the centripetal hero of the return who has
apparently completed his journey and now contemplates it serenely
from the safety of the native country he has reconquered. But the
cry of exultation dies in the writer's throat, and Du Bellay's
nostalgia for the return turns into its opposite, admiration for
'adventurous voyages'. Here is Odysseus wandering around the
Mediterranean, travelling over the 'inland sea' as if in a vicious
circle which is the projection of our own mind. Once more, wonder
is seen as the *arkhe* of poetry, the 'nursery of the craft':

Happy he who, like Ulysses, has made an adventurous voyage: and there is
no such sea for adventurous voyages as the Mediterranean—the inland sea
which the ancients looked upon as so vast and so full of wonders. And,
indeed, it was terrible and wonderful: for it is we alone who, swayed by the
audacity of our minds and the tremors of our hearts, are the sole artisans
of all the wonder and romance of the world.

This Homeric, Mediterranean Odysseus stands both at the
beginning and end of the ancient world, at the same time
constituting the *typos* of another Ulysses. 'Voices menacing,
seductive, or prophetic' sing to him 'among the black rocks

---

[2] J. Conrad, *Tales of Hearsay and Last Essays* (London, 1926), 142–3; and see
R. Ambrosini, *Conrad's Fiction as Critical Discourse* (Cambridge, 1991), 36–63.

seething in white foam', 'in the darkness above the moving wave'. These are clearly the voices of Homer's Sirens, who seduce with knowledge and poetry and represent the icons of death—our first shadow—at the centre of Odysseus' journey. But Conrad superimposes on them the 'voice heard at the beginning of the Christian era' by Thamus, the Egyptian pilot of a ship which, according to Plutarch's *De Defectu Oraculorum*, travelled from Greece to Italy.

One evening, near Paxi, the wind suddenly drops and a mysterious voice is heard calling Thamus, 'bidding him go and tell all men that the great god Pan was dead'. The supernatural voice actually announces not only the death of Pan, but the end of all oracles and the *Dämmerung* of the entire ancient world. It should be remembered that a respectable exegetic and poetic tradition exists, from Prudentius down to the Milton of 'On the Morning of Christ's Nativity', relating the death of pagan oracles to the birth of the Christian redeemer. When, in the dead calm, Thamus sights Palodes and repeats his message to the mainland, a great cry of lamentation goes up 'not of one person, but of many, mingled with exclamations of wonder'. Classical wisdom is dying, and the new, Christian 'sapientia' is being born. Once more, Ulysses is straddling two eras. But the 'great legend of the Mediterranean', Conrad writes, 'the legend of traditional *song* and grave *history* lives, fascinating and immortal, in our minds'.

The dark and terrifying sea over which the 'resourceful Ulysses' wandered is to become the familiar route of Carthaginian merchants and the pleasure-'ground' of the Caesars. From the beginning, then, it represents the historical home of 'that spirit of open defiance against the great waters of the earth' which constitutes the impulse behind every seafarer's vocation. It was this impulse which, leaving the Mediterranean and 'issuing thence to the west and south . . . as a youth leaves the shelter of his parental home', ventured out towards the Indies, discovered the coasts of a new continent, and crossed 'at last the immensity of the great Pacific, rich in groups of islands as remote and mysterious as the constellations of the sky'. Under the spell of the sea (the passion he analyses in his Note), Conrad retraces, in literature and in history, all the stages of Ulysses' journey which we as readers have reenacted in the present work. Significantly, as soon as he begins to reconstruct it he associates Dante's Ulysses with Odysseus: Ulysses' 'first impulse' towards the sea is nurtured in the tideless basin of the Mediterranean as if in the 'nursery of his craft', after which he ventures from gulf to gulf, from island to island, before launching himself 'into the promise of world-wide oceans beyond the Pillars of Hercules'.

Quite deliberately Conrad goes through the typological stages of the Odysseus-Ulysses figure, in a conscious reincarnation and attempt to read the most significant phases figurally in his own career as man, writer, and modern. He takes Ulysses as his cultural and literary model, as he states explicitly in chapter 39 when, after re-evoking the whole of European civilization, he moves to the personal level:

The truth must have been that, all unversed in the arts of the wily Greek, the deceiver of gods, the lover of strange women, the evoker of bloodthirsty shades, I yet longed for the beginning of my own obscure Odyssey, which, *as was proper for a modern*, should unroll its *wonders* and *terrors* beyond the Pillars of Hercules.

Homer's Odysseus and Dante's Ulysses are now once more superimposed, forming a single shadow which grows longer and longer until it covers the next 'figure', Dominic Cervoni, the captain of the *Tremolino*, the faint shadow and simultaneously the Homeric Tiresias and Dantean Virgil of Joseph Conrad. From the 'mezzo del cammin', which Conrad renders 'the middle turn of life's way', the writer looks back in search of his roots. Darkness lies over the past, peopled by a 'crowd' of 'grey', 'friendly' figures who, however, 'gaze sadly after us as we hasten towards the Cimmerian shore'. The 'selva oscura'—Dante's dark wood—is now suspended between two shadows, two mirroring mists of death. Between the 'greyness' of one and 'our already crepuscular sky' there emerges a 'figure glowing with a faint radiance' and trembling as the name of his ship, *Tremolino*, suggests. The new Ulysses, the astute and decisive Dominic Cervoni who would have been a worthy rival of Laertes' and Anticlea's unfortunate son, and who would have stopped for no Circe and no Polyphemus, thus emerges from Conrad's *nekyia*. Later, we learn from Conrad himself, he becomes Nostromo in one of Conrad's best-known novels, also appearing under his own name in *The Arrow of Gold*.

The *Tremolino* is sunk by its own crew, and Cervoni vanishes from sight, a 'strangely desolate figure', 'carrying an oar on his shoulder up a barren, rock-strewn ravine under the dreary leaden sky'. The last reincarnation of the *typos* takes us back to the Odysseus-in-the-future of Tiresias' prophecy, the Odysseus we took as our departure point at the beginning of this book.

The final message concerns humanity and its position in time: its illusions, 'desires, thoughts, and wonder' (in a word, poetic imagination) become, in their search for lost time, a means of matching our existential minuteness against the immensity of history and myth.

With the quality of our desires, thoughts and wonder proportioned to our infinite littleness we measure even time itself by our own stature . . . Imprisoned in the house of personal illusions thirty centuries in mankind's history seem less to look back upon than thirty years of our own life.

The immediate and the remote past form a shadow *continuum* and merge in the single image of a beginning, an *arkhe*, leading in the awed wonder which is the foundation of philosophy and of philomythy to Homer and the poetry of antiquity, and to Conrad and the fiction of modernity. We are here reading pure typology, high-quality figuralism: as if in a magic circle, they leap over the Ulysses of the Renaissance, of Dante, of Plutarch, and make the end coincide with the beginning, with the narrative excess and mysterious gap which open up to Ulysses his mythical future:

And Dominic Cervoni takes his place in memory by the side of the legendary wanderer on the sea of marvels and terrors, by the side of the impious adventurer, to whom the evoked shade of the soothsayer predicted a journey inland with an oar on his shoulder, till he met men who had never set eyes on ships and oars.

A master of the truth,[3] Tiresias shows Odysseus the road he must travel in time and space. Before his prophecy is fulfilled, however, a further step has to be taken. Side by side with Odysseus and Dominic Cervoni, their *anti-typos* and fulfilment *in literature* must be outlined in a personal and historical present which is also open to the future. Ulysses and the *Tremolino* captain appear side by side in the twilight of an arid land, like the 'unfortunate possessor[s] of the secret lore of the sea', carrying on their shoulders the sign of their difficult vocation, surrounded by silent and curious men. 'His back upon the sea', the writer Conrad bears the sign of *his* difficult vocation, carrying his 'few pages in the

---

[3] M. Detienne, *Les Maîtres de vérité dans la Grèce archaïque* (Paris, 1967).

twilight, with the hope of finding in an inland valley the silent welcome of some patient listener'.

The writer is a Ulysses embarked on his last journey; the reader lives in the inland valley, the saltless, sealess land. We could now compare this with our initial image: the *miraculum* which so perturbs Boethius, and the ships which come and go on the brink for a week or two. We have come, as the saying goes, a long way: the distance of a whole odyssey. At the end of it we are over the brink, beyond wonder, in an extreme and perpetually moving world which produces both *wonders* and *terrors*. If Odysseus is constantly journeying with his oar on his shoulder, he has not yet come to the land without ships. Writer and reader only meet in the realm of wish-fulfilment: it may be that they will meet in no other country.

We should be careful, then, not to embark on an aesthetics of pure reception, which would make reading—and reading in a particular moment in history, and a particular social climate—the only touchstone for viewing fiction.[4] We must, naturally, equally avoid considering modern literature simply as ruins of the sacred truth:[5] if Ulysses' journey is not over, he cannot meet the death which Tiresias promises will come from within, or far from, the sea. Poetry, ·which itself comes from death, goes beyond that ultimate limit; it waits in the inland valley which separates and unites writing and reading—the Dantean valley of the dark wood, between this world and the next.

It is this 'border country' and no-man's-land Conrad guides his 'writerly' steps towards: the heart of darkness, the Gulf, and the shadow-line. This is where history lies, in the valley of wonders and terrors. In *The Heart of Darkness* the shadows and 'the horror, the horror' of European civilization and its colonialism cry out from the deepest recesses of Africa, where Conrad's narrator Marlow travels, oar on shoulder, having navigated the Thames and the Congo River, like the author of *The Mirror of the Sea* in the 'Faithful River' section.[6] *Nostromo*, where Dominic Cervoni reappears in the guise of a dashing, daring Italian who gets rich by stealing the silver he himself has saved, seethes with the uprisings in Costaguana, South America, revolution, the drifting mine of the Sulaco silver,

[4] W. Iser, *The Implied Reader* (Baltimore and London, 1974); and see U. Eco, *Lector in Fabula*, (Milan, 1979); cf. J. Hillis Miller, *The Ethics of Reading* (New York, 1987).

[5] H. Bloom, *Ruin the Sacred Truths* (Cambridge, Mass. and London, 1989).

[6] See G. Sertoli, *Introduction to J. Conrad, Cuore di tenebra* (Turin, 1989), pp. v–xliii.

and the People—an embodiment of all the economic and political problems of the nineteenth and twentieth century.[7] The protagonist of *The Shadow-Line*, in 'late youth', finds himself captain of a ship which, in a desperately dead calm, he steers across the Gulf of Siam, his fever-ridden crew reduced to skeletons, and the boat haunted by the ghost of its crazed late captain, waiting like a Flying Dutchman or Ancient Mariner 'down there under the sea with some evil intention'. But the novella, as the Author's Note states, is a meditation on the rites of passage from youth to maturity, and the shadow-line separating the two; it is also a metaphor of 'the supreme trial of a whole generation': the Great War.[8]

The sea is the mirror of the earth and of the ego: 'calme plat, grand miroir | De mon désespoir', as the epigraph from Baudelaire puts it in the first chapter of *The Shadow-Line*. It is dominated by dead calm and darkness in the night-black Gulf of *Nostromo* and the wind-less Gulf of *The Shadow-Line*, symbolized in their *terra firma* equivalent in the darkness of England and the Congo in *The Heart of Darkness*. History lies in this metaphysical obscurity and humanity's anguished immobility:[9] fiction and poetry translate the existent into being in expectation, in illness, in corruption, and in the constant threat of death.

History infects the flesh, the mind, and the heart. A subtle and elusive but unyielding *shadow*-line separates youth from maturity, one generation from another, one age from the next, and the living from the dead, and the wonder from 'the horror'. Only a harsh, vigorous ethics and poetics can survive in such a context. The heroism of the sailors (and soldiers, in the case of the First World War) which deserves the writer's 'undying regard' consists in remaining loyal to their captain despite his being a virtual stranger to them: in their human solidarity 'on the brink', as Conrad writes, using Chaucer's word, in the Note to *The Shadow-Line*, 'of a slow and agonising destruction'. The duty of the captain, of the responsible man, and of the poet is to face that line and brink squarely, and steer himself, his ship, and his men over them

[7] See I. Watt, *Joseph Conrad, Nostromo* (Cambridge, 1988); C. Watts, *Joseph Conrad, Nostromo* (Harmondsworth, 1990).

[8] J. Berthoud, 'Introduction: Autobiography and War', in J. Conrad, *The Shadow-Line* (Harmondsworth, 1986).

[9] R. Roussel, *The Metaphysics of Darkness* (Baltimore and London, 1971); H. M. Daleski, *Joseph Conrad: The Way of Dispossession*, (London, 1977).

without succumbing to their terrors, and without being (ship)-
wrecked by their horror and darkness. Knowledge, experience, and
poetry are indispensable in pointing the way, but they will not be
sufficient: humanity can only hope to save itself within history
through the *virtute* counselled to his companions by Dante's
Ulysses.

In the most ancient, and perhaps now most neglected work of
literary theory extant, the *Poetics*, Aristotle maintains that poetry is
more philosophical and more serious than historiography, in that
the latter reveals actual events through the particular while the
former offers a vision of the universal by narrating facts which may
happen, and events which are possible within the bounds of the
probable and the necessary. Until now, while trying to keep poetry
and history within sight of each other, I have maintained this
distinction, and thus have talked about shadows. Conrad's fiction
indicates a way of finding a space, within our own time, in which
history and poetry can converge without losing either the parti-
cularized vision and factuality of the one or the seriousness,
potentiality, and philosophical nature of the other, thus keeping
alive the tension towards the universal, and the desire for truth,
which brings poetry, the love of myth, closer to philosophy, the love
of wisdom.

Conrad's Ulysses is from the beginning, as we have seen, a
legend of *song* and *history*. He is born out of wonder and memory,
but is alive to the horrors of the world; he embodies personal and
artistic experience, but also civilizations, and human spirit; he
comes from the sea, but moves towards the earth in order to return
to the sea. In the horror of the darkness he contains, poetry and
history—Sirens and the twilight of the oracles—meet on a shadow-
line which symbolizes the only survival strategy for modern
humanity.

Our own century presents us with at least one extreme instance
of how history and literature, real and possible events, meet in the
open wounds of Western civilization, in the boundless horror
invented not by poets or novelists, but by the 'engineers' of modern
society. This particular horror poses deeply disquieting questions
about the significance of and difference between the probable and
the necessary.

On 13 December 1943 a young, middle-class Italian Jew, newly graduated in chemistry, Primo Levi, was captured by the Fascists on the Piedmontese mountains, handed over to the Nazis who were occupying Northern Italy, and sent, with thousands of other men and women, to Auschwitz. Levi recounted his internment in a book published in 1947 which soon became known all over the world, *Se questo è un uomo* (*If This is a Man*).[10]

Life in a lager is ultimately, literally, unspeakable, and any account of it should be approached, as Levi himself does, with understatement, sobriety, and humility. There is no doubt, however, that the author quite intentionally narrates it as an *Inferno* and new Bible, and that it is as moving and silencing in its effect on the reader as the first cantica of the *Commedia* and the Book of Job: in short, that *Se questo è un uomo*, for all its basis in the historical particular, is a work of art.

The eleventh of the seventeen chapters in the short novel is entitled 'The Canto of Ulysses'. Levi recounts how one day he was chosen by Jean, the Alsatian Pikolo of the Chemical Commando, to go with him and fetch the hundred-pound-heavy pot of soup for their daily rations. The young but resourceful Jean makes the kilometre walk to the kitchens last as long as possible, so that, still unburdened, they are relatively free to talk about home, their mothers, and their studies without arousing undue suspicion. Pikolo loves Italy and expresses a wish to learn Italian; Levi immediately starts on a crash course.

All of a sudden *Inferno* XXVI comes to mind, and he tries to explain who Dante is, what the *Commedia* and 'contrapasso' mean, and what the functions of Virgil-Reason and Beatrice-Theology are. He begins to recite the Ulysses episode, trying to translate and gloss it. The greater horn of the ancient flame tosses and murmurs indeed, and ejects its voice. The translation is a disaster. After the 'Quando' which opens the account of his departure from Circe, memory fails Levi, and only useless fragments drift up to the surface. One line is salvaged, though, and produces an immediate reaction:

> Ma misi me per l'alto mare aperto.

Di questo sì, di questo sono sicuro, sono in grado di spiegare a Pikolo, di distinguere perché "misi me" non è "je me mis", è molto più forte e più audace, è un vincolo infranto, è scagliare se stessi al di là di una barriera, noi conosciamo bene questo impulso.

Of this, yes, of this I am sure. I am able to explain to Pikolo, to distinguish why 'misi me' is not 'je me mis', it is much stronger and bolder, it is a bond being broken, it is to fling oneself beyond a barrier. We know this impulse well.

Ulysses has become a prisoner of the lager. The deep open sea means 'the horizon that closes on itself, free, straight, simple', when all that remains is the smell of the sea, one of the 'sweet things' which are now 'cruelly remote' from concentration camp reality: poetry can both express present experience and re-create, with devastating longing, the past, uniting the other world and this, the real 'other'.

Memory fails him again. Levi is forced to recount the 'foolish flight' beyond the Pillars of Hercules in prose ('supreme sacrilege'), yet he realizes only now, only here, that the prohibition, 'acciò che l'uom più oltre *non si metta*' ('beyond which man may not go') explicitly denies Ulysses' impulse ('*misi me*'). It is as if poetry acquired greater significance in memory and in the sudden intensification amidst the death-in-life of Auschwitz; as if hermeneutics could be produced only in a moment of dire suffering.

Levi is seized by a frenzy of anxiety. There are so many things to be explained, but the 'orazion picciola', 'Considerate la vostra semenza', is paramount. He calls Pikolo's attention to the crucial passage, and finds that he is also calling his own: 'as if I, too, heard it for the first time, like a trumpet blaring, like God's voice'. For an instant he has forgotten who and where he is: this is 'God's message' to 'all suffering men', and the lager inmates in particular, not least the two of them, trudging along and daring to reason about such things with the soup pot on their shoulders. In a second, from within Auschwitz, Levi explodes the orthodox and traditional reading of the *terzina*. From the centre of the catastrophe of European civilization, present reality and the classical, humanistic culture of an Italian Jew make the pagan desire for knowledge and virtue coincide with the pre-lapsarian image and destiny of man in Genesis: not made to live as brutes ('fatti non foste a viver come bruti') but according to 'God's voice', after God's own likeness.

Levi's is an extraordinary, revolutionary interpretation which actually goes beyond the 'Romantic' reading discussed in Chapter 2.

No one would dare deny its basic truth. It is true for anyone reading the poem in extreme circumstances, in the other world: and against this truth it is perfectly futile to set philology or a reconstruction of the original epistemic and cultural context of the *Commedia*. Only the human being in history gives a meaning to the poetic text.

Yet even Levi's text is divided. Another mental blank forces him to skip the four *terzine* recounting the journey towards the Pillars, under the moon and stars. Here is the mountain again, dark on account of the distance, like those seen in the evening on the return train journey from Milan to Turin, 'sweet, fiercely remote things' 'which one may think of, but may not say', and the shipwreck. Levi tells us he would 'give today's soup to join "non ne aveva alcuna" with the end', but none of the lines from Dante whirling in his head will fit. As they approach the kitchens, the ship circles round, and with the poop aloft and the prow below, plunges down 'com'altrui piacque'. Levi holds Pikolo back:

E' assolutamente necessario e urgente che ascolti, che comprenda questo 'come altrui piacque' prima che sia troppo tardi, domani lui o io possiamo essere morti, o non vederci mai più, devo dirgli, spiegarli del Medioevo, del *così umano e necessario e pure inaspettato anacronismo*, e altro ancora, qualcosa di gigantesco che io stesso ho visto ora soltanto, nell'intuizione di un attimo, forse il perché del nostro destino, del nostro essere oggi qui . . .

It is absolutely necessary and urgent that Pikolo listen and understand this 'com'altrui piacque' before it's too late. Tomorrow either he or I may be dead, or never again see each other. I must tell him, explain to him about the Middle Ages, about *the totally human and necessary and yet unexpected anachronism*; and something more, something gigantic that I myself have seen only now, in the intuition of a second, perhaps the why of our destiny, of our being here today . . .

The stories of prisoners of Auschwitz, Levi had told us earlier, are all 'simple and incomprehensible', like Bible stories; all full of a tragic, surprising *necessity*. The anachronism in Dante's tale, the conflict between Ulysses' pagan past and the Christian present in hell—the clash between two different cultures—make *Inferno* XXVI the equivalent of the Bible and simultaneously of classical tragedy: tragic plots, Aristotle states, unfolding according to the necessary and the probable, the terrible, pathos-evoking events arising the one from the other *against all expectation*.

Here, where men (satanic 'others') have totally blurred the distinctions between probability, possibility, necessity, and un-expectedness, that anachronism also precipitates a mysterious and terrible theophany. 'Ulysses' (and Levi's) "virtue" and "knowledge" are put to the test, the definitive test, by the encounter with the insuperable limit of absolute Alterity.'[11] What is the 'something gigantic' which hides behind this vision? Why does it coincide with the cause and purpose (the 'perché') of Levi's, Pikolo's, and all the prisoners' presence in the lager, and with their destiny? Is Levi implying that the Holocaust 'pleased' 'piacque') Jahveh? Why, above all, does he not end the sentence, leaving us with the full burden of interpreting silence?

'Hier ist kein Warum', here there is no why, a guard had replied earlier on to Levi's innocent question. And no answer to these questions is given in the last book Levi wrote before his tragic death, *I sommersi e i salvati* (*The Drowned and the Saved*),[12] in which he returns to 'The Canto of Ulysses' to confirm the truth of the episode, and to maintain that culture and poetry were useful to him in surviving the lager because they allowed him to re-establish a link with the past, to consolidate his own identity, and to convince himself that his mind was still working.

The 'liberating and differential' function accorded literature and culture, a 'fleeting but not foolish respite', in *I sommersi e i salvati* is basically part of the same humanistic message that the 'fatti non foste a viver come bruti' already contains in *Se questo è un uomo*. It gives not a ghost of an answer, however, to the final question of 'com'altrui piacque'; and the fact that in this last book Dante's Ulysses is replaced to an extent by the Ancient Mariner is certainly significant. In the epigraph from the *Rime* Levi puts the Mariner's words into his own mouth: it is to him that 'That agony returns', and his 'heart' that 'burns' 'till [his] ghastly tale is told'. With his experiences in the concentration camp burnt into his flesh, too, the narrator is condemned to retell and relive his life-in-death.

No, *I sommersi e i salvati* has no answers to give: it only throws up new and disturbing questions. If the title is that of one of the chapters in *Se questo è un uomo*, thus establishing an ideal continuity between Levi's first and last work, the tragic end to his life, shortly

---

[11] G. P. Biasin, *I sapori della modernità* (Bologna, 1992), 199.
[12] *I sommersi e i salvati* (Turin, 1986).

after its publication, leaves a painful question open: which group did Primo Levi belong to—those who were sunk and covered by the waves (the *sommersi* like Ulysses and the millions who disappeared in the camps), or those who were saved, the *salvati*? The Ancient Mariner's is no fiction: *this*, precisely this, *is a man*. But did this man drown, or was he sunk by the Other?

An answer to this question, and to the preceding questions it automatically recalls, is intrinsically impossible to the human being, and silence, in cowed and humbled dignity, is the only reply a writer or reader can give. But it is the task of literature in history to put questions while knowing there can be no answers.

Levi's story gives meaning to mine. Its sense rises up from the damp, dark soil of Auschwitz like an all-enveloping shadow. The exaltation, the desire, and the tragedy of Dante's Ulysses are wounds that tear apart, now, the flesh of a human being. That the destiny of a mythical, fictional, pagan hero should, thanks to a piece of poetry canonized by the Italian secondary school curriculum, be borne on the shoulders of the children of Israel by a man called Levi constitutes the paradox of our history. But through the context in which it is inserted, this poetic fragment also points to the damnation of ideology—be it the lager and gulag systems, any absolute epistemic and cultural model, or any 'pure' or purely theoretical hermeneutics of books and the world.

Humanistic culture, the love of nature, art, and music, in George Steiner's opinion have not stopped the hand of Europe's bloodier butchers;[13] but, as Levi testifies, they have at least helped the butchered. And in some way we are all victims. History is not, as Paul de Man would have Benjamin say, a 'motion', an 'errancy of language which never reaches the mark', the 'illusion of a life that is only an after-life'.[14] History is real and human—possibly too human; and it contains a place and a task for poetry. The place is Conrad's shadow-line; the task to 'cercare l'uomo',[15] to look for man, and help him face the supreme alterity of the abyss.

It is by starting from this zero degree in which real, possible, probable, necessary, and surprising events merge into the same

---

[13] G. Steiner, *Language and Silence* (Harmondsworth, 1979), 83.

[14] P. de Man, 'Walter Benjamin's "The Task of the Translator" ', in *The Resistance to Theory* (Manchester, 1986), 92. The essay de Man discusses is Benjamin's 'The Task of the Translator', in *Illuminations*, ed. H. Arendt (New York, 1968), 69–82.

[15] F. Calvo, *Cercare l'uomo* (Genoa, 1989).

text, that literature can still mean something. If shreds of words are worth, as Levi states in *Se questo è un uomo*, a portion of soup—and in Auschwitz, as he underscores in *I sommersi e i salvati*, that means 'blood', life's blood—then there is still a hope for literature within history. Dante had indeed 'remembered the future'.[16] And Levi, when he finally joins the soup queue, embodies and fulfils the past. In the sordid-looking crowd, among shouts of 'Kraut und Rüben', announcing a soup of cabbage and turnips, a line returns to close the chapter and offer us a possible conclusion:

Infin che 'l mar fu sopra noi richiuso.

[16] H. Fisch, *A Remembered Future: A Study in Literary Mythology* (Bloomington, Ind., 1984).

8. *Ulysses, the Sirens, and the Pheasant: Word, Enigma, and Silence*

As if another sail went on
Straight forwardly through another night
And clumped stars dangled all the way.

In the last two chapters I looked at two possible conclusions to my narrative: the one ontologically comic, the other able, within history, to restore hope to modern literature after the darkness and shadow in Conrad, and the inferno in Levi. In this chapter I shall posit three different endings, not necessarily alternatives to these original two, for Ulysses and his story.

It is not, of course, a question of proposing a solution or of establishing a 'truth' which is universally valid, supposing that were possible. Everyone has to feel the urge to find their own truth, and then settle with it 'come fera in lustra', like an animal in its den, to use Dante's words in *Paradiso* IV; desire must then propel us out again, because 'doubt, like a shoot, springs from the root of the truth'. Dante considers this desire to be 'nature | that urges us to the summit from height to height'. Through its rational intellect—and, I would add, its poetic intuition—humanity has access to some sort of truth. 'E giugner puollo' ('and it can gain it'), he insists, adding a line that reveals all the passionate cerebrality of a 'mind in love':[1] 'se non, ciascun disio sarebbe *frustra*', 'else all desire were vain'.

As moderns (and we have already had occasion to note this in the present work), we find ourselves in the existential and historical condition of the inhabitants of Dante's Limbo: 'sanza speme vivemo in disio', living with desire but without hope. I hope I have demonstrated that a gleam, at least—that which Levi saw in Auschwitz—is left us; and above all, that desire, *desio*, is the bridge between Limbo and Paradise which we are endlessly crossing.

The Word, Enigma, and Silence prophesied by Ulysses in this

---

[1] K. Foster, 'The Mind in Love: Dante's Philosophy', in J. Freccero (ed.), *Dante* (Englewood Cliffs, NJ, 1965), 43–60.

chapter are, of course, equally shadows. I ask the reader, as Statius asks Virgil when they meet in *Purgatorio* XXI, to 'understand the measure of the love that burns in [us] for [them]' and to 'forget our vanity' while for the last time I 'treat shades as solid things'.

Let me begin with a number of aphorisms to define the terms of discussion. They are all from Wallace Stevens's *Adagia*.[2] On the one hand, the poet is 'the priest of the invisible' and poetry is a 'search for the inexplicable'. On the other, 'poetry is often a revelation of the elements of appearance'. Its aim is to round life off, make it whole, redeem, and act as intermediary between people and themselves (and not between humanity and some other world), giving some idea of the vitality and vibrancy of life.

Poetry erects a bridge between these two banks of the invisible and the apparent, making them meet on an almost imperceptible threshold. To quote another of the *Adagia*, poetry is 'a pheasant disappearing into the brush'—a creature which is glimpsed and immediately lost to view, a receding towards density and shadow, a disappearing in the split second between being and non-being: a real, living thing of flesh and blood, ready to take flight but always escaping and blurring, as if it were merely a water-colour, into the (paint) 'brush', the very means of expression itself, a blot of *silence* which immediately precedes and succeeds the *word*.

In this chapter I want to look at this threshold between the visible and the ungraspable, examining, as far as is possible, the ontological state of poetry (or at least some of the major instances from the present century) and the particular form of knowledge it offers us. I shall attempt to fix the pheasant as it disappears.

Stevens insists that poetry creates a world ('mundo') where all that belongs to reality and all that belongs to the imagination are one and the same thing. The perception of this unity on the threshold constitutes the 'state of clairvoyant observation accessible, or possibly accessible to the poet or, say, the acutest poet'. Imagination is the 'necessary angel' which brings humanity the values and principles of order through the 'supreme fiction' of poetry.[3] In a world where belief in God is no longer possible, the

[2] All quotations from *Adagia, Notebooks, Sur Plusieurs Beaux Sujets* are from *Opus Posthumous*, ed. M. J. Bates, rev. edn. (London, 1989).
[3] W. Stevens, *The Necessary Angel* (London, 1960); 'Notes toward a Supreme Fiction', in *The Collected Poems* (New York, 1982), 380–408.

ultimate *credo* has to be in a fiction 'which you know to be a fiction'. The most exquisite truth consists in knowing it to be a fiction but still believing in it of our own free will.

Poetry creates on the one hand 'fictitious existence on an exquisite plane'; on the other, the 'greatest piece of fiction' ever produced by humanity is Greek mythology, which means that there exists an essential affinity between the two. Ulysses and the pheasant belong to the same universe. And to the Ulysses Stevens celebrates in two of his major poems, written towards the end of his life, I shall be returning shortly.

For the moment we should set sail towards the Sirens. It is superfluous to state how largely they figure on Ulysses' horizon, the sinister, spell-binding gleam of poetry, knowledge, and death: we have noted it in Homer, Dante, Columbus, Tasso, and Conrad. In our own century's literature they are an essential *locus*: figurally, the beginning and end of poetic discourse, Word and Silence.

T. S. Eliot makes Ulysses' voyage begin[4] from the confrontation with the Sirens, predicting the end of the odyssey but at the same time starting on what is to become a Divine Comedy of the Word. In *Prufrock and Other Observations* (1917), the first published collection of his poems, it is precisely the song of the Sirens which ends 'The Love Song of J. Alfred Prufrock', the work which inaugurated modernism in poetry in English.

Prufrock is a representative inhabitant of our Limbo. While content to wander through 'half-deserted streets', 'one-night cheap hotels', and 'sawdust-restaurants', he finds himself immured in the room where 'women come and go | Talking of Michelangelo'. Preparing for tea, he puts off all decisions, wriggles out of asking himself uncomfortable questions, postpones all action and defers all reality, avoids both murdering and creating—all 'the works and days of hands | that lift and drop . . . on [his] plate' a fundamental question. He surfaces from his apathy and social ennui, however, to question continually whether he, sublimely, 'dare disturb the universe', 'force the moment to its crisis', and 'presume', and more absurdly 'part his hair behind', and 'dare to eat a peach'.

Having, on the other hand, 'known them all already', the eyes closed to all but the 'formulated phrase' and the voices 'from a

---

[4] D. Manganiello, *T. S. Eliot and Dante* (London, 1989), 17–39.

farther room', Prufrock is near-convinced that it would not have been worth it 'to have squeezed the universe into a ball | To roll it towards some overwhelming question'. He is in a suspended state, one of Dante's slothful: neither a prophet nor a poet, nor even a Hamlet, he opts for the role of 'attendant lord', 'full of high sentence', like Chaucer's Clerk of Oxford, 'but a bit obtuse'; at times, indeed, almost ridiculous. Unable to say just what he means (far less sing a love-song), he only mutters his monologue because, like Ulysses' neighbour in Dante, Guido da Montefeltro, he believes no one has returned alive 'da questo fondo', from this depth.

Yet this radically insecure being who lives without hope is capable of his own soul-searing desire. Walking along the beach, at the end of his long confession, he hears the mermaids singing and, although knowing that their song is not for his ears, the force of nostalgic passion is overwhelming:

> I have seen them riding seaward on the waves
> Combing the white hair of the waves blown back
> When the wind blows the water white and black.
>
> We have lingered in the chambers of the sea
> By sea-girls wreathed with seaweed red and brown
> Till human voices wake us, and we drown.

Prufrock is well aware that he is no Homeric Odysseus—in his presence, the mermaids sing 'each to each'—but he is unable to shake off the vision of them riding the waves towards the 'alto mare aperto'. Even he, who like the Muses and the Sirens has known and experienced everything, feels regret for the poetic illusion of the past, the wild flight over the waves and the accompanying voice of the wind. The seduction of the myth is unable, however, to dispel awareness of historical and existential reality: for centuries lulled to sleep in underwater palaces by the Sirens' fairy-tales, humanity is now awoken by 'human voices', and drowns.[5]

The logic of the *mythos*, then, is inverted. These Sirens sing only to each other: poetry is a dream closed around itself and the past, towards which we can feel only nostalgia. The voices we hear are those of our fellow-humans, and they make us drown, like Dante's Ulysses.

---

[5] See E. R. Curtius, 'T. S. Eliot', in his *Essays on European Literature*, trans. M. Kowal (Princeton, NJ, 1973), 355–99.

This hinted death by water in 'Prufrock' reappears to form the fourth section of *The Waste Land*. Here 'Phlebas the Phoenician, a fortnight dead' represents the whole of humanity; casting off all memories of life, his bones 'picked in whispers' by underwater currents, he moves backwards through age and youth before 'entering the whirlpool'.

In the first redaction of *The Waste Land*,[6] before Pound's savage pruning, these ten lines of Phlebas's funeral epitaph were preceded by a long account based on those of Dante's and Tennyson's Ulysses.[7] Here the sailor, 'attentive to the chart or to the sheets', is an Odysseus who has 'much seen and much endured', and, although drunk like Baudelaire's traveller, also retains, even ashore, 'something inhuman, clean and dignified'. He sets sail with 'a light, fair breeze' from the East Coast of the United States past the Dry Salvages. After a few days the wind drops and everything begins to go wrong. The journey comes more and more to resemble that of the Ancient Mariner. The crew begins to complain, and the 'sea with many voices', like Tennyson's, moans around the ship 'under a rainy moon', while the 'suspended winter heaved and tugged, | Stirring foul weather under the Hyades'.

Like Dante's Ulysses, Eliot's sailor is forced to steer by the light of the stars. Suddenly a strange wind drives the ship beyond 'the farthest northern islands', 'beneath invisible stars'. In the Conradian 'horror of the illimitable scream | of a whole world about us', no one dares to speak. One night the protagonist thinks he sees 'in the fore-cross trees | Three women . . . with white hair | Streaming behind, who sang above the wind | A song that charmed my senses'. 'Frightened beyond fear, horrified past horror, calm', the sailor rationalizes that the nightmare might end on waking. But at dawn a 'different darkness' (cf. Conrad again) flows above the clouds, while 'A line, a white line, a long white line' appears on the horizon like a wall or Poe-like barrier. *Hic*, to reader's and protagonist's surprise, *sunt ursi* ('My God man there's bears on it'). Then, 'not a chance'. After shreds of memory, the ship sinks:

[6] T. S. Eliot, *The Waste Land: A Facsimile and Transcript of the original Drafts Including the Annotations of Ezra Pound*, ed. V. Eliot (New York, 1971), 54–69.

[7] In his 1929 'Dante', Eliot discusses the differences between Dante's and Tennyson's versions of Ulysses, underlying Tennyson's self-consciousness, flatness, and 'forcing', and emphasizing, by contrast, Dante's 'readability' and 'depth'. See *Dante* (London, 1965), 23–5.

And if Another knows, I know I know not,
Who only know that there is no more noise now.
(ll. 82–3)

Phlebas the Phoenician, 'handsome and tall as you', drowns in the whirlpool with only the awareness of ignorance and silence, mute with the knowledge of Dante's *Altrui*.

On this journey (which again, at a crucial moment in modern culture, contains all the literary *typoi* of Ulysses encountered so far in our critical *excursus*), there is room only for a poetry of death beyond the illimitable scream of the whole world: darkness, the shadow-line, the extreme north, disaster, perdition, alterity, and nothingness. The word is utterable only to recount the other world, or as an epitaph oblivious to even the most 'breve carta'. The Sirens are again like Conrad's: seducing the senses, they terrify like the life-in-death nightmare, pre-announcing empty awareness, non-knowledge, and a degree zero of the poetic voice.[8]

Section One of *The Waste Land* ('The Burial of the Dead') shows Phlebas's death by water as predicted by the 'wicked pack of cards' of the modern prophetess, Madame Sosostris: humanity's inescapable, tragic destiny. The shipwreck still, however, holds out the slenderest of hopes, an 'ambiguous salvation':[9] that Ulysses, undergoing a metamorphosis 'into something rich and strange', can be reborn like the shipwrecked survivors of Prospero's tempest (Madame Sosostris, a twentieth-century Sibyl of Cumae, uses Ariel's song to describe the drowned Phoenician sailor: 'those are pearls that were his eyes').

Within the context of *The Waste Land*, this chance of salvation is basically left to the reader, to our ability to establish intertextual links and to accept to some extent, each from his own cultural and religious standpoint, the message of regeneration offered in the rites described by modern anthropology which Eliot uses as a sub-frame for the poem. But when, in 'Marina', Eliot's (and of course Shakespeare's) Pericles has his daughter restored to him by the sea, and finds a life to live 'in a world of time beyond' himself, and with

[8] See D. Donoghue, 'The Word Within a Word', in *The Sovereign Ghost* (London, 1978), 183–206.
[9] S. Sabbadini, *Una salvezza ambigua: Studio sulla prima poesia di T. S. Eliot* (Bari, 1971); cf. also F. Moretti, 'Dalla terra desolata al paradiso artificiale', in *Segni e stili del moderno* (Turin, 1987), 195–234.

this 'the hope' and 'the new ships', it is the poet in person who changes the basic significance of the odyssean journey.

In the first version of *The Waste Land* Phlebas set out from the Atlantic coast of New England, immediately passing a group of rocks called the 'Dry Salvages'. Here, in the *Four Quartets*, one of which is called 'The Dry Salvages', he is transformed into Ulysses for the last time, following the pheasant only to put it definitively behind him.

This is a new, Dantean, and to an extent Tennysonian Ulysses who becomes increasingly like Dante the pilgrim, the protagonist of the *Commedia* travelling across the great sea of being from time to eternity. This navigator sets out 'in the middle way', 'nel mezzo del cammin', and right from 'East Coker', the second *Quartet*, is aware that old age—the last lap, the 'small wake' of the senses—must not be a 'deliberate hebetude', and 'wisdom only the knowledge of dead secrets'; he also knows that the 'knowledge derived from experience', so ardently desired by Dante's Ulysses, possesses only a 'limited value'.

The task of 'old men'—and old sailors—is to be 'explorers' for whom the 'here' and 'there' are of no importance: Ulysseses who 'fare forwards' towards a more complete communion with being, and towards the end which is beginning:

> Old men ought to be explorers
> Here and there does not matter
> We must be still and still moving
> Into another intensity
> For a further union, a deeper communion
> Through the dark cold and empty desolation,
> The wave cry, the wind cry, the vast waters
> Of the petrel and the porpoise. In my end is my beginning.

Poetry points the way beyond itself ('The poetry does not matter', 'East Coker' II proclaims), towards the shores of eternity, in the relived, re-cognized, and transcended here and now.

In the third *Quartet*, 'The Dry Salvages', the sea voyage, through the ocean's flotsam, fog, and 'many voices', is a navigating in time 'older than the time of chronometers':

> Between midnight and dawn, when the past is all deception,
> The future futureless, before the morning's watch
> When time stops and time is never ending;

And the ground swell, that is and was from the beginning,
Clangs
The bell.

When night falls, 'in the rigging and the aerial, | Is a voice
descanting'; not the voice of the Sirens, the poetry of the world and
knowledge which conceals death, but a living 'descanting' of
metaphysical and, for Eliot, transcendental truth. This is the voice
of a Dantean Ulysses purified by Heraclitean and Indian wisdom.
With the 'orazion picciola' pronounced 'not in any language', and
'not to the ear, | The murmuring shell of time', but to the soul,
Ulysses now exorts *us* to 'considerate la vostra semenza' ('consider'
is Eliot's word too): i.e. the being which 'lies beneath' as a 'substance' subsumes existence within the time of death ('And the time
of death is every moment')—on the continual threshold, 'The point
of intersection of the timeless | With time':

> O voyagers, O seamen
> You who come to port, and you whose bodies
> Will suffer the trial and judgement of the sea,
> Or whatever event, this is your real destination.
>
> .   .   .   .
>
> Not *fare well*,
> But *fare forward*, voyagers.

The true destination is beyond the port or shipwreck, beyond the
events of existence, yet within life and history, in a suspension of
time which in 'Little Gidding', the fourth *Quartet*, is 'midwinter
spring', 'sempiternal though sodden towards sundown', within and
beyond the death of the four elements. In this last *Quartet* the
tongue of fire from which Dante's Ulysses speaks and in which he
burns becomes a purgatorial, pentecostal flame which purifies,[10]
and a form of speech not available to the living: 'the communication
| Of the dead is tongued with fire beyond the language of the
living'.

Beyond the language of the living. The poetry of essence, and for
Eliot of love and a Christian God, dies to the word—to the
language which, for all its purifying at the school of Mallarmé,
remains a mere 'dialect of the tribe'—to be born again as the Word:

---

[10] 'Foco che li affina' from *Purgatorio* xxvi. 148 (applied to Arnaut Daniel), returns at
the end of *The Waste Land*, l. 427, and as 'refining fire' in *Little Gidding*, II, five lines
before the end of the section.

human, but son of the divinity made flesh, the *Logos* of the ineffable.[11] Now every sentence is right, every word in its rightful place, the result of 'an easy commerce of the old and the new' without gaps, ambiguity, excesses, or awkwardness. 'The common word exact without vulgarity, | The formal word precise but not pedantic', are in 'complete consort', perfect harmony, and 'Every phrase and every sentence is an end and a beginning, | Every poem an epitaph'.

The seal poetry places on earthly existence is that of a Word which, in death, goes beyond death. Ulysses will continue to explore:

> We shall not cease from exploration,
> And the end of all our exploring
> Will be to arrive where we started
> And know the place for the first time.

Through the known and the unknown gate, the Word takes us where no Columbus can ever travel, to 'the last of earth left to discover' which 'is that which was the beginning'. In 'the stillness between two waves of the sea', Ulysses, the supreme poet and new Dante, bends, a tongue of flame, into the 'crowned knot of fire' where 'the fire and the rose are one'.

This is no pheasant disappearing into the brush. Eliot's is no fiction, but an extremely particular approach which we earthlings can only observe, like a miracle which requires an almost inhuman religious or poetic faith. If, for us, the journey ends with Montale on *this* shore, eroded by patient, deliberate waves, and if with Beckett we believe that 'Yes, there is hope, but not for the majority of us', then we ourselves must recognize that 'taluno sovverta ogni disegno, | passi il varco, qual volle si ritrovi'; that some-one subverts all design, crossing through the passage, and finding himself such as he wanted to be, a new Glaucus or new Dante, sailing from time to eternity. This of course requires a desire which is both extreme longing and iron determination: 'Perhaps infinity is gained only by an act of will'—in Montale's words, *Forse solo chi vuole s'infinita.*[12]

---

[11] See H. Gardner, *The Art of T. S. Eliot* (London, 1949), chs. II and VII; H. Kenner, *The Invisible Poet: T. S. Eliot* (London, 1960), chs. V and VI; H. Gardner, *The Composition of Four Quartets* (London, 1978).

[12] E. Montale, 'Casa sul mare', in *Ossi di seppia: L'Opera in versi*, ed. R. Bettarini and G. Contini (Turin, 1980), 91–2.

To those left asking themselves if everything disappears in these mists of memory, the lesson given by Wallace Stevens may be useful. After touching on the Ulysses theme in 'Prologues to What is Possible', in 'The World as Meditation' (1952),[13] he lands us directly mid-fiction, mid-myth, and in a situation which is para-Homeric but not Dantean. We find ourselves in Ithaca, in the royal palace, and indeed in the very room in which Penelope had waited for her husband through twenty long years: a time stasis, then, of constantly repeated minutes projected into expectation without end—as if the two tremendous decades could not and must not come to an end. Ulysses is introduced to us, albeit indirectly, as the '*interminable* adventurer'. In this present without a *telos*, as a parenthesis of the Homeric myth which totally invades it, Stevens's tale unfolds.

One central interrogative forms the base-note for the whole poem: 'Is it Ulysses that approaches from the east?' The question pulls every inch of ontological and mythical ground from under the reader's feet: we know Ulysses could be disguised, and go unrecognized, but we had always believed it was still Ulysses. In a flash we are well beyond Homer's one, no one, and one hundred thousand. In answer to the initial question we are offered an apparently well-founded, solid image of reality: winter is over and the trees are 'mended'. The world is here, now, immanent, tangible, ordered, and ready for the approach which we expect to turn into arrival. No sooner have we recovered from the initial uncertainty, and the idea of trees being 'mended' like a mechanical object gone wrong, than the opening question becomes an equally mysterious answer. Someone moves on the horizon—on the final threshold between the visible and the invisible, the indefinite line between the conscious and the unconscious; but, on contact with the material and colour surrounding Penelope, this 'someone' appears as a form of fire: a sheer transparency of air, light, and warmth. What is now called a 'presence', and defined 'savage', is sufficient to stir Penelope's world: expectation and desire are incandescent, and the flame now singes the material fibres, and the fibres of her being:

[13] Texts in *The Collected Poems*; and see L. L. Martz, *Wallace Stevens: The World as Meditation*, in M. Borroff (ed.), *Wallace Stevens*, (Englewood Cliffs, NJ, 1963), 133–50; L. Beckett, *Wallace Stevens* (Cambridge, 1974), 198–203.

Is it Ulysses that approaches from the east,
The interminable adventurer? The trees are mended.
That winter is washed away. Someone is moving

On the horizon and lifting himself up above it.
A form of fire approaches the cretonnes of Penelope,
Whose mere savage presence awakens the world in which she dwells.

Horizon and room, rising and approaching, presence and impalp-
ability. A disappearing pheasant, poetry evokes the invisible in the
visible: the spring sun which burns and enamours, and the Dantean
'alba' which conquers the small hours of the morning. If this is not
Ulysses, it is the dawn of the world, its *fiat lux*.

The creator of this world, and its inhabitant, is Penelope. It is
she who has 'composed a self' with which to welcome Ulysses, and
'imagined' them together once more, 'two in a deep-founded
sheltering, friend and dear friend'. To this world of human
imagination, which alone comforts, protects, and cherishes, there
corresponds a world as 'inhuman' meditation, more ample than
Penelope's: a world in which the trees have been mended after
winter's breakage.

Both universes are created out of meditation, however: both are
fictions. There are no winds to guard Penelope like dogs. There
are no grounds for believing in a Nature which oversees human
affairs in the guise of the elements or living spirits. Nature mends
the trees as an 'essential exercise' of meditation parallel to
Penelope's. In her world, the woman awaits fulfilment: the
presence of Ulysses, without gifts and useless 'fetchings'. His arms
will be 'her necklace and her belt', the 'final fortune' of a desire
which is no longer just hers, but belongs to both. The two
existences form in the imagination, firm companions, rooted in the
'deep-founded sheltering' of the dearest friendship.

This is the consolation Stevens offers: poetry which redeems and
completes life, health which heals the mind and crowns human
happiness. No greater homage has ever been paid to the plot which
gleams throughout the *Odyssey* and which, for all the travelling,
transforms it, as Stevens's epigraph from Georges Enesco suggests,
into a permanent and unresting dream. 'Poetry', Stevens's *Adagia*
proclaim, 'is a purging of the world's poverty and change and evil
and death. It is a present perfecting, a satisfaction in the
irremediable poverty of life.'

Although poetry knows—as Penelope knows, and as we ourselves know—that the ontological question cannot be shirked, and that uncertainty is at the root of our knowledge; that this could be Ulysses, but that it could also be simply the sun's warmth, the meeting sustains and encourages the whole human planet. Ulysses and Penelope, the sun and the day, 'beat' together. This, then, both is and is not Ulysses:

> But was it Ulysses? Or was it only the warmth of the sun
> On her pillow? The thought kept beating in her like her heart.
> The two kept beating together. It was only day.
>
> It was Ulysses and it was not. Yet they had met,
> Friend and dear friend and a planet's encouragement.
> The barbarous strength within her would never fail.

Penelope's barbarous strength creates the fiction which constitutes all that is real. Talking to herself while she brushes her hair, she becomes the Maker: *poietes*. She patiently repeats the name of her patient husband, unforgetting, keeping alight the 'form of fire' which continues to approach.

This, then, is a 'poetry of the human', a revelation of nature and a declaration of the relationship between humanity and its world. It is also, however, vibrant with that same liminal quality observed in Eliot's *Quartets*: the suspension and reminder, 'the thing seen and the thing unseen'; a fable which fulfils and satisfies,[14] but only through Eliot's 'hints and guesses', and which comes to us like the form of fire: a poetry of approach but not of arrival, of *enigma*, not of reply. It looks out at the world, Stevens notes in the *Adagia*, 'somewhat as a man looks at a woman', and at the same time 'resists the intelligence almost successfully'. Ulysses is a pheasant disappearing into the *brush*, which is why we are impelled to hunt for him.

In the *Notebooks* Stevens writes that two archetypes of poetry exist, Homer illustrating the first, narrative kind, Plato the second, reflexive one. In 'The World as Meditation' Stevens practises the former, like Demodocus and Phemius, the poets of *mythos* in the *Odyssey*. In one of his last poems, 'The Sail of Ulysses', from 1954, he seems to be working within the latter, enacting the *logos*. A

---

[14] F. Kermode, *Wallace Stevens* (London, 1989), 114.

Tennyson-like monologue,[15] it is focused not on Penelope but on Ulysses himself: not, here, during his Homeric return, but as a Dantean 'symbol of the seeker' who nightly stalks the vast ocean in the guise of his sail.

'When we are born, we cry that we are come | To this great stage of fools', Lear mutters (or howls) when he finds his old friend Gloucester ruined and blinded. 'We come | To knowledge when we come to life', Stevens's Ulysses meditates in the fifth section of the 'Sail'. 'As I know, I am and have | The right to be'; this is the poem's gist, beyond Descartes' 'Cogito' and towards the reverse of the biblical Adam's position. Humanity has the right to be because it knows, and knows good and evil. Knowledge is not death but the only life, 'the only sun of the only day, | The only access to true ease | The deep comfort of the world and fate'.

Naturally, the burden of knowledge is not light; it can only come out of human solitude, and only in solitude find the strength of being which constitutes knowing, our 'luminous companion', the 'triumphant vigor', 'that which keeps us the little that we are'. In this 'little', inside poverty and shadow, poetry is born. For the 'true creator', 'he who waves purpling wands' and 'thinks gold thoughts', happy in the meaning which, wrenched from chaos, is visible in the design, 'the lamp of knowledge' burns, 'enlarging like a nocturnal ray | The space in which it stands, the shine | Of darkness'.

A similar halo of the here and now contains the *Dasein*,[16] the order in which humanity has the right to be as it is, absolute within itself, and freed of the mystic. There, outside logic, humanity can receive a life beyond present knowing, lighter than 'the present splendor': a gift or 'divination' which holds no maps of paradise but simply comes as a series of 'misgivings dazzlingly resolved in dazzling discovery':

> The great Omnium descends on us
> As a free race. We know it, one
> By one, in the right of all. Each man
> Is an approach to the vigilance
> In which the litter of truths becomes

---

[15] H. Bloom, *A Map of Misreading* (Oxford, 1975), 159. The text of the poem is printed in *Opus Posthumous*.

[16] See F. Kermode, 'Wallace Stevens: Dwelling Poetically in Connecticut', in *An Appetite for Poetry* (Cambridge, Mass., 1989), 79–96. As stated in my Preface, I owe a great deal to Kermode's book.

> A whole, the day on which the last star
> Has been counted, the genealogy
> Of gods and men destroyed, the right
> To know established as the right to be.
> We shall have gone behind the symbols
> To that which they symbolized, away
> From the rumors of the speech-full domes,
> To the chatter that is then the true legend,
> Like glitter ascended into fire.

'Glitter ascended into fire': this could be the Eliot of the *Quartets*. The register and image are similar, the ontological desire the same, and the expression is equally purified in the Dantean tension. Here, however, the 'master of knowledge', the master of the world and himself, is man, his mind creating the cosmos 'in a verse, | A passage of music, a paragraph | By a right philosopher': 'the living man in the present place'. His only legacy and destiny is truth—not 'Plantagenet abstractions' but the particular thought, 'the difficult inch' supporting the vast arches of space, the 'little confine soon unconfined | In stellar largenesses': the particular 'bent' to the universal in the 'relative sublime'. The 'full flower of the actual', one of the *Adagia* proclaims, 'not the California fruit of the ideal': in short, the Aristotelian *tode ti* filtered through American transcendentalism, in the destitution of Hölderlin and Heidegger[17] and, above all, glimpsed from that 'small wake' of old age, the final threshold.

Inevitably, in this poor-man's version, the Sibyl of truth is no longer a woman gleaming like the dew or like pearls but a 'blind thing fumbling for its form', 'lame, | worn, and leaning to nothingness'; a woman looking down into the street, and also 'a child asleep in its own life', the cowed but tranquil warning of the inhuman which will soon be arriving:

> The englistered woman is now seen
> In an isolation, separate
> From the human in humanity,
> A part of the inhuman more, and yet
> An inhuman of our features, known
> And unknown, inhuman for a little while,
> Inhuman for a little, lesser time.

[17] See H. Bloom, *Wallace Stevens: The Poems of our Climate*, (Ithaca, NY and London, 1977).

In the breathing-spaces of the soliloquy, while the journey nears its final passage, the great sail of Ulysses comes 'alive with an enigma's flittering', in a double shadow. Another sail is projected over the first, which thus becomes an abstraction into which the particular of another 'relative sublime' merges:

> As if another sail went on
> Straight forwardly through another night
> And clumped stars dangled all the way.

We can go no further. A poem, Stevens says, 'reveals itself only to the ignorant man', and neither author nor reader of this book would claim the epithet. There is only one thing left to consider. In one of Stevens's last poems, 'Of Mere Being', he speaks of 'A palm at the end of the mind | At the edge of space', which represents being pure and simple.[18] On it a bird with 'fire-fangled' feathers is singing 'a foreign song', without 'human meaning' or 'human feeling'. This both is and is not the phoenix, is and is not a pheasant. While the wind 'moves slowly' through the branches, its feathers dangle down.

The Enigma is one of the conclusions to my narrative. In 'The Immortal', the first story in *The Aleph* (1952), Borges furthers the mystery and doubles our already considerable perplexity. In June 1929, in London, the polyglot antiquarian Joseph Cartaphilus, a 'wasted and earthen man'[19] from Smyrna, sells the Princess of Lucinge a six-volume *Iliad* in Pope's translation. Shortly afterwards Cartaphilus dies at sea on his return journey to Smyrna and is buried on the Island of Ios, where Homer's grave is supposed to be. The last volume of the *Iliad* is found to contain a manuscript in English, and the author proceeds to give a 'literal' translation.

The protagonist-narrator, Marcus Flaminius Rufus, a Roman, is stationed in Egypt with the imperial troops of Diocletian. One day, at dawn, from the mountains beyond the Ganges an exhausted horseman appears, covered in blood, stating that he is seeking in the west, 'where the world ends', the river of immortality on the

---

[18] See J. Hillis Miller, 'Wallace Stevens' Poetry of Being', in R. Harvey Pearce and J. Hillis Miller (eds.), *The Act of the Mind* (Baltimore, 1965), 143–62; H. Bloom, *Poetry and Repression*, 267–93; J. Hillis Miller, *The Linguistic Moment* (Princeton, NJ, 1985), 3–58 and 390–422.

[19] All quotations are from Jorge Luis Borges, *Labyrinths*, ed. D. A. Yates and J. E. Irby (Harmondsworth, 1970).

banks of which stands the City of the Immortals. The man then dies. Rufus embarks on an expedition to the west; he crosses the desert, passes Atlas, loses his men, and finds himself, alone and desperate for water, before a stream which flows from the splendid City of the Immortals. He drinks. Inexplicably, he pronounces a number of words in Greek, from the catalogue of the ships in the *Iliad*.

Surrounded by troglodytes, he enters the city, a senseless labyrinth of buildings. One of the primitive inhabitants, who reminds him of Odysseus' dog, Argos, takes to following him around. One day, in pouring rain, Rufus calls the man 'Argos'; the man amazingly stammers out 'Argos, Ulysses' dog', and then quotes the line in the *Odyssey* describing the animal. The Roman asks him how much he knows of the Greek poem. 'Very little,' he replies in hesitant Greek, 'less than the poorest rhapsodist. It must be a thousand and one hundred years since I invented it.'

The troglodyte is Homer, the stream that of immortality, and the perfect City of the Immortals was destroyed at their hands and replaced by the crazed labyrinth Rufus has already marvelled at. The immortality mortals so long for is simply this; somewhat like Swift's Struldbruggs, the troglodytes are forgetful, incapable of understanding and speaking, and totally unaware of the physical world, and live in caves—a return to the beginning, in a pseudo Earthly Paradise of cave-dwellers. Homer tells Rufus how, in old age, he had undertaken his final journey, 'moved, as was Ulysses, by the purpose of reaching the men who do not know what the sea is nor eat meat seasoned with salt, nor suspect what an oar is'. Once he reached the City, he had advised the inhabitants to destroy and rebuild it.

The Immortals have reached a perfection of tolerance and wisdom. They know that 'in an infinite period of time all things happen to all men'. Homer had composed the *Odyssey* because 'If we postulate an infinite period of time, with infinite circumstances and changes, the impossible thing is not to compose the *Odyssey*, at least once. No one is anyone, one single immortal man is all men.' Homer and Rufus decide to search for the river which removes Immortality. They depart for the east, going separate ways in Tangiers.

The protagonist travels through time; in 1066 he fights at Stamford Bridge in the battle between the English and the Vikings which takes place shortly before the Battle of Hastings; in the thirteenth century he transcribes the seven journeys of Sinbad; in 1729 he discusses the origins of the *Iliad* with a professor of rhetoric by the name of Giambattista; in 1929 he is on the coast of Eritrea. Recalling the far-off period on the shores of the Red Sea as tribune of Rome, he happens to drink from a river. A thorn-tree rips the back of his hand, and the blood begins to ooze out. He is once more happily mortal.

After a year he rereads the manuscript and realizes that the story is unreal in that it mixes the events of two discrete people, Rufus and Homer. The end approaches; all images have disappeared from memory, and only words remain: 'I have been Homer, shortly I shall be No One, like Ulysses; shortly I shall be all men; I shall be dead.'

The images of the story are those now familiar to us: a journey towards the westward limits of the earth, the new world of the City, and the earthly paradise. They are altered, however, by the vortex of enigma Borges throws his reader into, and stretched, first in space, to the point of snapping, the geographical co-ordinates overlapping and interlocking: Cartaphilus towards the east, and death; towards immortality, but finding death, the rider from the east; towards immortality in the west, Homer and Rufus, who finally return east to die. Space stretched to its extremes then dovetails into time: London and Smyrna, 1929; Egypt, third century AD; England, 1066; Bulaq, thirteenth century; Koloszvár and Leipzig, 1638; Aberdeen, 1714; 1729, the discussion with 'Giambattista' (Vico, the note suggests); 1921, the journey towards Bombay and his stay on the Eritrean coast.

Time is annihilated by its own convolutions. In between, the absurd and unremembering immortality which leads back to the irrational barbarity of humanity's origins and, by prolonging life infinitely, encircles history in eternal returns, coincidences, echoes, omens, and repetitions—circles where the possible becomes the inevitable. Only death makes men precious and pathetic ghosts, forever on the point of vanishing like dreams, shadows whose actions have the value of the irrecoverable and the casual.

Poetry is tradition turned in on its own, inverted canons—a literary infinite:[20] from Pope's *Iliad* comes Homer's *Odyssey*; Rufus

---

[20] M. Blanchot, 'L'Infini litteraire: L'Aleph', in *Le Livre a venir* (2nd edn., Paris, 1959), 116–19. And see L. A. Murillo, *The Cyclical Night* (Cambridge, Mass., 1968); R. Paoli, *Borges: Percorsi di significato* (Messina and Florence, 1977).

writes like Pliny the Elder, De Quincey, Descartes, and George Bernard Shaw; Cartaphilus creates Sinbad and speaks with Vico. Lastly, myth gapes over its own abysses, in a parody of its metamorphoses and its figuralism: Argos, Ulysses' dog, becomes Homer; Homer is Ulysses; Ulysses is Sinbad; the 'I' has been Homer and Ulysses and Sinbad and a thousand others, and will be No one. At the end of the final journey, out of history, poetry, and myth, the themes of my book, words alone remain: 'words displaced and mutilated words, words of others'.

In a sonnet in the collection *El otro, lo mismo* (1964), entitled 'Odyssey, Book XXIII',[21] Borges uses an ironic paradox to get to the ontological and gnoseological basis of the mystery. We find ourselves at the end of Homer's story, and beyond the perennial moment of Stevens's 'World as Meditation'. Revenge has been taken against the suitors, Ulysses has repossessed his kingdom and his queen, in spite of the gods, the winds, and 'the clangour of Ares'. Penelope sleeps on his chest, in a bed which is finally shared. But half-way through the tenth line, the serenity of this long-sought *telos* is suddenly disturbed, not by the thought of the final journey, but by a radical question:

> . . . ¿pero dónde está aquel hombre
> Que en los días y noches del destierro
> Erraba por el mundo como un perro
> Y decía que Nadie era su nombre?

but where is that man | who in the days and nights of his exile | wandered through the world like a dog | saying that No one was his name?

Odysseus is finally cut in two, beyond any momentary duplication in 'The World as Meditation', or the doubling of the shadow in 'The Sail of Ulysses': on the one hand Ulysses the king, now; on the other No one, the wandering dog, in the past.

As in all his works, however, Borges is doing here something more subtle and perverse, shifting the burden of cognition and recognition on to the reader. In the first nine-and-a-half lines he offers a factual story which we know quite well to be a poetic fiction. He tells us how events unfolded, and we are perfectly

---

[21] Texts of this, of 'Los Enigmas', and 'Edipo y el Enigma' in *El otro, lo mismo* (Buenos Aires, 1964).

content to accept this account on the basis of the Homeric *mythos*. Then, against all expectation, he pitches his *pero* against everything he has just stated, and vitiates it with his question. By asking not 'who' but 'where' 'that man' is, Borges is thrusting us into the realm of endless speculation, among the enigmas which constitute the title of another poem in *El otro, lo mismo*. How can we decide *where* that man is who is clearly 'the other, the same', different from the one present and yet identical? How are we to recognize a link between No one and Ulysses?

The only possible way is by establishing an intertextual connection with the episode in the *Odyssey* where Odysseus tells Polyphemus to call him Nobody. There is not the slightest doubt that this is what Borges expects of us: his literary game forces us to interpret one poetic fiction through another, older, canonical one.

If, though, we stuck out for the orthodox process of knowledge, taking one object to be recognized at a time, i.e. reading one text only, the one before our eyes, then we should be unable to establish any precise link between Odysseus and No one. The same page presents two people totally distinct in space, time, and name. The gap between them is enormous: the one, his *nostos* over, has returned home, a king; the other is an exiled wayfarer wandering round the world in the guise of a dog.

And how, in any case, are we to recognize No one? All we learn from the sonnet—and which we know from reading the *Odyssey*—is that this man *said* his name was No one. Are we to believe him, as poor Polyphemus did, at his peril? To believe, beyond Stevens, in the make-belief, the fiction, knowing it to be the fiction of a fiction? What we are being asked to do is to licitly recognize a being from the mere knowledge of his presumed *name*.

When Dante's Virgil ordered Ulysses to say '*dove*, per lui, perduto a morir gissi', where he had gone to die, the interrogative-imperative put enormous strain on the classical and medieval epistemes, also raising, as we saw in Chapter 2, an overwhelming hermeneutic question which the narrative fails to answer. When Borges asks *where* the man who claimed to be called No one now is, he is splitting the text in two and making interpretation possible only through intertextual 'markers': he kills off Odysseus, makes his identity a yawning gap of alterity, undermines the very possibility of the epistemological process, and ends the poetic fiction with a far more radically insoluble Enigma than Stevens's.[22] This Enigma comes, as it were, before that put by the Sphinx to all wayfarers, and to Oedipus himself: not *which* animal walks with four legs when young, two when mature, and three when old, but where it 'is' in time and space. Discovering the 'ingent form of our being' would be certain annihilation, 'Edipo Y El Enigma', another sonnet in the same collection, announces. Ulysses has entered a labyrinth which will hold him forever, and in which he is already unable to pronounce a single word. The end of this adventure is a 'poor and immortal' poetry, a green, eternal Ithaca; but at the same time, as Borges states in 'Arte Poética',[23] the same, other river of the same, other Heraclitus:

> Cuentan que Ulises, harto de prodigios,
> Lloró de amor al divisar su Itaca
> Verde y humilde. El arte es esa Itaca
> De verde eternidad, no de prodigios.
>
> También es como el rio interminable
> Que pasa y queda y es cristal de un mismo
> Heráclito inconstante, que es el mismo
> Y es otro, como el rio interminable.

They tell how Ulysses, tired of marvels, wept for love when he glimpsed his own Ithaca | green and humble. Art is that Ithaca | of green eternity, not of marvels.

It is also like the interminable river | which passes and stays and is the mirror of one same | unconstant Heraclitus who is the same | and another, like the interminable river.

Inside the Enigma, let us now move on to our fifth possible conclusion: Silence. Silence comes from the Sirens of a writer who is crucial to our century, Kafka. In his perpetual, paradoxical *midrash* of the whole Hebrew and Western tradition, Kafka subjects the Sirens to the logic of the absurd on two occasions: in 1917, the year Eliot's *Prufrock and Other Observations* was published, he wrote 'The Silence of the Sirens', and returned to it briefly in a letter in 1921.[24]

In the first passage, consisting of eight paragraphs, Kafka

---

[22] S. Yurkievich, 'Borges, poeta circular', in *Fundadores de la nueva poesía latinoamericana* (Barcelona, 1973), 117–38; R. Xirau, 'Borges: de la duda a lo eterno dudoso', in *Poesía y conocimiento* (Mexico City, 1978).

[23] Text in *El Hacedor* (Buenos Aires, 1960).

[24] Texts in *Franz Kafka, Parables and Paradoxes* (New York, 1961), 88–93.

proceeds by degrees. He announces at the beginning that the story is *proof* of the fact that inadequate and even infantile ploys can suffice to save us from danger: Odysseus, to save himself from the Sirens, merely stopped his ears with wax (first misreading of the original, in which he stops the ears of his companions), and has himself tied to the mast. The comment analyses both actions; any mariner could have done the same, other than those the Sirens had already enchanted at a distance. The whole world knew, *however*, that none of this would have been sufficient: the song of the Sirens penetrated every known thing, and the passion of those who heard them would have broken more than chains and mainmasts. *But*, '*although* he had *probably* heard of it', Odysseus never gave it a thought. He trusted blindly in his wax and chains and, innocently gleeful at his little ploy, sailed on towards the Sirens.

This presentation in the second paragraph may well lead us to expect a 'psychologistic' conclusion: Odysseus is not only astute and resourceful, but closed within himself. He will escape from the Sirens because he believes in the power of wax and chains to save him. Our expectation is soon thwarted, however: 'Nun haben *aber* die Sirenen eine noch schrecklichere Waffe als den Gesang, nämlich ihr Schweigen'—'*but* the Sirens have a weapon which is still more fatal than their song, namely their silence', Kafka writes in the third paragraph. It might never have happened, *but* it is still conceivable that someone has escaped from their singing: from their silence, *however*, never. No earthly power could withstand the sense of triumph felt in defeating the Sirens with one's own resources, nor the overriding exaltation. The silence of the Sirens—this second, astonishing manhandling of the myth which goes far beyond Pascoli's or Eliot's in 'Prufrock', is, then, the internal reflection of a victory for mankind? Or its external consequence?

Neither. In the fourth paragraph Ulysses approaches them and they refuse to sing, *either* because they think only silence can defeat an enemy of this kind, *or* because the expression of bliss on Ulysses' face, all intent on his wax and his chains, simply makes them forget. The presence of the two alternative hypotheses immediately subverts the rationality of the explanation the same hypotheses were intended to furnish, and the gap created by the dilemma can only be filled with further speculations and a *mise-en-abîme* of exegesis. The Enigma breeds enigmas.

Odysseus *however*, Kafka continues in the fifth paragraph, 'if one may so express it', did not hear their silence. He believed they were singing, unheard by him alone. Once distorted, the perversion of the traditional poetic fiction is total. Neither their singing nor their silence is now important: what counts is the unfounded presumption of the 'I'. Odysseus sees their throats rising and falling, their deep breathing, and their eyes full of tears, *but* thinks all this is part of the songs which, unheard, die around him. Immediately afterwards, *however*, everything disappears from his sight as he gazes into the distance; the Sirens *literally* 'vanished before his resolution', and at the very moment he was closest to them, 'he knew of them no longer'. Kafka's Odyssey is at the opposite pole from that of Goethe's Faust: in the supreme instant of encounter, when he should be saying to the moment 'stop, you are so beautiful', Odysseus is barely aware of the seduction, ignores the beauty offered him, fails to understand even his own gaze, forgets everything, and, instead of knowledge, acquires total ignorance.

This, however, is not just the story of Odysseus; its most remarkable characteristic, besides the narrator's absolute and schizophrenic omnipotence, and the feelings of the hero, is that, for the first time in Western literature, we hear the Sirens' own point of view. *But*, 'lovelier than ever', in the sixth paragraph the Sirens stretch out their necks and turn, their 'ghastly' hair flowing in the wind, and 'forgetting everything cling with their claws to the rocks'. Having become monstrous once more after the hero's passage, they no longer desire to seduce: 'all that they wanted was to hold as long as they could the radiance that fell from Ulysses' great eyes'. Those with binding powers are now themselves bound. It is now the man who bewitches, a specular Siren; and in this inversion of identity— the radiance belonging now to the human being—lies the final destruction. '*If* the Sirens had possessed consciousness they would have been annihilated at that moment', the seventh paragraph states. *But*—and this is the paradox which seemingly doubles back into normality—the Sirens stay as they are: quite simply, Odysseus got away.

A 'codicil' to all this has been handed down to us, Kafka concludes, and he gives it in his final paragraph. Odysseus was so guileful that not even the goddess of fate could 'pierce his armour'. *Perhaps* he had really noticed that the Sirens were silent, and opposed his pretence to them and the gods as a sort of shield.

Lastly, Kafka returns to the Sirens in the second passage, comparing them with the seductive voices of the night. They now sing, not to bewitch but to bewail their ugliness and sterility:

> The Sirens, too, sang that way. It would be doing them an injustice to think that they wanted to seduce; they knew they had claws and sterile wombs, and they lamented this aloud. They could not help it if their laments sounded so beautiful.

Poetry is lament, and then silence. Memory gives way to oblivion. Subject and object of seduction and desire are inverted. The light of humanity prepares the way for the annihilation of song. Cunning is simulation, an extreme defence of the self against the entire universe, a happiness closed in on itself. Knowledge is *méconnaissance*, and topples over into ignorance. And everything is stated totally blandly: abnormality is completely normal. Wonder has disappeared. The myth is taken up and torn apart in a swift succession of fictions, possibilities, hypotheses, and glosses on tradition. The narrative is transformed into exegesis, *midrash*.[25]

Any interpretation of Kafka's story will be irremediably divided. Those emphasizing the Sirens' silence will read it as a consequence of modern humanity's deafness, a pitching of the instruments of human technology (represented by the wax and chains) against the now mute forces of nature, in the knowledge that poetry reflects the silence of being, and no longer 'sings' but offers itself as a simple comment.[26] Others will equally legitimately claim that the main significance of the two passages lies in Odysseus' cunning and his excessive precautions, which enable him to use his pretence as a shield to hide his secret: that he belongs to the same species as the Sirens, and to their world of beauty and death; and that he, too, possesses a voice which is a desperate lament at his own inhumanity.[27]

Neither is completely satisfactory. The silence of poetry and metaphysics as an image exerts a strong attraction which modern humanity will resist with difficulty. Equally attractive, for those living 'without hope in desire', is the idea of beauty in literature as simply a raw cry at humanity's sterility and monstrous being-in-

---

[25] See F. Kermode, *The Genesis of Secrecy* (Cambridge, Mass. and London, 1979).

[26] The interpretation is Walter Benjamin's, quoted by G. Baioni, *Kafka: letteratura ed ebraismo* (Turin, 1984), 227 and n. 56.

[27] With this reading Baioni himself answers Benjamin in *Kafka*, 226–9.

death. It seems to me important, however, to observe that the imaginary and logical structure of the story is constitutionally adversative, actively contradictory, and openly hypothetical: every sentence negates the preceding one with a *but* or *however*, and contorts its phrasal syntax with further *yet*s, *perhaps*es, *or*s and *probably*s. This is language against itself: negating while stating, and establishing rational connections only to destroy them with continual strokes of the glottis. Every causal plot is thus undermined by the purest *logos* in the instant the *mythos* is undergoing radical alteration.

The story throws itself open to infinity. Ulysses is an Enigma without reason which we want to penetrate at all costs precisely on account of this mystery. He is perpetuated in stories which in their turn are interpretations of other stories. And Kafka's paradox explains why the shadow of Ulysses becomes surrounded by more consistent shadows, and lengthens over the centuries.

On the other hand, the story shuts like a clam at any attempt at integral exegesis. As any reading tends to become multiple and contradictory interpretation, it has to face the epistemological wall of indetermination and complementarity.[28] When observing atoms and their phenomena, Heisenberg maintains, expounding the principle of indetermination, it is conceptually impossible simultaneously to determine the position and speed of a particle with absolute precision: there exists a precise limit to precision, and an inevitable threshold of uncertainty. In the same field, according to Bohr's theory of complementarity it is impossible to produce a rigorous localization in time and space, and simultaneously a rigorous causal description of phenomena. The same principles hold in the universe of Kafka's Sirens: a threshold on which literature and science meet in the present century. The narrative comprises a sequence of paragraphs with only apparent causal links, and these paragraphs, like atoms, are in their turn broken down into particles possessing contrary values and moving in a different direction. The demonstration *proves* the validity of the assumption and at the same time reveals it as a mere pre-text, while the text itself changes internally, expanding into authorial exegesis and pre-empting the reader's own. When adding his 'codicil' to

---

[28] J. D. Barrow, *The World within the World* (Oxford, 1988), 137–41; and see the conclusion to Chapter 5 above.

'The Silence of the Sirens', i.e. adding an interpretation of his interpretation, Kafka actually states that at this point the human intellect is beyond understanding and intelligibility.

Isaiah's and Christ's preaching was expressed in prophecy and parable—in enigma—'that seeing they may see, and *not* perceive; and hearing they may hear, and *not* understand; *lest* at any time they should be converted' and saved.[29] Kafka's parable works on a similar logic: Odysseus neither sees nor hears. What the story foreshadows in the final instance, prefiguring both the death of poetry and being, and the 'song' of human inhumanity, is the Silence of Interpretation. If it is true that poetry can meet with human indifference, and be destroyed by it, it is equally true that reading, criticism, and exegesis, which prolong the life of poetry, have intrinsic limits. Faced with the pain which the Word and all its Enigmas inflict, there comes a moment when they all must fall finally silent.

---

[29] Mark 4:12, and see Kermode, *The Genesis of Secrecy*; G. Baioni, *Kafka: Romanzo e parabola* (3rd edn., Milan, 1980); R. Alter, *Necessary Angels* (Cambridge, Mass., 1991).

INDEX